THE UNFRACTURED FAIRY TALE LIFE OF
EDWARD EVERETT
HORTON

LON & DEBRA DAVIS

Published in the USA by:
BearManor Media
1317 Edgewater Dr #110
Orlando, FL 32804
www.bearmanormedia.com

Library of Congress Cataloguing in Publication Data :
Davis, Lon & Debra
The Unfractured Fairy Tale Life of Edward Everett Horton
Includes bibliographical references and index/
Perfect ISBN 979-8-88771-683-1
Case ISBN 979-8-88771-684-8
1. Horton, Edward Everett, 1886–1970
2. Comedians—United States—Biography
3. Motion picture actors and actresses—United States—Biography.

The front cover photo is courtesy of the Edward Everett Horton Collection; the back cover photo is courtesy of Steve Cox.

Edited by Scott H. Reboul
Book design by Robbie Adkins
www.adkinsconsult.com
BearManor Media, Orlando, Florida
Printed in the United States of America

Dedicated to our loyal publisher
BEN OHMART
a true champion of the obscure,
the overlooked, the unpublishable

Books by Lon & Debra Davis

Silent Lives: 100 Biographies of the Silent Film Era (2008)
Stooges Among Us (2008)
King of the Movies: Francis X. Bushman (2009)
Flirtation Act: The Story of a Boy, a Girl, and Vaudeville (2016)
CHASE! A Tribute to the Keystone Cops (2020)
Ma and Pa Kettle on Film (2020)
Stumbling into Film History (2024)
The Unfractured Fairy Tale Life of Edward Everett Horton
(2025)

Lon & Debra Davis have been collaborating on writing projects since 1978, the year they met in college. Film buffs since childhood, they continue to share their mutual love of classic cinema by researching and writing books on the subject. They have also co-edited more than two hundred academic books on the performing arts, American history, and literature. Their acclaimed documentary film, *This is Francis X. Bushman*, is shown occasionally on the Turner Classic Movies network (TCM). It is also available on Blu-ray from Flicker Alley in Los Angeles. Lon & Debra and their Bengal cat, Willoughby, reside in the Pacific Northwest.

Table of Contents

Edward Everett Horton Collection

THE UNFRACTURED FAIRY TALE LIFE OF
EDWARD EVERETT HORTON

Edward Everett Horton

ACKNOWLEDGMENTS

We would like to extend our sincerest thanks to our publisher and this book's dedicatee, Ben Ohmart, for encouraging us to write about Edward Everett Horton. Ben is the one who initially put us in touch with our favorite designer, Robbie Adkins, with whom we have collaborated on five books since 2020. Another friend and collaborator is Barry Thompson, a professional videographer and editor, who created a compilation of numerous clips from Eddie's career. A new friend, Jeffrey L. Carrier, arranged for us to interview Jerry Vermilye, a ninety-three-year-old actor and author, who spoke frankly about his experience as the stage manager of one of Eddie's touring shows in 1954. Jeffrey also shared the remembrances of his late friend and collaborator Patsy Ruth Miller, who co-starred with Eddie onstage and in six films. Another silent film star, our late friend Diana Serra Cary (once known professionally as Baby Peggy), also shared her impressions of Eddie during the filming of *Helen's Babies* (1924).

We are enormously grateful to the following individuals for granting permission to quote from their published works : Jeremy Carr (and *Film International* editor Matt Sorrento) for "There Seems to Be a Slight Mistake"; Leonard Maltin, for his *Classic Movie Guide*; Steve Massa, *Lame Brains and Lunatics 2*; Keith Scott, *The Moose That Roared*; Anthony Slide, *Eccentrics of Comedy*; Eve Golden, *Bride of Golden Images*; Dan Callahan, "Double-

Takes"; and Sarah Clothier, *The American Film Institute Catalog of Feature Films*. Steve Cox, Steve Massa, Jordan R. Young, and the enigmatic perfectionist behind www.doctormacro.com generously contributed some beautiful stills.

In this increasingly impersonal world it is a pleasure to interact with real, live people. We have been fortunate to deal repeatedly with some genuinely helpful archivists, including Mary Huelsbeck at the Wisconsin Center for Theatre and Film History; Edda Manriquez at The Academy of Motion Picture Arts & Sciences on Vine Street in Hollywood; and Jessica LaBozetta of the American Heritage Center, located on the campus of the University of Wyoming. It is at the latter institution that Edward Everett Horton's papers are housed. Contained within 37 boxes, measuring 38 cubic feet, the collection was donated posthumously to the AHC by Eddie's sister, Mrs. Hannabelle Horton Grant.

As always, many thanks to Phil Hall, Richard Skipper, Stu Shostak, Mike Gebert, and Jordan Rich, whose superb podcasts and radio shows provide us with international exposure to publicize our books.

And finally, we greatly appreciate Scott H. Reboul for lending his estimable editing skills to this endeavor. Scott is more than an editor, more than a friend. He is a one-man cheering squad, whose insights, enthusiasm, and eagle eye make completing a book a satisfying, stress-free experience.

Thank you kindly, one and all.

Lon and Debra

Eighty-four-year-old Edward Everett Horton in his final role, that of a ninety-seven-year-old doctor, on the CBS primetime comedy series The Governor and J.J., *in 1970. His co-star is his former protégée Julie Sommars.*
Jordan R. Young

PROLOGUE

To the very end, he was a working actor. He was eighty-four when he played his final role, although he didn't look it—he looked older. His face was deeply lined, his tousled hair was snow white, his aquiline nose was crinkled, and his tiny mouth was puckered with age. "Nobody's older than I am," he told an interviewer in 1968. "Oh, a few people are, but they are not in circulation. They're generally in asylums or old men's homes."[1] Perhaps, but there was a kind of indestructability about Edward Everett Horton. As he liked to say : "I'm still using the same face, the same gestures, the same voice I was using back in 1927."[2]

---

1   Bernard Rosenberg and Harry Silverstein, *The Real Tinsel*, NY: The Macmillan Company, 1970, p. 219.
2   Peter Noble interview with Edward Everett Horton, London, England, 1970.

And why not? It was a great face, they were eloquent gestures, and oh, what a voice! It was like butter with a little acid in it. Sweet, but with an edge. He spoke with pure American Yankee elocution, often with the decisive tone of one who is not to be trifled with. There were also those masterful double-takes; the end-of-the-world exclamations of "Oh, dear, this is *terrible!*" Even his name was unique : a triple-barreled moniker that set him apart from the ordinary. And while there were those who formally addressed him as Edward Everett, or Mister Horton, his friends called him Eddie. If you'll forgive our familiarity, we consider him to be a lifelong friend as well.

What struck us as we researched this remarkable actor's prolific, sixty-year career was just how different the world of entertainment was then compared to now. At twenty-four and with no previous experience, he was able to find a lucrative full-time position as a stage manager and occasional understudy. Most big cities in 1910 had one or more professional stock companies requiring actors of range. Instead of being left to fend for themselves, young hopefuls were taught the craft of acting. Eddie was forever grateful for the training and opportunities he was blessed with by the renowned Broadway star Louis Mann, whose stock company was the first one he joined. Working for such an entity allowed an actor to go from play to play, without fear of unemployment. Lesser-known actors in the 21st century, regardless of how talented they may be, enjoy no such advantage.

Entering the film industry in the 1920s was difficult, but not as difficult as it is in the 2020s. A producer apparently saw Eddie in a play and thought he would be a natural in pictures. Surviving examples of his silent film comedies reveal a likable fellow, well suited to the medium with his physical agility, facial expressions, quirky mannerisms, and aptitude for pantomime. Although this is the most overlooked part of his career, Eddie headlined seventeen silent features and eight two-reel comedies, the latter produced by Harold Lloyd.

The 1930s marked the peak of Eddie's popularity. In that decade he appeared in a total of sixty-four full-length films, a dozen of which were released in 1935 alone! He was earning good money and holding onto it, save for those occasions when he splurged on a questionable antique or two. Never limiting himself to any one medium, he brought his dithering character to radio. During television's formative days, he took part in everything from game shows to dramatic anthology programs to narrating the "Fractured Fairy Tales" on *The Rocky and Bullwinkle Show*. And with summer stock a staple of American entertainment, Eddie toured with a play every season for decades, doing one-night stands in cities big and small.

We are honored to be the authors of this first book devoted solely to Edward Everett Horton. By no means a tell-all, it is more of an appreciative career record of a consummate artist. Incredibly, he never wanted for work—or for money. It was as though he had been kissed by the goddess Dionysus. He epitomized the trouper, that hallowed term applied to a stalwart member of the taxing business of entertainment. That's not to imply that he was without foibles. Like many successful actors, he could be self-absorbed and diva-like. But then, God has yet to create a perfect mortal.

And now, here is the unfractured fairy tale life of Edward Everett Horton.

A Horton family portrait. Isabella and Edward Everett Sr. with their first-born, Edward Everett Jr., c. 1891. The Edward Everett Horton Collection

ACT I

Scene 1: Once Upon a Time . . .

Before Edward Everett Horton Jr. there was Edward Everett Horton Sr., his father. And before Edward Sr. there was Edward Everett, one of the great American orators of the antebellum and Civil War eras. He was also a diplomat, a senator, a governor (of Massachusetts), a secretary of state, an instructor at Harvard, and that university's president. In 1863, he was the opening act for Lincoln's Gettysburg Address at the dedication ceremony of the Gettysburg National Cemetery. He spoke for two hours; Lincoln's speech contained a mere 272-words, beginning with "Four score and seven years ago." In a letter to the Great Emancipator, Everett stated: "I wish that I could flatter myself that I had come as near to the central idea of the occasion in two hours as you did in two minutes."[3] It was after this accomplished yet humble gentleman that Maryland-born Edward Everett Horton Sr. was named. Born on May 11, 1860, he was the youngest of six brothers, all of

---

3   https://www.history.com/topics/american-civil-war/gettysburg-address.

whom were also named after prominent Americans. They were George Washington Horton, Millard Horton, Henry Peter Clay Horton, Herbert Berkeley Horton, and Winter Davis Horton.

Edward Everett Sr. must have had newspaper ink in his veins. He had worked his way up from being a reporter on a small Baltimore newspaper to become a compositor for the *New York Times*. In 1900, he was put in full charge of a contingent sent with linotype machines and printing equipment to form the *Times*'s edition of the Paris Exposition. Fifteen years earlier, he met twenty-five-year-old Isabella Stephen Diack (b. October 27, 1859, in Matanzas, Cuba), who had come to America from Kilmarnock, Scotland. They married on April 2, 1885, and settled on Willow Street in Brooklyn, New York; they eventually purchased the 1857 Italianate-style townhouse at 316 Carlton Avenue. On March 18, 1886, the couple welcomed their first child, whom they named Edward Everett Jr. According to Eddie, he was something of a child prodigy, "and yet lived to outgrow it."[4] At the age of one, he said, he could recite one hundred nursery rhymes. Over the next seven years he was succeeded by three siblings, in order of appearance : George, Hannabelle, and Winter Davis.[5]

Outside of his work, Edward Sr.'s favorite activity was going to the theatre. He was mesmerized by the stage stars of that time : Joseph Jefferson as Rip Van Winkle, William Gillette as Sherlock Holmes, and Maude Adams as Peter Pan. His favorite actor was

---

4   Marie Canel, "Edward Everett Horton Learned to Like the Oregon Mist," *The Oregonian*, September 30, 1934.

5   George was born on September 30, 1887; Hannabelle, on August 13, 1890; and Winter Davis, on June 3, 1893.

Edwin Booth, the son of Junius Brutus Booth, and the brother of the infamous John Wilkes Booth, Abraham Lincoln's assassin. Edward Sr. shared his love of histrionics with his young son, despite his stern wife's objections. "My mother was horrified,' Eddie recalled. "She was a Scot and had no use for the theatre. She thought he was ruining 'that boy.'"[6]

Isabella may have enjoyed going to plays more than she liked to admit. When five-year-old Eddie was recuperating from a severe case of whooping cough in the home of relatives in Carbondale, Pennsylvania, she took him to see E.H. Sothern and Julia Marlowe in *As You Like It*. To protect the still-ailing child from the harsh winter weather, Isabella outfitted him in leather leggings with silver buttons up to his knees. As the elegant Marlowe, portraying Rosalind, made her entrance dressed in tights, Eddie said loudly enough for everyone to hear, "Look, Mama! She's wearing *my* leggings!"[7]

Eddie's brother George was the scholar of the family. He was a graduate of Yale, where he had majored in bacteriology. As Eddie said proudly, "George was with DuPont for a while. He isolated some sort of germ afflicting chickens."[8] Eddie's own educational record was hardly so impressive. Self-described as a "diffident, shy kid,"[9] he attended kindergarten in Brooklyn. He then went to P.S. 11, and from there to Boys' High School. The benefits of a formal

---

6   *The Real Tinsel*, p. 220.
7   Jeanne Stein, "'Fusspot' and 'Fortune's Fool' Edward Everett Horton," *Focus on Film* no. 1 (1970), p. 31.
8   Noble interview, 1969.
9   "Famed Actor Edward Everett Horton Was Born and Bred in Brooklyn," https:// stuffnobodycaresabout.com/2019/01/07/edward-everett-horton/.

education were lost on him. His intense dislike for school caused him to drop out and take a job. Earning the weekly sum of twelve dollars, he worked as an office boy for the telephone company. In any given week, he stated hyperbolically, he was assigned no fewer than twelve thousand chores. After enduring these appalling, slave-like conditions for nearly a month, he decided the working world just wasn't for him. At this point, the directionless young man decided to go back to college. To appease his worried parents, he said he wanted to be a teacher, a dentist, or a banker, although privately the idea of those professions—or *any* profession—filled him with dread.

His parents briefly pulled up stakes and moved to Maryland, where they lived for three years, and where Eddie went to the Baltimore City College. Before he could graduate, the itinerate Horton clan returned to Brooklyn. Eddie enrolled at Oberlin College in Ohio, where he majored in German. Exactly what he hoped to gain from studying that language is unknown. We do know, however, that he took his subject seriously. During his three years at Oberlin, he lived with a German family, speaking their native language exclusively.

It was at this time that the stage began to occupy his thoughts. He corralled some of his peers and went about constructing some original one-act plays. When the junior prom was announced, he thought it might be nice if he and his troupe were to coincide the event with a presentation of one of these plays. Eddie and his fellow thespians gathered in the women's gymnasium, where they constructed a stage that had little footlights in front with candles behind them. At no time did it occur to Eddie to seek permission to present the play. As the troupe was nearing an end to their labors, the dean of women made a surprise appearance.

"*Mister* Horton," she said pointing at the makeshift stage, "what is *this?*"

As the fledgling Belasco stammered out an explanation, the dean was shaking her head. "Oh no, no, *no,*" she said disapprovingly. And just like that, the show was canceled.[10]

This was Eddie's first taste of show business.

During the three years Eddie was boarding with the German family, his own parents learned of his interest in the theatre. "That annoyed them no end,"[11] he said amusedly. His father was secretly half-pleased that his son was joining the same profession as his hero Edwin Booth, although for the record, he said, 'We didn't send you to college for *this.*'[12] Eddie understood; he later said that he felt as though his parents were paying for his education under false pretenses. "Anyway," he explained, "if I was getting theatre in a strict school like Oberlin, my word, *something* had to be done. My parents thought maybe I'd better stay home and go to the Polytechnic Institute in Brooklyn. I was there a whole year, majoring in German, English, and history." He also tried his hand as a playwright, penning *Meridon*, in which he took the part of Mrs. Gwendolyn Brooks. It wasn't long after this that Polytechnic did

10   *The Real Tinsel*, p. 220. David J. Belasco (1853–1931) was an American theatrical producer, impresario, director, and playwright.
11   Ibid., p. 219.
12   Ibid., p. 220.

away with its art courses and became a purely technical school, which it remains to the present day.[13]

Eddie's third, and final, attempt at higher education was at Columbia College, located on 116th Street in New York City. His fraternity brothers of Phi Kappa Psi were early witnesses of Eddie's comedic abilities. As he recalled : "I was running around with a bunch of fellows there, and one of them said, 'Why don't you try out for the Columbia show? You can tell stories and everything.' I auditioned and was given a part right away in *The Varsity Show of 1909*."[14] Recalled Eddie : "The show that year was a musical comedy about European Royalty and Newport, Rhode Island, aristocracy."[15] The director, Frank Stammers, also knew a potential star when he saw one. He befriended Eddie and served as his mentor and unsolicited agent.

"This was really the first time I ever stood on a stage," Eddie explained. "The rehearsals started, the music started, the dialogue came along as did the dancing, and finally we opened the show. Ran it for two weeks at the old Waldorf Astoria, when it was down on Thirty-Fourth Street. By the time Saturday night came, I was almost as good as I thought I was."[16]

Eddie was cast in an important role, that of Tessie, the Newsstand Girl. A reporter from *The Brooklyn Eagle* enthusiastically described Tessie's elaborate ensembles.

---

13   It is known presently as the New York University Tandon School of Engineering.
14   *The Real Tinsel*, p. 220.
15   Stein, p. 31.
16   *The Real Tinsel*, pp. 220–221.

His make-up as the Newsstand Girl in the tightest of short skirts and the queerest of blouses was rich and rare. According to the play the Newsstand Girl is soon disguised as the Millionaire's Daughter. Then Mr. Horton appeared in gowns that were simply extraordinary. Especially so was his Salome costume.[17]

It seemed to his parents and teachers that this potentially bright young man was unable to take anything seriously. For example, he was something of a prankster. Before a sizeable crowd of onlookers, he climbed to the top of the campus's service building. Upon reaching the summit, he threw down a dummy, alarming those who believed he had fallen to his death. The school's board of directors did not share his sense of mischief.

"After that, to put it gently, Columbia and I came to an amicable parting of the ways," Eddie said. "They were just as glad to see me go as I was to get out."[18]

The time had come for him to pursue acting on a full-time basis. Being able to earn a living by treading the boards was not the pipe dream it often is now. In the early part of the 20th century virtually every major city had opera and stock companies. Small-time vaudeville theatres were ubiquitous as well, providing those with specialty acts a place to be seen and the opportunity to improve and make a living. Eddie found temporary employment in the chorus of an amateur Gilbert & Sullivan opera company on Staten Island, performing *The Mikado*. That lasted for three or four weeks. From there, he went looking for his next job.

---

17   *The Brooklyn Eagle*, as quoted in Brooklyn online article.
18   *The Real Tinsel*, p. 221.

By his own admission, Eddie was not a talented singer, but as he explained, "You didn't need voice training in those days. I found out, too, that if I sang with all the rest, no one could tell what I was singing, and I couldn't help being on key. I was in the baritone section. In this second chorus, I had a very unusual experience. It was in a musical comedy that had been quite successful in New York, called *The Newlyweds and Their Baby*. They were going out all over the United States. They needed one chorus boy who had to be a certain height [six feet] because the chorus started with a big bruiser and came down to a little fellow at the end. They needed someone to be the second guy. He had learned this from a member of the little opera company, who said, "What are you doing, Edward?"

"Well, I don't know that I'm doing *any*thing," he answered.

"Listen," the informant continued, "get down to the Irish Athletic Club, near the Hudson River on Fifty-second Street and … Is that the best suit you have?"

"Yes."

"Oh," he said. "Go anyway and see what happens."

Eddie, it turns out, was just what the casting director was looking for. He got the part without having to audition.

"Now, as a chorus boy, you were supposed to know certain steps because there was no choreography in those days," Eddie said rather questionably. "You went forward and back, and you did this, that, and the other thing. All these boys knew the steps, so I had to learn them quickly. Now, the fellow ahead of me was a very big bruiser with the largest hands and the biggest feet in all of human captivity. I tried to keep out of his way while doing these steps, watching over here and watching over there, because I knew if he ever stepped on me, my career would be ruined. But he didn't, and we finally got along all right. That chap was Wallace Beery!"[19]

Scene 2 : Footlights

Returning to New York City in 1910, Eddie soon discovered that an aspiring actor was dead in the water without an agent. "You had to have somebody working for you," he said. "So I decided on an agent named Chamberlain Brown."[20] "I used to get up to that office in the morning when it first opened," Eddie vividly recalled. "Somebody would come out, glance at me, and be less than encouraging. Finally, other actors and actresses would come in, all beautifully dressed, with their hair combed, wearing tight shoes, and, oh, gee! I would sit there, and then it would be lunchtime, and I had about thirty cents to spend. I'd go out, have lunch, and come back. I did this for three days. I stayed until they were locking up. Nobody paid any attention."

That changed after the third day. Mr. Brown was locking up when he noticed the tall, thin young man still waiting patiently to be noticed.

19　Ibid. Wallace Beery (1885–1949) was a film actor known for his gruff-but-lovable characters, including that of a washed-up boxer in *The Champ* (1931), for which he won an Oscar.

20　Ibid. A ubiquitous presence on the American theatre scene of the early 20th century, Chamberlain Brown (1892–1955) was an actor, a producer of Broadway shows, a publisher of theatrical periodicals, a radio host, and a casting agent. He and his brother ran the Chamberlain and Lyman Brown Theatrical Agency, handling the careers of the greatest names in show business. Their extensive collection of papers is held by the New York Public Library.

"What do you want?" he asked.

"I'm looking for a job," Eddie replied.

"Are you an actor?"

"I'd like to be."

"What have you done?"

"I haven't done anything special."

"If you haven't done anything, we can't do anything for you here."

"Well, I had a part in the varsity show at Columbia University."

"Oh?" he said. "What's your name?"

"Edward Horton."

"Here, you take this card and tomorrow morning you get over to the stage entrance of the Lyric Theatre in Brooklyn. Go right in on the stage. Go there about nine or nine-thirty. There you'll meet a very fine, well-known actor, a great star, who is looking for a young man to be in his play."[21]

Eddie was so excited he could hardly sleep that night. In the morning, exhausted but exhilarated, he arrived at the Lyric and entered through the stage door. The well-known actor—the great star—was wearing a fur hat, a fur coat, and an oversized necktie. In front of him were six or seven fellows, each one holding the same white card Eddie had been given.

"I had thought I was going to be the only one there. I went to the back of the line. He was taking these cards and listening to

---

21   Ibid., p. 222.

what the fellows said. As I got nearer, I'd hear them say, 'Bought and Paid For,' 'Paid in Full,' 'Butterfly on the Wheel.' I thought, 'Golly, there's no use in my staying here. I can't say *anything*.' I wanted to go away. Then I thought, '*No!* I'm already here. I must see what's going to happen.' It got to be my turn, and I handed him the card.

"All right, all right, let's have it," he said, someone jadedly.

"There's nothing, sir."

"*What*?"

"Nothing."

"What do you mean, *nothing*?"

"I have nothing to say."

"You haven't done *anything* in the theatre?"

"No, sir."

"You want to be an actor?"

"I am very anxious to be."

"Well, well, well. Perhaps we could teach you. But right now I need a stage manager. I'll pay you twenty dollars a week—and if you're good, I'll let you act, too."

Then, turning to the others, he said, "Thank you, gentlemen."[22]

This was Broadway star Louis Mann. Born in New York City on April 20, 1865, he made his theatrical debut as a child actor. In 1896, he appeared at the Herald Square Theatre on Broadway,

____

22   Ibid.

in the George Dance and Ivan Caryll production *The Girl from Paris*. On October 16, 1899, Mann and his new leading lady, Clara Lipman, opened in the original production of *The Girl in the Barracks*, which ran for only thirty-one performances. Undaunted by this misfire, the couple soon married and went on to become a widely respected team. Lipman wrote twenty-two plays, five of which starred her husband. Mann was well known for his portrayals of excitable, confused, lovable heroes. He was also one of the last great actor-managers of that era.

Eddie hit the ground running. His responsibilities as a stage manager included checking on the props and sound effects; making sure the actors were on time and knew their parts; and generally ensuring that each performance ran as smoothly as possible. As Eddie recalled : "I had only been getting twelve dollars, and oh boy, I was there with a script and watching everything. Finally, he let me write some letters for him. I had some very fine notepaper."[23]

"Mostly," Eddie recalled, "I watched Louis Mann. He was a great artist, oh, a *great* artist. He was fabulous. He was a dialect comedian, you know. It was just as if I had gone to school to be with him. Eventually, he wouldn't come to rehearsals at all. He'd say, 'Horton, you know the play.' And I could imitate him, and I'd do all the other parts. It was a great experience. Whatever I know about the theatre, I learned from Louis Mann."[24]

At the end of the second week, Mann asked, "Horton, how much did I say I was going to pay you?"

---

23   Ibid., p. 223.
24   Ibid.

"Twenty dollars," Eddie answered.

"Well, make it forty."

"My *word*! *Forty* dollars!" Eddie recalled joyfully. "I couldn't believe it. I haven't had that much money since."[25]

As promised, Eddie was cast in bits, walk-ons, and even had a line or two in most of the plays he oversaw, both on Broadway and

Broadway star Louis Mann

on tour. His Broadway debut, on June 29, 1910, was in *The Cheater*, a farce adapted by Louis Mann from a German play called *Der Doppelmensch*. In a supporting role as a portly porter was John Bunny, who would soon become world-famous as one of the silent screen's first major American comedians.

Eddie knew that if he was to advance as an actor he would need to play more prominent roles. Louis Mann had reservations about his protégé's acting ability; he felt he lacked experience, which was undeniable. Unsure if his boss was serious or merely being flippant, Eddie was told that he may have missed his calling as a streetsweeper. It was a difficult decision but, without any bridges burned, he resigned from the Louis Mann Company. Now

---

25 Ibid.

on his own, Eddie was cast as "Jake's Friend" in David Belasco's production of *The Governor's Lady*, but the part amounted to little more than the walk-ons he had been playing for three years. His luck would change dramatically when he was hired as the juvenile lead for the Orpheum Players Stock Company in Philadelphia's Chestnut Street Theatre. This was followed, in 1912, by a stint with Beaulah Jay's Company, also in Pittsburgh. He was given his first official leading role, that of a German doctor, appearing opposite Blanche Yurka in *The Typhoon*. One of his co-stars, Thurston Hall, approached him after a rehearsal and said, "Edward, I could no more play a Japanese prince than I could play Sarah Bernhardt. Why don't *you* play the Japanese prince, and *I'll* play the German doctor?"

"Well, I did," said Eddie. "I tackled the part of the Japanese prince. At that time, at the University of Pennsylvania, there was a fabulous Japanese student named Sato, who was surrounded by very interesting Japanese friends. He had the whole top of the dormitory, and everybody said he was a prince. I contacted him about the play. He read it over and gave me, phonetically, what he felt this Japanese prince would say, and on the opening night, who was in the audience with all his Japanese friends but Mister Sato. They gave me a little party after that."[26]

Another memorable experience for Eddie was playing in the melodrama *A Fool There Was*, a 1909 Broadway play by Porter Emerson Brown; this was based on an 1876 poem by Rudyard Kipling

---

26   Ibid., pp. 223–226.

called "The Vampire," which had been suggested by a painting by Philip Burne-Jones. The first of the poem's five stanzas reads :

> A fool there was, and he made his prayer
>
> (Even as you or I!)
>
> To a rag and a bone and a hank of hair,
>
> (We called her the woman who did not care),
>
> But the fool he called her his lady fair—
>
> (Even as you or I!)[27]

The play's leading character is an intensely erotic woman whose unholy purpose in life is to lure decent men away from their wives and children.[28] Eddie, cast as the poor schlemiel who falls for the dark-eyed beauty's charms, gave it all he had in what he described as a "dramatic, hysterical"[29] part. Instead of engendering the sympathy of the audience, the theatre rocked with laughter. It was then, he later said, that "I realized I *must* be a comedian. The audience made me realize it."[30]

One might imagine that a single man in his twenties would be painting the town red with his surplus of cash. That simply wasn't Eddie's style. In fact, the majority of his income was being sent home to help fund his brothers' and sister's education; his father

---

27   https://www.poetryverse.com/rudyard-kipling-poems/vampire.
28   The Fox Film Company had its first major hit with a five-reel version of *A Fool There Was* (1915), starring screen vamp Theda Bara.
29   Stein, p. 32.
30   Ibid.

wasn't especially well-heeled, but Eddie was clearing sixty dollars a week.

As Eddie's career gradually showed promise, his father said to him, "I think you're making a mistake, Edward. Anybody—*anybody*—can be Edward Horton, but no one, *no one else*, can be Edward *Everett* Horton."

After thinking it over for a moment, Eddie smiled and said, "I think I like that."[31]

Sadly, Edward Everett Horton Sr. did not live to see his son achieve worldwide fame; he died, aged fifty-five, on November 15, 1915, while visiting his son George at his home in Mountain Grove, Missouri.[32]

"About this Edward Everett Horton," producers would say, "is he any good?" The standard answer to that was "Well, he gets three figures."[33] That was all they needed to hear. Another offer came in, this time from the owner of a theatre in Portland, Oregon. To procure Eddie's services as an offbeat leading man, he was willing to pay him $125 a week.

"So, I went up to Portland and played the Keith Theatre there with Dorothy Dalton as the leading woman," he said. "She eventually married Arthur Hammerstein, Oscar's brother.[34] She and I

---

31   *The Real Tinsel*, p. 220.
32   Edward Everett Horton Sr. was laid to rest in Hillcrest Cemetery, Mountain Grove, Wright County, Missouri. His plot number is NW Orig. 118-2.
33   Ibid., p. 226.
34   Eddie is referring to Oscar Hammerstein II, not Oscar's father.

played together for thirty weeks. Oh, she was lovely. I played in Portland for eighty-eight consecutive weeks."[35]

Eddie had not relished the idea of a long engagement in the Pacific Northwest; he had heard from numerous sources that it rained there all the time. Not long into his stay, he began to appreciate the peaceful coolness of Oregon's often misty conditions. In addition to becoming acclimated to the weather, he undertook a job that was in no way associated with the theatre. He had arrived in Portland during the fall of 1917, just as the United States was preparing to join the war effort in Europe. Feeling patriotic, he approached the administrator of a government-run agency and asked if there was any volunteer work for which he might be suited. To his surprise, he was entrusted to deliver government-controlled foods (sugar, for example) to Portland's various cafés and restaurants. Eddie found immense personal satisfaction in fulfilling his task. Indeed, he claimed that, for the first time, he felt like an everyday citizen, not merely a make-believe actor in greasepaint. "I enjoyed every moment of it and loved the town that saw in me something of a business executive," he told *The Oregonian*.[36] He later stated that he applied his newly acquired acumen to the production of plays and managing his own theatre without falling into bankruptcy.

When he was asked to give a talk to a large assembly of high school students, Eddie accepted the invitation without hesitation. We'll let him tell us what happened that day.

---

35 *The Real Tinsel*, p. 220.
36 Canel.

"I was very much impressed by the attention I was receiving. When I came to the end of my fifteen allotted minutes, I hadn't quite finished with the story of my life, so I asked my audience if they wished me to go on. The applause was deafening, and so I went on for about ten more minutes. In the hall later when I was signing autographs, I spoke to one youngster whom I had noticed as paying more than particular attention and thanked him for the tribute. 'Oh, that's okay," he remarked dismissively, 'but if you'd carried on for five minutes longer, I wouldn't have had to report for geometry.'"[37]

From Portland, the thirty-year-old rising star went to Pittsburgh and then all over the country in different plays, always getting bigger parts and a better salary. In 1919, at the invitation of Thomas Wilkes, Eddie went to Southern California to star in that West Coast impresario's famed stock company. For a weekly salary of $225, he would be replacing leading man Lewis Stone.[38] Located at 845 South Broadway in Los Angeles, the Wilkes-Majestic Theatre was built in 1908; it boasted sixteen hundred seats. Eddie would be instrumental in filling those seats for several years to come. His debut at the Majestic was in *Never Say Die*, a prophetic title for the driven young actor. With tongue firmly in cheek, he

---

37   Virginia Irwin, "He's Having the Time of His Life," *Everyday Magazine*, January 15, 1940.

38   Lewis Stone (1879–1953) went on to become a rather mature leading man in silent films. Beginning in 1937, he was cast as the wise Judge Hardy in MGM's Hardy Family series.

said, "I had already played it five times before, so I *almost* knew the lines. I followed that with *An Ideal Husband* [by Oscar Wilde]."[39]

Predictably, Eddie excelled in comedies. Two of his oft-used bits of business, the double-take and the foot-stamping temper tantrums, were perfected when essaying the titular role in *Clarence* by Booth Tarkington. Clarence has been described as "a patient, slyly witty 'poor soul,'"[40] a character introduced on Broadway by Alfred Lunt.[41] Eddie played that part for forty-four consecutive weeks in Los Angeles.

Publicity for The Nervous Wreck, *Los Angeles, California, c. 1923. Edward Everett Horton Collection*

Wilkes employed an effective strategy that made stars out of his various featured players. Casting them in new plays that proved successful in Los Angeles and San Francisco, he would then transfer the show and its leading man to New York. This formula

---

39 Noble interview, 1969.
40 Stein, p. 32.
41 Alfred Lunt (1892–1977) was an American actor, best known for the light comedies he and his English wife, Lynn Fontanne (1887–1983), performed to much acclaim on both sides of the Atlantic.

worked brilliantly for two of his discoveries, Richard Bennett (the father of Joan and Constance Bennett) and Fred Keenan (Ed Wynn's father-in-law and Keenan Wynn's grandfather), but not for Eddie. The show was *The Nervous Wreck*, written by Owen Davis, the noted playwright who had recently been awarded the Pulitzer Prize for his serious play *Icebound*. Eddie and his leading lady, Frances Howard (the future wife of Samuel Goldwyn), traveled across the country to Atlantic City for the opening. *The Nervous Wreck*, based on a short story by E.J. Roth, was said to be a vehicle that played to Eddie's strengths. His character, a hysterical, self-centered clerk from Pittsburgh, goes to an Arizona ranch for a rest-cure. Feeling much more relaxed, he becomes involved with the rancher's daughter, a dalliance that does not sit well with the girl's fiancé. Audiences responded favorably to the featured comic artist, as did the critics. One especially impressed writer compared Eddie to Sidney Drew.[42] So, what was the problem, then? It was that Wilkes had a falling out with his influential associate, producer Sam Harris. Harris insisted that Otto Kruger[43], not Eddie, be cast for the New York opening. In one of the few negative aspects of his fairy-tale career, Eddie was soon on a train, heading ignominiously back to Los Angeles. Wilkes even insisted that the frugal actor pay his own fare.

---

42   Sidney Drew (1863–1919) was a light comedian who worked onstage and in films with his first and second wives, Gladys Rankin (1870–1914) and Lucille McVey (1890–1925); they were billed, rather austerely, as Mr. and Mrs. Sidney Drew. Sidney was an uncle of John, Ethel, and Lionel Barrymore.

43   Otto Kruger (1885–1974) began his acting career as a matinee idol on Broadway in 1915. In movies, he was often cast as a smooth-talking villain, as in Alfred Hitchcock's spy thriller *Saboteur* (1942). He is especially memorable in two films from the fifties: Fred Zinnemann's *High Noon* (1952) and Douglas Sirk's *Magnificent Obsession* (1954). He was also active in radio and television.

"That was supposed to be my big chance,"[44] Eddie told an interviewer late in life.

Scene 3 : Silent Movies Calling

One day in 1922, a thirty-six-year-old producer and director named Jess Robbins paid a visit to Eddie at the Majestic. A true movie pioneer, Robbins had supervised the filming of Charlie Chaplin's two-reelers for the Essanay Film Manufacturing Company in Niles, California. He also directed Stan Laurel and Oliver Hardy in their first film together, *The Lucky Dog*, c. 1921. In addition, Robbins was supposedly the first to use reflective lighting in his productions. As he told Eddie, "I think you'd do wonderfully in pictures, Mister Horton. Would you like to make one?"

Eddie was cautiously interested. But how on earth could he give all that was required to succeed simultaneously on stage *and* in the movies?

"Oh, that's all right," Robbins replied. "We'll make them in the daytime when you're not playing or rehearsing. You just come down and we'll shoot around you if we have to. We'll give you one hundred and fifty dollars a week."

One can almost see the dollar signs in Eddie's dark brown eyes. Imagine—$150 a week *more* than he was already getting! In his mind, he would soon be joining the lofty ranks of such prominent men of business as John D. Rockefeller and Henry Ford.

"So I decided to do it," he said.[45]

---

44   Ibid., p. 33.
45   *The Real Tinsel*, p. 226.

Eddie looks rather dashing in this early publicity portrait of the rising film star. Steve Massa

Robbins was then working for Vitagraph. Established in 1897, the Vitagraph Company of America was founded by Albert E. Smith and Stuart Blackton in the Midwood (also known as Flatbush) area of Eddie's hometown of Brooklyn. In its early years, Vitagraph's leading players were matinee idol Maurice Costello,

Edward Everett Horton Collection

the physically disparate comedy team of John Bunny & Flora
Finch, Norma and Constance Talmadge, Clara Kimball Young,
Viola Dana, and Mr. & Mrs. Sidney Drew. In 1912, Smith and
Blackton opened a West Coast branch of Vitagraph in the Los
Feliz area of Los Angeles. Eddie would make his first feature film
there, *Too Much Business* (1922). Robbins wanted him to play an

athletic bank teller, somewhat along the lines of the swashbuck-ling Douglas Fairbanks.[46]

To hear Eddie tell it, his debut in motion pictures was a trial by fire. "They thought they'd give me something to do the first day so that no matter *what* lay in the future, it could never be worse," he said. "I was called upon to report down to the L.A. Athletic Club. They put make-up on me. In those days, in silent pictures, it was sort of thick and yellow all over. I had never appeared on the street in make-up before in my life. It was something I wouldn't do. Nevertheless, I had to do it, and then I had to walk down to the corner of Seventh and Broadway. It was teeming with people, walking by on the street and riding in trolley cars. I was to wait until I saw a dolly coming along with a box on it that looked as if it might contain an upright piano. But in it was a camera. I am to get in back of that box, keep about twenty or thirty feet behind it, and walk slowly to the front of it. If people stopped me, I was to appear as though I was talking to them."[47]

Did this make the neophyte photoplayer nervous?

"*Nervous?* I was *shivering*."[48]

The following day, he sat down with Robbins to view the rushes. Until that time, Eddie considered himself to be passably good-looking, even handsome. It therefore came as a rude awak-ening to see his face magnified on the screen, ninety-six times its actual size. That wonderful, imperfect face—with the knitted

---

46   Ibid. p. 227. Eddie was physically fit and therefore more than able to "[jump] around and all that. I used to play handball a lot."
47   Ibid.
48   Ibid.

brows, those frightened eyes, the generous nose, and that crooked smile—would make him one of the most sought-after character actors in the business. Even so, he once confessed to a newspaper columnist : "The first thing that I think of when I see one of my pictures is how I look. Consideration of the setting comes second. And believe it or not, a tie askew or a collar point turned up can spoil his whole picture for an actor. I don't know how many actors would admit that, but if they tell you the truth, it is that—in movies—*looks* come first; acting, second."[49]

Eddie was doing what he loved most : performing in good plays for enthusiastic audiences. "The theatre is delightful," Eddie often said. "It is the only thing I ever wanted. I used to have the key to the stage door of the Majestic Theatre. I'd get down there at seven in the morning. In my dressing room, I had couches and things to drink. It became known as Majestic Alpha, and everybody in the world was always welcome."[50]

Unlike many of his colleagues in the performing arts, Eddie remained, as always, very much aware of the bottom line : "I was in that theatre for six years, starting at two hundred a week. Then they put in a Sunday matinee after about the third week and gave me two-fifty."[51] Whatever his salary, Eddie was worth it. His versatility allowed him to do straight dramatic leads as well as comedies, although his particular company much preferred acting in dramas. Comedy was hard work. Eddie elaborated on

49   Irwin.
50   *The Real Tinsel*, p. 228.
51   Ibid., p. 226.

this theatrical phenomenon : "If you weren't getting laughs and you *knew* it was a funny show, you had to get together and say, 'What's the matter? What can we do? How can we be funny?' In a dramatic play, if you didn't remember a line, you just stood perfectly still, not moving a muscle, and people would say, 'Oh, what an actor! For *five minutes* he didn't say a *word*. You could hear a pin drop. *Marvelous!*' You couldn't do that in a comedy. You *had* to keep going."[52]

What exactly is the difference between farce and comedy? According to Eddie : "A comedy is a play written for the stage that could be played either as tragedy or comedy. It depends on the tempo. It's written around a situation that could happen, and it is treated either for laughter or for tears. A farce is something that couldn't possibly have happened but is played so that it seems to be happening while you're looking at it."[53]

Eddie was confident in his abilities just as he was the first to admit his limitations. One weakness was his singing voice : he didn't have one. "I can't *talk* a song," he said, "I have no sense of rhythm at all." Despite that, he was routinely cast in musicals, although in speaking roles only.

One of "the nicest times I ever had in the theatre," he said, was appearing as the governor of Louisiana in the Victor Herbert oper-etta *Naughty Marietta* in San Francisco at the newly constructed Curran Theatre in 1922. As he recalled of that experience : "They assured me that I wouldn't have to sing, but when it comes to the

---

52   Ibid., p. 227.
53   Ibid., p. 233–234.

end of the play, there's a long speech, leading into about eight bars of the big finale number that I *had* to sing—or somebody else would do it. Anyway, it was the day prior to opening night … We were having our dress rehearsal, and everyone had on their costumes, and a big orchestra of sixty people was out there. Suddenly, it was time for my speech. When it came time to sing, I said, 'I can't hit the key.' And Ed Lester, who was the director and producer, said, 'Just go into anything.' And I said, 'No, no, no, no. It would be much funnier if I hit the key; if I didn't, it wouldn't be funny.' So, they gave me a chord in the orchestra and, of course, it was hopeless; they tried it on the oboe, and I couldn't hear that, and they tried it on the violin, and finally, one of the chaps in the tenor section behind me, said, 'Mister Horton, I have what they call *absolute pitch*, and I know exactly what the note is. So, when you do your part, just lean back and I'll give it to you in your ear.' I said, 'Alright, but not tonight at the dress rehearsal; we've spent enough money on it, but tomorrow night if we get it, fine, if we don't get it, fine.' So, the next night came. … I do my speech, and hit the note right on the key, you know? *That was the only night I got it!*"[54]

British music hall performers, many of whom were women, brought their specific style to American shores. "They were fabulous," Eddie said with enthusiasm. "They had comedy songs that had us rolling in the aisles, they were so funny. They were all founded on a very sad, and kind of pathetic, little incident. For instance, 'There was I, waiting at the church, waiting at the church, waiting at the church. When I found that he had left me in the

---

54   Noble interview, 1969.

lurch, Lord did it upset me. All at once, he sent around a little note. Here's the very note. This is what he wrote. 'Can't get away to marry you today. My wife won't let me.' Oh, they laughed. That's kind of a sad thing. Almost tragic. Then there was another one : 'John took me around to see his mother, his mother, his mother. When he'd introduced us to each other, she sized up everything I had on. She put me through a cross-examination till I fairly boiled with aggravation. Then she shook her head, looked at me, and said, 'Poor John, poor John.' Well, that's sad, too, but it was very funny. That was also Chaplin's secret. He came out of the same English music-hall tradition at about the same time. So did Stan Laurel. Wasn't he marvelous?"[55]

One encounter Eddie had at the Majestic involved someone who would one day loom large in the movie capital. He described his visitor as "a nice-looking chap—well dressed and everything, but on fire! He had a play for me to read and he wanted to know if I would listen to the first act. Well, I did, and it was pretty good, but I didn't know how to encourage him because I had nothing to do with the selection of plays. He wanted to know if he could come again when he finished the second act. Well, he did. Two or three weeks later, he came down again. I told him all I could do was to suggest it. I never knew what happened because that was the last time I saw him, but I have never forgotten his forceful personality and how ambitious he was. I found out that he later went

---

55   *The Real Tinsel*, pp. 233–234.

Photo courtesy: Doctor Macro

into pictures and got to be the head of Twentieth Century-Fox. His name is Darryl Zanuck."[56]

Director James Cruze[57] worked in the fledgling movie industry as an actor, a producer, and director at several studios before finding his niche with Paramount Pictures. Cruze gained prominence by helming *The Covered Wagon*, a realistic Western that became an instant critical and commercial hit in 1923. Another box-office success that year would be *Ruggles of Red Gap*, with a screenplay by Anthony Coldeway and Walter Woods, which was adapted

---

56 Ibid., pp. 228–229.
57 James Cruze (1884–1942) was born Jens Cruz Bosen in Ogden, Utah, of Mormon parents. He went on to direct more than a hundred films, mainly during the silent era. His first known acting job was at Lubin Manufacturing Company in 1910. The following year, he signed with Thanhouser, where he made the vast majority of his films.

from the 1915 novel by Harry Leon Wilson. *Ruggles of Red Gap* had a proven track record in print, on stage, and in film. The novel was a runaway best seller upon its original release; a Broadway musical version immediately went into production, and moviegoers were delighted by a film version in 1918, starring the long-forgotten Taylor Holmes. "The story concerns a British gentleman's gentleman who discovers a 'new birth of freedom' in a small Western American town in the early 20th century."[58] Eddie, who was ambivalent about the flickers, was actually excited by this project; he believed (correctly) that he was born to play the veddy proper Ruggles. Actors' Equity, however, attempted to stand in the way of the deal.

"They claimed that I had no right to go," he recalled. "I said, 'I have a two-week clause, and I want to make a picture.' Mister Cruze said, 'All right, we'll pay them to let you go for two weeks.'"[59] During that fortnight, Cruze, Eddie, and a top-flight supporting cast (made up of various players from *The Covered Wagon*, including Lois Wilson, Ernest Torrence, and Charles Ogle) made *Ruggles of Red Gap*. Red Gap, in this instance, was the little town of Eureka, in Northern California. Stated Eddie : "The interiors were shot in a great big house all made of scrolled wood, very viciously Victorian, but rather handsome. That was very, very interesting indeed. It was a lovely picture."[60]

---

58   Wes D. Gehring, *Leo McCarey: From Marx to McCarthy* (Lanham, MD : The Greenwood Press, 2005), p. 65.
59   *The Real Tinsel*, p. 229.
60   Ibid., p. 227.

It no doubt was, but we'll likely never see it. No prints are known to exist.

Eddie found ample employment in Hollywood, and didn't seem to mind having to juggle his stage and movie careers.

"I was in that Majestic Theatre morning, noon, and night, rehearsing a new show all the time, leaving to make a picture, and then coming back," he said. "I was very pleased to get to know someone like May McAvoy or Louise Fazenda. I'd have parties and invite them out. In fact, when I made a picture with Lily Pons, *Hitting a New High*, I had a very big party in my banquet hall."[61]

In Manhattan, Eddie was also famous for his champagne breakfasts for a dozen or more friends at a time, including Tallulah Bankhead and Dorothy Parker. Still, he couldn't help but feel like a second-class citizen in Hollywood. "They had very little use for stage actors," he explained; "they had these marvelous silent stars like Valentino, and they just ignored the stage actors. We were on the wrong side of the tracks at all times—and we knew too much."[62]

That may have been true to some extent, but Eddie was well compensated for bringing Broadway to Los Angeles. Six years after aligning himself with the Majestic Theatre he was raking in $1,250 a week from his stage work alone. And with his reputation as a polished screen comedian growing apace, his agent began fielding offers of long-term contracts from the major studios.

---

61   Ibid.
62   Noble interview, 1969.

"The movie people would offer me five hundred or maybe seven-fifty and ask if I would sign a seven-year contract," Eddie stated. "I would think, 'Wait. Suppose I'm no good in the motion picture business and they rent me out to another studio where they give me parts I can't play? Anything to get rid of me. *Here* I am my own boss.' So far I have always been a freelance player. Even when I got to make big pictures I was never under contract to *any* studio."[63]

One of Eddie's few extant silent features is *Helen's Babies*, a 1924 comedy-drama, based on the 1876 novel by John Habberton; it was produced by Sol Lesser and directed by William A. Seiter. The following plot description is based on the authors' repeated viewings of the film.

Eddie plays Harry Burton, a wealthy bachelor and a noted authority on the subject of child rearing. When he announces to his sister, Helen Lawrence (Claire Adams), that he will be staying at her palatial home for an extended period of time, she sees this as an opportunity to get away with her husband, Tom (Richard Tucker). Helen and Tom have two small daughters, Toddie (Baby Peggy) and Budge (Jeanne Carpenter). They are nice little girls, but they are all but bursting with the endless curiosity and unfocused energy of extreme youth. What the vacationing couple does not realize is that Harry has no real knowledge of youngsters—he's not even particularly fond of them. The only reason he authored *How to Rear Children* is that his boss ordered him to. Reluctantly taking on the job of babysitter for his nieces, things

---

63   *The Real Tinsel*, p. 229.

Eddie, Clara Bow, and Baby Peggy in a scene from Helen's Babies *(1924).*
Author's Collection

do not proceed smoothly. The girls go through his belongings and take foolish risks that lead to trouble.

Thoroughly exasperated, Uncle Harry writes a scathing letter to his sister and brother-in-law in which he threatens to abandon the girls unless the parents return home immediately. Before he mails this blistering missive, he is interrupted by a visit from a neighbor named Alice (the irresistible Clara Bow, before she was dubbed Hollywood's "It" Girl). An admirer of his writings on children, she invites him to her home for dinner. Smitten with this vivacious young woman, Harry shreds the letter and sets about to win her affections. He arrives at her door, a box of flowers in hand. At least, that's what he *thinks* is in the box. Unbeknownst to him, Toddie had secretly replaced the flowers with her doll. When Alice opens the box, she is delighted with what she perceives as a comical gesture. As Harry flirts with Alice, his charges run away to follow a stray dog. When word of their absence reaches them, Harry and Alice begin a frantic search. Meanwhile, the girls are playing with the dog on some railroad tracks and are almost hit by an oncoming train. Two passengers on that train are the returning Helen and Tom. Later, back in their own home, the distraught parents vent their rage onto Harry. It is obvious, however, that the girls are extremely fond of their uncle. Suffused with tenderness, Harry picks up both children and takes them upstairs to tuck them in for the night. At one point, Toddie slips out of bed and opens the door to her room. Standing there are Harry and Alice, locked in an embrace.

Eddie, Clara Bow, and Baby Peggy had a wonderful rapport, both on and offscreen. When asked his opinion of his youthful co-star, Eddie replied, "How could I help smiling? She was only three years old!"[64] When we asked our good friend Diana Serra Cary—the former child star known as Baby Peggy—what she remembered about working with Eddie, she cheerfully stated that she liked him very much. "He treated me as a fellow professional, not as a child," she said.[65]

In 1927, one of the titans of the film industry, Harold Lloyd, decided to invest in Eddie. He had seen his work and felt he would be ideal in two-reel shorts. Unlike some comedies of that

---

64   Stein, p. 33. Incidentally, Baby Peggy was five, not three, when she appeared in *Helen's Babies*. She was born on October 29, 1918. She died at the age of 101, on February 24, 2020.

65   Telephone conversation with Diana Serra Cary, n.d.

time, these would not involve pie-throwing slapstick. As William Fraser, president of Lloyd's Hollywood Productions, states in the April 23, 1927, issue of *Exhibitors Herald* : "Horton is best in the situation-gag of comedy, and that is the kind of stories he will be given."[66] Eddie was in excellent hands. Lloyd hired only the best gagmen, crew members, and stock company players. Visually speaking, the films are an absolute treat, on par with the stunning transfers of the box set of Harold Lloyd's features, which was put out by the late star's estate in the early 2000s. According to Eddie, "They paid me to make one every month, then help for a month in preparing the next."[67] It's true : he did not approach these films as a mere actor; he had definite ideas about the types of stories that would best showcase his burgeoning screen character, that of a well-meaning but not overly bright fellow who finds himself in embarrassing predicaments.[68]

"One of the two-reelers was a Western, my idea," Eddie recalled. "I didn't write it, but I gave them the idea. I would be a grown-up Little Lord Fauntleroy, who lives with my two very well-to-do aunts. But I'm Ferdie, who is very nervous. I mustn't play with rough people and mustn't make noises on the street. I'm leading a very cloistered, very sheltered life, very snooty, very snobby, wearing glorious clothes. Finally, my aunts find out that I have been visiting a soda fountain where I have been known to sit and talk to a blonde. So something has to be done. They're going to send Ferdie

---

66	Quoted in Steve Massa, *Lame Brains* and *Lunatics 2* (Orlando, FL: BearManor Media), 2022.
67	Stein, p. 33.
68	That description could also apply to the characters played by Charley Chase.

out to their brother's in the far West. Their brother has a hotel out in Death Valley or Devil's Gulch, way out in Colorado, and they think it would make a man out of me to go there. Well, I get out there and I discover that this hotel is a nightclub, the likes of which has never before been seen—all these women with no clothes on. I'm a little bit shocked, but I assume that as soon as they know I'm annoyed, they'll stop all that piano playing. I want to see the proprietor. Now, the proprietor is the bad man of the comedy. I go into his office in the back of a shack and there is this fellow wearing a frock and combing his wavy hair. I take one look at him, and I say, 'I'm sorry, sir, but you can never wear a tie like that with that kind of coat.' So I rip off his tie, take off my bow tie and put it around his neck, and get behind him to tie a bow. Well, all this fellow's life he'd been trying to tie a bow tie and he's never been able to. So he and I are buddies right then. Finally, I get the cowboys to take some baths, and I get them to smoke tailor-made cigarettes. And soon I'm out on a horse and enjoying the cowboy life too."[69]

That film, *Find the King* (1927), was completed, with a number of changes to the above scenario. There are seven additional titles. Eddie had a theory as to why Harold Lloyd authorized the making of these two-reel shorts in the first place : "Possibly Lloyd wanted his regular crew kept intact or working—he had to pay them—while he took a long vacation."[70] Eddie was dismissive of the shorts, stating, "They were never released because the talkies arrived."[71]

---

69   *The Real Tinsel,* pp. 232–233.
70   Stein, pp. 33–34.
71   Ibid., p. 33.

In fact, the films *were* released, but they were upstaged by a series of clunky, experimental talkies. It would be nearly a century before the Horton two-reelers finally achieved some recognition. This was due to the combined efforts of Ben Model and Steve Massa. Previously unseen silent films, both comedies and dramas, are released on DVD through Model's label, Undercrank Productions. The digital restoration of these films, in tandem with the Library of Congress, is funded by online kickstarter campaigns, to which scores of silent film aficionados donate. In all the projects of this nature that Undercrank has taken on, the Edward Everett Horton two-reelers received the most interest and were financed in record time. The two-disc set was released in 2021 and has been deservedly praised by the silent film community.

Jeremy Carr, who teaches film studies at Arizona State University in Tempe, has written an insightful treatise on this series of short films. Entitled "There Seems to Be a Slight Mistake," it was originally published in *Film International Magazine*, to correspond with the DVD set's release. With Jeremy's kind consent (and that of his editor, Matt Sorrento), we herewith present excerpts from his fine monograph.

> *No Publicity*, from 1927, was directed by N. T. Barrows and features Horton as a newspaper photographer tasked with capturing a snapshot of young socialite Sally Lawrence (Ruth Dwyer, who here and in 1928's *Scrambled Weddings* is quite striking). Sally is game, but her snooty companions, gathered in "Snob-haven," are less keen on the exposure. This is especially the case for Sally's dowager aunt, played to stuffy perfection by Josephine Crowell (she'll also reappear in this collection). Horton's covert

Eddie the photographer in No Publicity *(1927). Steve Massa*

maneuverings are thwarted at every turn, and he eventually finds himself donning the guise of a dowdy temperance speaker brought in to lecture on "What is wrong with our girls?" Rather convincing in the part (drag was a staple of Horton's early comedy), he stumbles and sweats his way through the impromptu speech, trying to appease the liberated Sally as well as the conservative ladies assembled for the luncheon. And of course, the real orator ultimately shows up.

One foil after another interferes with Horton's assignment in *No Publicity*, but as in several of these films, he soldiers on, just trying to do his job. He relies on a determined resourcefulness that defines his characters throughout this collection, and this cleverness and affinity for comically fruitful improvisation likewise occur in *Find the King*, directed by J.A. Howe and also released in 1927. Horton and Howe begin by having some fun at the expense of another blue-blood crowd, as Horton's wealthy, strait-laced aunts can't quite come to terms with their distracted nephew preoccupied with card tricks. But from this aris-

In Dad's Choice *(1928), Eddie fails to make a favorable impression on his future mother-in-law, played with deft comic skill by Canadian-born actress Josephine Crowell (1859–1932).*
Steve Massa

tocratic pitch, the film transitions to a wild west setting as Horton is, rather unsuitably, sent off to tend to some family business, namely a gambling hall. Though he clearly doesn't belong in this rowdy saloon (merely *looking* out of place is part of Horton's fundamental shtick), the venue is much more fun for the bemused young man, but it's also more dangerous than he reckoned. Horton's natural impudence and best of intentions allow him to bluff his way through another madcap milieu, and thanks to the skill of his sleight of hand, he remains knowingly prudent and surprisingly slick.

Howe also directed Horton in *Dad's Choice*, from 1928, where the star attempts to woo Sharon Lynn. Starting off in an urban environment teeming with mass chaos, the film is ripe for the mistaken identities and amusingly erroneous assumptions that are an additional hallmark of these collected shorts. Routinely flustered, Horton manages his way through seemingly unavoidable mishaps and owing to some perceptive staging by Howe, he overcomes a series of gags shrewdly introduced and extended until the final payoff (an uncooperative dog steals the show during one such skit). With multiple locations arrayed as the film continues, including a vehicular pursuit that is well-filmed but fairly standard in terms of silent comedy, resulting in a nimbly hectic mobile marriage, *Dad's Choice* is somewhat less consistent in its dispersal of humor, whereas *Behind the Counter* (also from 1928 and directed by Howe) is, by comparison, dependent on a central, fertile setting, a narrative context in which Horton performs best. Appearing alongside Dorothy Dwan and Oscar Smith, Horton is an anxious and generally hapless department store employee, and the retail backdrop is skillfully established to generate any number of havoc-inducing calamities. *Behind the Counter* also has the most prominent bit of camera movement in these collected films, a bold visual gesture that comes out of nowhere and is never again repeated, and it boasts a genuinely surreal touch as a mannequin head begins to melt and misshapen on a radiator, sending Horton and company into a tizzy as they confront real burglars and imagined ghosts.

Horton is primarily outdoors for 1928's *Horse Shy* and *Vacation Waves*. In the former, he is exceptionally bumbling as he prepares for a fox hunt, despite an aversion to horses (he is predictably assigned the most rambunctious one), and his comedy is exceptionally physical, combatting everything from an ordinary saddle to a fitful mechanical apparatus. With the same high production values evident in all eight films, *Horse Shy* even features some low-key special effects, which are arguably funnier because of their obvious simplicity. In *Vacation Waves*, Horton simply wants to get away for a fishing trip, but like the meddlesome wildlife in *Horse Shy*, here he is continually obstructed by his wife's mother and younger brother. Even after he finally manages to board his boat, no easy task in itself and another of Horton's more persuasively

In a scene cut from the release print of Horse Shy *(1928),
Eddie attempts to prepare himself for his first ride on a horse.
Co-stars William Gillespie and Anita Cavalier stop by to offer
support.* Steve Massa

physical endeavors, he is routed by the film's prop-infused disruptions.

"Pardon me, there seems to be a slight mistake." This quote from *Scrambled Weddings* could well have been applied to any of these assembled films, as Horton is regularly the victim of diverting misunderstandings and false interpretations. Such is the case at the very beginning of *Scrambled Weddings*, where Horton discovers the prone body of his friend on the floor, a gun placed next to the apparent corpse. Not to worry, though, he's just drunk. And the gun? It's just a cigarette holder. Horton again finds himself in a twisted romantic entanglement, thanks in part to this irresponsible buddy of his, and as a young bachelor in love, the appearance of Horton, born in 1886, is itself somewhat incongruous. But that works fine, and to comedic effect, as this embattled man-child attempts to rectify the amorously convoluted state of affairs with his characteristic, albeit haphazard, quick thinking.

The films collected for this set would have been lost if not for Harold Lloyd, who kept the negatives in his vault. They were later donated and preserved by the Library of Congress but the decomposition still apparent in *Scrambled Weddings* and the last film featured, 1928's *Call Again*, remains a minor impediment — in *Call Again*, it's so bad that a title card is inserted to explain a pivotal plot point, obscured by the decay. Regardless, this impurity doesn't prevent the film from advancing a standout sequence in which Horton, on his way to meet his girlfriend, follows an older lady who also intends to board the same bus. She mistakes his trailing for corrupt stalking and the hilarious sequence alone would have been worthy of an entire short.

Eddie's silent films, although well done and entertaining, do not represent the actor at his optimum. We appreciate his prowess at pantomime and his surprising agility, but we miss that distinctive voice. Fortunately, he was at the perfect age and had the precise tools needed for the coming apex of his career.

ACT II

Scene 1: The Talkies

Like most of his fellow actors who left the East Coast for the West, Eddie fell prey to the warm embrace of Southern California. What may well be the best investment of his life, he purchased a twenty-two-acre parcel in the San Fernando Valley, at 5521 Amestoy Avenue, in the district of Encino. Eddie shared his rather unusual vision of the house with an architect : "It should give the suggestion that it was a very old manor house that different families, through the years, have added onto while attempting to keep the architecture about the same, but not doing it too successfully."[72]

The colonial house was huge, with seventeen rooms and fourteen working fireplaces. A number of Eddie's relatives resided in California. As he liked to say, "Take my relatives out of California and what have you got?"[73] Eddie was generous with his family. His mother, his brother George, and his sister Hannabelle would live

---

72   James Reid, "Lord of Belleigh Acres," *Motion Picture Magazine* (July 1937).
73   Irwin.

The ranch house at Belleigh Acres.

Eddie and one of his dogs at home, c. 1928. Throughout his life, Eddie had many dogs and just as many cats.

Both photos are courtesy of The Edward Everett Horton Collection

on the estate, which he dubbed Belleigh (pronounced *belly*) Acres, for the rest of their lives.

While Eddie was contentedly nesting in the Hollywood landscape, the industry itself was in a state of chaos. Sound had been introduced to the movies. *The Jazz Singer* (1927), a part-talkie starring Al Jolson, is often credited as the first sound movie. It was not, but it was significant in the industry's transition. At one point in that film, Jolson ad-libs some dialogue, particularly in the scene with Eugenie Besserer, the actress playing his mother. The spontaneity of these offhanded remarks struck a chord with audiences, giving them a foretaste of dialogue's potential in films.[74] Within two years' time, sound would be the industry standard.

That's all well and good, but what was to become of the gods and goddesses of the silent screen? Hearing them speak—perhaps with a lisp or a squeaky voice or a Jersey shore accent—would instantly turn them into mere mortals, no different than those paying a quarter to see them. In addition, the early sound-on-disc recordings were generally quite poor, reproducing only the higher registers of a star's voice. The first contract players to receive their walking papers were those whose accents reflected their foreign birthplaces : Pola Negri (Poland), Karl Dane (Denmark), and Vilma Bánky (Austria-Hungary), among others. Of course, there were those individuals whose voices broadened their appeal, so perfectly matched were they with their already-established personas. Laurel

---

74   Deaf though he was, Thomas Edison (1847–1931) wanted his movies to talk from the outset, in the 1890s. At this, the inventor's genius failed him: his talking picture device never worked properly. D.W. Griffith (1875–1948), known as "The Father of Film," successfully employed synchronized sound sequences in his 1921 feature *Dream Street*, released six years before *The Jazz Singer.*

& Hardy come to mind, as do Greta Garbo, Boris Karloff, Joan Crawford, Billy Haines, Anna May Wong, Gloria Swanson, Erich von Stroheim, Wallace Beery, Lon Chaney, Buster Keaton, Norma Shearer, W.C. Fields, Marie Dressler, and of course, Rin-Tin-Tin. Master pantomimist Charlie Chaplin simply refused to join the talkie revolution. His 1931 film, *City Lights*, was silent with a synchronized score and sound effects. Another director who defied the trend of endless dialogue was F.W. Murnau, who has gained a cult following for his 1922 German Expressionist film of *Nosferatu*. Like *City Lights*, Murnau's silent film *Tabu : A Story of the South Seas*, was released in 1931, just a few days before the forty-two-year-old filmmaker was killed in an automobile accident.

Earlier in our narrative, Eddie commented that the movie industry had little use for stage actors. That was *then*. Now, with sound being all the rage, Broadway performers were being lured away from the theatres of the East to sign with the studios of the West. Actors, after all, should know how to speak, and speak properly. Having been on the stage since 1909, Eddie was about to prove once more that he was in the right profession at the right time. And indeed, the addition of sound in motion pictures would be of incalculable benefit to his career.

The truth is, acting in silent films made Eddie uncomfortable. "How I longed to talk!" he said. "Speech became more dear to me every single moment. While playing before the cameras, I would think of the most engaging lines to say, and I just *had* to *speak!*"[75] His voice, which was soft, hesitant, and slightly effeminate— "a

---

75   Stein, quoting from Eddie's 1929 article in *Theatre Magazine*, p. 34.

sort of a choir boy's voice,"[76] as he described it—coupled with perfect diction and grammar—was ideal for the prissy characters he played. His theatrical training had wiped out any trace of his original Brooklynese.

"I developed a certain method of speaking, a certain method of enunciation," he explained. "I can speak pure Castilian Brooklynese if I have to, but you don't hear it very often, you hear 'dem bums,' but that's not Brooklynese. The Brooklynese of my day was derived from the Dutch umlaut sound. You had a kind of saying that illustrates how it goes, you see? 'I soitenly blew out gravy. It's a boid; she lives on Thoity-Second street, next to Thoity-Thoid." I learned to speak poifect, er *perfect*, English at the university. But

Eddie shushes his co-star May McAvoy in the early talkie The Terror *(1928).* Steve Massa

76   Noble interview, 1969.

that's the soft sound, the Brooklyn of today isn't the real Brooklyn. The real Brooklyn is sort of a forgotten language, like Aramaic."[77]

The first all-talking feature was *The Lights of New York* (1928), starring May McAvoy. Eddie was cast in the *second* all-talking picture, a six-reel Warner Bros. / Vitaphone sound-on-disc production called *The Terror*, also starring May McAvoy. The plot involves a killer who inhabits an old English country house that now serves as an inn. The guests are deeply disturbed by some mysterious noises, including eerie organ music. A murder occurs and mayhem reigns late into the night, ultimately leading to the discovery of The Terror's true identity. The film received mixed reviews in America and disastrous ones when it was released in the United Kingdom three months later. British reporter John MacCormac wrote in a piece for *The New York Times*:

> The universal opinion of London critics is that "The Terror" is so bad that it is almost suicidal. [Those who have seen it] claim that it is monotonous, slow, dragging, fatiguing and boring, and I am not sure that I do not in large measure agree with them. What is more important, Edgar Wallace, who wrote the film, seems to agree with them also. "Well," was his comment, "I have never thought the talkies would be a serious rival to the stage."[78]

For many seasoned moviegoers, accustomed to full orchestras providing live musical accompaniment, talkies were at best a novelty and no real threat to silent films. As many theatres had yet to be wired for sound, silent versions of most major releases were also made available.

---

77   Ibid.
78   John MacCormac, "The Terror" [review], *New York Times*, November 18, 1928.

"There had been one or two little [sound] two-reelers before them, and I was in one of those [*Miss Information*] with Lois Wilson," said Eddie. "The producers didn't seem to know what they had, since *The Jazz Singer*, which was really the *third* feature-length [part-] talkie, hadn't come out yet. In those days, there was no boom that followed you all around. The microphones hung down, all wrapped around with material to make them look like part of the backdrop. We had three or four cameras. In a great big ensemble scene these cameras were sort of like coffins with tarpaulins so that you couldn't hear the buzz of the camera. They were on turnstiles or something like that. We were instructed not to talk until we felt ourselves in the center of the camera. So the scene would go around : 'You see this man?'… Camera turns … 'Yes' … Camera turns … 'You know what happened?' … Camera … 'No' … Camera … 'Killed' … Camera … 'What?' … Camera … 'Who did it?' … Camera. Of course, then they took it all and cut it up and put it together again. We didn't think anything could be better than that. It was the last word in progress.

"Making pictures was quite exciting in those days because it was a brand-new field. It was not like the theatre, but it was exciting because everybody was excited. Along came *The Jazz Singer*, and that was the beginning of history. The other two, somehow, were thought to be tricks. But Jolson started it. I've been at this business ever since."[79]

By 1930, sound-on-film recording had improved substantially over earlier attempts. Filmmakers like Lewis Milestone

---

79   *The Real Tinsel*, pp. 227–228.

A sound stage at the Vitaphone studio (formerly Vitagraph), Brooklyn, New York, c. 1929. Author's collection

began experimenting with new techniques to heighten the emotional impact of a given scene. It was at this critical period when Milestone tackled the difficult topic of the recent world war in his 152-minute epic, *All Quiet on the Western Front*. Critics raved about Milestone's directorial genius, adding that Arthur Edeson's brilliant camera work and C. Roy Hunter's expert recordings of the sounds of war placed the viewer smack in the middle of the battlefield. The Academy of Motion Picture Arts and Sciences named *All Quiet on the Western Front* the Best Picture of 1930; Lewis Milestone won the Oscar for Best Director.

Producer Howard Hughes was so impressed by Milestone's accomplishment that he asked him to direct an adaptation of *The Front Page*, Ben Hecht and Charles MacArthur's hit 1928 Broadway play. The resulting film perfectly captures the gritty behind-the-scenes machinations of a prominent Chicago newspaper during the Prohibition era. The superb ensemble cast is headed by Adolphe Menjou as Walter Burns, the paper's bellicose editor-in-chief. His ace reporter, Hildy Johnson (Pat O'Brien), has gone soft: he's planning to marry some dame, in this case his sweet-natured fiancée, Peggy Grant (Mary Brian). The manipulative Burns will stop at nothing to prevent the nuptials from taking place. There is a suspenseful subplot involving a pathetic little white man named Earl Williams (George E. Stone), who is to be hanged for having killed a black cop. Williams has an impassioned supporter in streetwalker Molly Malloy (Mae Clarke). The supporting cast features such seasoned character actors as Slim Summerville, Frank McHugh, and Walter Catlett. Eddie, who was personally requested for the movie by Milestone, plays Roy V. Bensinger, an effete poet who reluctantly shares the newsroom with the gruff, cynical reporters. It is in Bensinger's rolltop desk that a wounded Earl Williams hides following a jailbreak. *The Front Page* remains a remarkable film, with its crackling dialogue and literal gallows humor. It also has one of the greatest closing lines in theatre history. The story has been revived, and at times reimagined, most successfully by Howard Hawks as *His Girl Friday* (1940), but the original continues to hold up well. And thus far, no actor has bettered Eddie's performance as the fussy Bensinger.

Scene 2 : The Play's the Thing

Eddie may have been busy cranking out one film after another, but his true interest remained with the stage. Using his experience from the Majestic, he also managed the Hollywood Playhouse. It was presided over by acting coach Neely Dickson. Described by *Modern Screen Magazine* in 1940, the playhouse was "in a wooden building, an overgrown barn once used by Mae West's manager for trying out new plays. Inside stretch[es] a large stage and 190 seats. Inside, also, stretches Miss Neely Dickson, elderly and bespectacled, and tired after a long day of work. The office walls surrounding Miss Dickson are thick with old photos of men like Conrad Nagel, Lawrence Tibbett, [and] Edward Everett Horton, who received their initial career impetus from her."[80]

With years of experience at both the front and back of the house, Eddie was well prepared to be a theatre manager. "I didn't have any money," he said, "but I had courage and faith in myself. I leased the Vine Street Theatre."[81] He later moved his productions to the Majestic, where he had worked for years for Thomas Wilkes. Eddie also engaged his brother Winter as his manager and co-producer. Due to Eddie's guidance, the Majestic became one of the most successful live venues of its time. Kyle Crichton wrote of Eddie in the July 18, 1936, issue of *Collier's* :

> Since becoming his own master, he has not presented one play which was in any way a compromise with local taste. Every Horton vehicle has been a play sound of construction, skillful of execution and intelligent of subject

---

80　*Modern Screen Magazine*, 1940.
81　Stein, p. 34.

matter, and the production on his stage is always evident of meticulous care and knowledge. Only Horton has ever been able to make Los Angeles turn out for Shaw and this feat was accomplished when he presented "Arms and the Man."[82]

Eddie did not turn his back on comedies. He presented several of the farces he had played during his stock company days, and headlined revivals of such favorites as *Clarence* and *The Nervous Wreck*. There were also West Coast premieres of Broadway shows, including *Private Lives*, which Noël Coward personally granted Eddie permission to stage in Los Angeles.

"I was going to do a play called *Her Cardboard Lover* in my own theatre now, acting *and* directing," he explained. "I was wishing for a certain type of leading woman, someone very patrician and elegant. A charming woman did come down to see me. She had been playing the lead in Denver. She and her husband had just arrived. She said, 'Mister Horton, I've never played comedy. I've played *Six Characters in Search of an Author* in New York.' I said, 'I think you'll be delightful in this part.' Her name was Florence Eldridge; she was great in the part, oh just great. Her husband was Freddie March, who eventually got a chance to do *The Royal Family* at another theatre [the El Capitan, operated by Franklin Pangborn], playing the [John] Barrymore part and playing it so much better than Barrymore. He was immediately put under contract and went right on up and up and up."[83]

---

82 *Collier's*, July 18, 1936.

83 *The Real Tinsel*, p. 229. Born in Racine, Wisconsin, Fredric March (1897–1975) was one of the screen's most dependable actors. He was the recipient of two Academy Awards, one for his vivid portrayals of *Dr. Jekyll and Mr. Hyde* (1931) and for his affecting role as a mature World War II veteran in *The Best Years of Our Lives* (1946).

Florence Eldridge enjoyed working with Eddie and, in time, the two became close friends. She was the lead in his production of *Among the Married*, a comedy by Vincent Lawrence. In the casting phase, Florence suggested a friend of hers as the second female lead. She was a twenty-two-year-old dark-haired beauty named Mary Astor. Eddie listened to her read a few lines of dialogue and hired her on the spot. As Astor wrote in her autobiography :

> I was a silent actress, and I had almost a year of *not* being the busiest, highest-priced leading woman in the movies. My pride had taken a beating. However, within a week of being in Eddie's production, I had offers from studios that had previously turned me down.[84]

Various actresses of the silent screen—including Marie Prevost, Lois Wilson, and Laura La Plante—were given the opportunity in Eddie's productions to prove they had good speaking voices and that there was a place for them in the talkies. While casting a production of Ferenc Molnar's *The Swan*, Eddie needed someone with a pronounced comic presence to play the Queen's sister. Actress Adele Ritchie heard about this and approached Eddie. "I hoped she wasn't going to ask me for the part," he recalled. "She just wasn't the type, and I didn't know how to turn her down. But anyway, she said, 'Eddie, would you let a friend of mine try out for the part?'"

Her friend was Marie Dressler.

---

84   Mary Astor, *My Story: An Autobiography* (Garden City, NY: Doubleday & Co., 1959).

"Well, of course, I knew Miss Dressler—why, who could forget *Tillie's Punctured Romance*?[85] Miss Dressler did an excellent job [in *The Swan*]—and as soon as she got an offer to be in sound films, she left the company flat. She also told the press and anyone who would listen that she had been discovered for her big comeback in films 'in a small Los Angeles stock company.' *Small stock company, nothing*! Why, it was the most important theatre in California!"[86]

"Prophet of Honor," an article in *Picture Play Magazine* dated October 1930, paid tribute to Eddie for presenting examples of the legitimate theatre to what was basically a town of farms and churches. According to the article's author, Margaret Reid, the Edward Everett Horton "known to picture fans is a faint, adulterated shadow of the Horton who reigns over The Majestic Theatre on Ninth and Broadway in Los Angeles. He is to our village what Alfred Lunt is to New York."[87]

No matter how lauded one is by the public, there is still that nagging desire to receive approval from key figures in one's past. For Eddie, that individual was his first boss, his mentor and idol Louis Mann. The Broadway star was in Los Angeles just long enough to attend one of Eddie's performances. After the show, Eddie waited impatiently to hear his reaction.

---

85   *Tillie's Punctured Romance* (1914) is the first feature-length slapstick comedy, produced and directed by Mack Sennett for the Keystone Film Company, and starring Marie Dressler (1869–1933). The six-reel film, which also starred Charlie Chaplin (1889–1977) and Mabel Normand (1893–1930), was based on Dressler's Broadway musical *Tillie's Nightmare*.

86   Stein, pp. 35–36.

87   *Picture-Play Magazine*, October 1930.

Mann cleared his throat. "The chandelier in the second act was crooked and, as a one-time stage manager, you should have seen to it that it was straightened." Then, almost as an afterthought, he said he liked the production.[88]

When a young Boris Karloff asked the great character star Lon Chaney for advice on how to succeed in pictures, Chaney's answer was "Do something that few others would care to do, and then do it better than anyone else."[89] Having a specialty was vital, whether in drama or comedy. Ed Wynn, billed as "The Perfect Fool," had his high-pitched giggle. Jack Benny got more laughs by pausing than most comedians do by talking. Billy Gilbert made his name with a hilarious sneezing routine. Eddie's gimmick was that long-established comic device known as the double-take. The rather prosaic definition of a *double-take* is "an actor's reaction to something, followed by a delayed, more extreme reaction." Just imagine a baggy-pants comedian seeing an alligator or a pretty girl. He looks once perfunctorily, and then looks again, this time with a snap of the neck. After that, he will likely run away from or run toward what he just saw. Eddie's version of the double-take was far more subtle. It was about his character's delayed reaction to something that is said to him. So distracted is he by the slightest thing that when someone makes an untoward statement, he is initially smiling and nodding in agreement; then, when his addled brain catches up to the true meaning behind the statement, he gives his

---

88   Stein, p. 35.
89   *Boris Karloff: The Man Behind the Monster* (2021). Sara Karloff relates the story involving Lon Chaney imparting advice to her father.

critic a second look, a double-take—and his smile is replaced by a look of peevishness. He even perfected what he called "The Verbal Double-Take." British interviewer Peter Noble, a great admirer of Eddie's comedic techniques, once asked him for a demonstration, for which he provided the setup.

> **Noble.** Edward Everett Horton, I think your performances are terribly disappointing, and I must say I don't think you have a great deal of talent.

> **Eddie.** (*Pleasantly*) Really? Well, I uh … (*suddenly cognizant*) Oh, *really?*

> **Noble.** (*Laughing appreciatively*) *That's* what I mean![90]

Scene 3 : Radio

By 1932, the world was mired in the Great Depression. At the outset, 25 percent of America's wage earners were out of work, while millions of others faced a steep reduction in pay. Everyone, it seemed, was dead broke. Everyone, that is, except Eddie, who was rolling in dough. Listening to him boast about the lucrative nature of his career, the authors were reminded of the titular, gold-hoarding character in George Eliot's 1861 novel, *Silas Marner*. It therefore came as a revelation to us when we unearthed a newspaper article from 1934, written by the reliable Hollywood correspondent for *The Oregonian*, Mary Canel. Having gotten to know Eddie through her interviews with him, she wrote the following.

> Edward Everett Horton is known as one of the most charitable actors in the film colony. It's not at all uncommon for him to get excited about some needy case that's

---

90 Noble interview, 1969.

suddenly come to his attention and to leave the company and director waiting while he walks off the set to arrange for his chauffeur to take money and gifts to the people in need. This is one subject Mr. Horton declines to discuss, and [no] word of his numerous charities was gained from co-workers on his many pictures.[91]

Network radio became a national craze during the 1930s. It was, after all, a source for news and entertainment, and what's more, it was free! Rather primitive in its early years, the medium improved exponentially, offering big-name entertainers, full orchestras emanating from hotel ballrooms, compelling stories, ingenious sound effects, and a wide variety of specialized programming. In the words of radio's great wit, Fred Allen :

> Radio in the '30s was a calm and tranquil medium. Oleaginous-voiced announcers smoothly purred their commercial copy into the microphones enunciating each lubricated syllable. Tony Wons was cooing his soothing poems. Bedtime stories were popular. Radio was one unruffled day from Cheerio in the early morning through to Music to Read By at midnight. Radio was fraught with politeness. No voice was ever raised in public.[92]

Once again, Eddie's understated humor was hand-in-glove with the style of the times. Listeners had the attention spans then to sit in an easy chair, light up a Lucky, and listen to *Mercury Theatre on the Air*, hosted by *wunderkind* Orson Welles and featuring audio dramatizations of classic works of literature. There were musical programs, featuring Rudy Vallée, Kate Smith, Russ Columbo, Al Jolson, and the world's first multi-media star, Bing Crosby. There

---

91   Mary Canel, *The Oregonian*, September 30, 1934.
92   Fred Allen, *Treadmill to Oblivion* (Boston: Little, Brown, 1954).

were soap operas with organ interludes, mysteries, serials, and pro-gramming geared to children, housewives, and farmers. Everyday citizens became better acquainted with their patriarchal president, Franklin Delano Roosevelt, by way of his famous "Fireside Chats." And, most wonderful of all, there were the comedies, including *The Jack Benny Program*, *The Fred Allen Show*, *The Bob Hope Pepsodent Show*, and *The Chase & Sanborn Hour* with Edgar Bergen & Char-lie McCarthy. Eddie appeared on many such programs, bringing his fussbudget movie character to the airwaves.

In the course of his career, Eddie impressed many of his col-leagues, some of whom were later compelled to mention him prominently in their memoirs. Mary Jane Higby, a soap opera star

Broadcasting on NBC Radio with (left to right) James Cagney, Rudy Vallée, and Carmel Myers, October 25, 1934. Jordan R. Young

whose career dates back to 1932, devoted several pages to him in her 1968 book, *Tune in Tomorrow*. Her first big break came when she landed an audition to appear opposite Eddie on *The Shell Show*. The twenty-three-year-old actress awakened on the day of the appointment with a runny nose and a sore throat. Never once did she consider cancelling. If she got the job it would pay $25, money she desperately needed. One positive side-effect of the cold was that it had added a husky quality to her usually "light, silvery voice."[93] She also had the benefit of being coached in the ways of comedy by her father, a professional, albeit unemployed, actor. She was a bit starstruck when she was informed that she would be doing the reading with Edward Everett Horton, whom she enjoyed very much. The scene they would be performing was from *Private Lives*. Following her reading, Eddie rewarded her by saying, "Splendid, splendid" in "that charming way of his." Seated in an anteroom, Mary Jane overheard Eddie and two of the agency men behind closed doors, conferring about which of the aspirants should get the job. At one point, Eddie said firmly, "You'll never get a contralto quality like the one you just heard—a beautiful voice—good actress, too."

"Oh, that dear, dear man," Mary Jane said to herself. She was, however, concerned that her "contralto quality" was as temporary as her cold. But there *was* the matter of that $25 … and, fortunately, she got the job. There followed many run-throughs of the script : "He liked to rehearse," she said.[94] When the night of the broad-

<hr>

93   Mary Jane Higby, *Tune in Tomorrow* (New York: Cowles, 1968).
94   Ibid.

cast arrived, Eddie and his discovery were seated in the performers' dressing room, reading over their lines. In the distance, they could hear George Stoll's orchestra begin to play the show's theme. About twenty minutes later, one of the producers stuck his head in the door and said, "You'd better come out now; your spot's coming up." Eddie, feeling confident, held up his script and said to his co-star, "Well, we won't need this, will we?" and then tossed it aside. Not wishing to contradict him, she followed suit. As they walked toward the microphone, she began to shake. Violently. If she blew this opportunity, she knew, her career would die aborning.

> When I opened my mouth, I found that my laryngitic baritone had risen to a nasal whine. My head felt hot and stuffy and the huge arc lights were making rainbows before my runny eyes. I was shivering with cold and the terror of forgetting my lines. The minute Mr. Horton began to speak, however, everything came right with my world. He was such a surefooted actor, I knew that no matter what happened he could bring the thing off. It was like a strong, steadying hand. Halfway through the skit a wave of panic broke over me again. The words sounded unfamiliar. I was completely lost. Then Mr. Horton looked right at me and threw me a cue that I recognized as part of the script. I replied with my line, and we went on. He had been ad-libbing and with fine effect. His digressions did not interrupt the flow of a well-written scene by Noël Coward. The scene had already been so tortured and truncated to fit into radio's arbitrary time pattern that any inspiration breathed into it from any source could act only as a restorative.[95]

Mary Jane Higby built on this inauspicious beginning a wonderful career as a soap opera queen, appearing regularly on *Our Gal*

---

95   Ibid.

Sunday, *Stella Dallas*, and *John's Other Wife*. She also considered herself fortunate when she was able to work with Eddie again. One of the many aspects of his acting prowess forever amazed her:

> He didn't change the little sketches, but he embroidered around them and always with good, solid laughs as a result. He never left the other actors up in the air. He changed things only within his own speeches, and always came back solidly with the cue. He also had what seemed to be a built-in time mechanism. In the programs I played with him afterward we never once ran over or under the allotted time. In those early days of radio he was one of the big names most in demand.[96]

Scene 4 : Pre- and Post-Code Hollywood

In Hollywood, an actor can hardly be considered established unless he has enemies, or at least dissenters. Although he was most likely unaware of it, one of Eddie's adversaries was RKO's executive sales manager, Ned Depinet. In an RKO studio memorandum, Depinet complained about David O. Selznick's insistence that Edward Everett Horton, a free-lance actor, be paid $3,500 per week for his work on *The Roar of the Dragon* (1932). According to Depinet, "Horton is not worth $3,500 per week or anything like that amount. While he is reputed to be an excellent actor, he has not five cents' worth of box office and for many people, myself among them, he does as much to ruin a picture as to help it."[97]

Fortunately, Eddie was not limited to working for RKO. Paramount was a much friendlier-seeming place, producing madcap features starring The Four Marx Brothers, Mae West, W.C. Fields,

---

96   Ibid.
97   *The AFI Catalog of Feature Films*, 1931–1939.

Jack Oakie, Burns & Allen, and Charlie Ruggles. Someone at the studio thought this was the time for a film of Lewis Caroll's youth-oriented fantasy novels *Alice's Adventures in Wonderland* and *Through the Looking Glass*, published in 1865 and 1871 respectively. They tell the tale of a twelve-year-old girl named Alice, who enters a portal wherein she encounters a series of surrealistic characters. This seemingly unfilmable story has been lensed more than fifty times, dating as far back as 1903 and as recently as 2016. Paramount's 1933 version of *Alice in Wonderland* had a screenplay by Joseph L. Mankiewicz and William Cameron Menzies, and was directed by Norman Z. McLeod.[98] The film was intended as a vehicle to feature virtually all of their contract players.—e.g., W.C. Fields as Humpty Dumpty, Cary Grant as Mock Turtle, Edna May Oliver as the Red Queen, Louise Fazenda as the White Queen, Alison Skipworth as Duchess, Sterling Holloway as Frog Footman, Richard Arlen as Cheshire Cat, Ned Sparks as Caterpillar, et al. There are *so* many guest stars, in fact, that the first four minutes of the seventy-six-minute film are taken up with identifying the players. Eddie, a bibliophile if there ever was one, was well acquainted with the original editions of the Alice books and always felt he resembled Sir John Tenniel's illustrations of The Mad Hatter. This was enough motivation for him to actively campaign, for the first and only time in his career, for a role in a film.

---

98   Norman Z. McLeod (1898–1964) is best known for directing some of the finest screen comedies of the 1930s and '40s, including the Marx Brothers' *Monkey Business* (1931) and *Horsefeathers* (1932); W.C. Fields's *It's a Gift* (1934); Cary Grant's *Topper* (1937); Danny Kaye's *The Secret Life of Walter Mitty* (1947); and Bob Hope's *The Paleface* (1948). In 1961, Rod Serling coaxed McLeod out of retirement to direct an episode of *The Twilight Zone*, "Once Upon a Time," written by Richard Matheson and starring Buster Keaton.

Eddie as The Mad Hatter in Alice in Wonderland *(1933).* Doctor Macro

Sir John Tenniel's illustration from Through the Looking Glass *(1871).*

He would come to regret it.

As he later explained, "They made everybody wear such heavy make-up and such cumbersome costumes, nobody could be identified. … Why, everyone knows I look like The Mad Hatter and Charlie Ruggles' face looks just right with little whiskers—as it is—for the March Hare. Well, they ruined the whole picture."[99]

Embodying the eponymous Alice is nineteen-year-old newcomer Charlotte Henry. Indicative of just how competitive the movie industry was even then, she was but one of seven thousand young ladies vying for the role. Unfortunately for Miss Henry, her career went down the rabbit hole along with the picture.[100]

Many mainstream films of the early thirties contain risqué themes, images, and suggestive dialogue. One especially notorious example is *Smarty* (1934), a Warner Bros. feature directed by Robert Florey and starring Warren William as Tony Wallace, Joan Blondell as his wife Vicki, and Eddie as Vernon Thorpe. The following is a summary of the sixty-five-minute film.

> Despite Tony Wallace's plans to celebrate his wife Vicki's birthday by taking her out to dinner and the theater, Vicki decides to spend the evening playing bridge with some friends, including her admirer, Vernon Thorpe. During the evening she and Tony quarrel and, exasperated, he hits her. Vernon is outraged and encourages Vicki's decision to divorce Tony, volunteering to act as her lawyer. Realizing that Vernon is in love with her, Vicki thinks the divorce is good fun, while Tony sees it as the end of his happiness. As soon as the divorce is granted, Vicki marries Vernon. She is not ready to let go of Tony, however, and invites him to

---

99 Stein, p. 37.

100 Robert J. Rhodes, "'Alice' Finds that Wonderland Proved Just a Myth, After All: Charlotte Henry, Who Tasted Fame and Fortune Six Years Ago in Child Film Fantasy, Is Trying to Convince Hollywood She Can Act," *The Times* (Hammond, Indiana), Thursday, July 28, 1939.

dinner. Meanwhile, she insists that Vernon grant her every whim. At her request, he leaves work to spend the afternoon with her at a dress shop, but when he disapproves of the dress she wants, thinking it is too revealing, she buys it anyway, intending to wear it at dinner to impress Tony. Bonnie (Joan Wheeler), a young married woman, is pursuing Tony, so he invites her to come to dinner with him. Two other friends, George (Frank McHugh) and Anita (Claire Dodd), are also invited. Tony and Bonnie arrive before Vernon, and Vicki invites Tony to her room to talk. She teases Tony until he admits that he is still in love with her. When Vernon arrives and sees that Vicki is wearing the dress he ordered her not to buy, he asks her to change her clothing. After they argue the point a while, she refuses to go to dinner at all. Their quarrel ends when Vernon slaps her, to Tony's amusement. After Tony and Bonnie leave for a nightclub, Vicki sneaks out to wait for Tony in his apartment. Her plans are somewhat thwarted when Tony brings Bonnie back with him, but when Bonnie goes into the kitchen to make some eggs, Vicki reveals her presence to Tony, telling him she has left Vernon. Meanwhile, Vernon is calling everywhere looking for his wife. When Vernon and Anita show up at Tony's, he denies that Vicki is there, but she calls them into the bedroom, where they see her wearing a bathrobe and sitting on Tony's bed. After Vernon decides to divorce her for infidelity, Tony agrees to take her back and promises to hit her if she causes him trouble in the future.[101]

Smarty, released in the United Kingdom under the more provocative title *Hit Me Again*, was considered by *The Hollywood Reporter* to be "a light, happy, irresponsible little comedy, that twinkles and grins and occasionally even gets a little slapstick. It's lots of fun

---

101   *The AFI Catalog of Feature Films*, 1931–1939.

and is as inconsequential as the foam on a beer glass."[102] Others forcefully disagreed, particularly the Catholic League of Decency. Their objection was that the film trivializes adultery, divorce, and (presumably) domestic abuse. Motion picture censorship had been an issue since 1922, a time when Hollywood was rocked by various scandals.[103] In order to protect the studios from being driven out of business for violating innumerable decency laws, a censorship czar was chosen. He was Presbyterian elder Will H. Hays, the postmaster general under former president Warren G. Harding and former head of the Republican National Committee. At an annual salary of $100,000, he would serve for twenty-five years as the president of the Motion Picture Producers and Distributors of America.

In 1930, the Hays Office published the Motion Picture Production Code, a set of rules that filmmakers were asked to follow to create clean movies for the masses. Very few in the industry took these strictures seriously. As writers and directors continued to push the proverbial envelope, the louder came the protests. Now, with the threat of a Catholic ban on the offending studio's product, the money men began to pay attention. This, after all, could hurt their profit margin. Given the choice between being censored

---

102 'Midnight Alibi' Excellent; 'Smarty' Corking Comedy, *The Hollywood Reporter*, January–June 1934—via archive.org.

103 Lon Davis, *Silent Lives*, p. 300. Popular comedian Roscoe "Fatty" Arbuckle was falsely accused of manslaughter in the death of a bit player named Virginia Rappé. It took three separate trials before Arbuckle was pronounced innocent, but the damage to his career was irreparable. Roscoe's friend Mabel Normand was the unlikely suspect in two shootings: of director William Desmond Taylor and society playboy Courtland S. Dines; both cases remain unsolved. Leading man Wallace Reid, who was seriously injured while on location, died of a morphine overdose. The heroic Reid was misleadingly branded a "drug addict."

by the government or the self-regulating Code, they chose what they believed was the lesser of two evils. On July 1, 1934, the Code officially went into effect. To enforce it, Will Hays hired a hardline Catholic and antisemite named Joseph L. Breen. Two years later, *Liberty Magazine* stated that Breen's appointment had given him "more influence in standardizing world thinking than Mussolini, Hitler, or Stalin."[104] Films like *Smarty* were out, and a more cautious approach to filmmaking was in.[105]

The Code listed three "General Principles," including : "No picture shall be produced that will lower the moral standards of those who see it. Hence the sympathy of the audience should never be thrown to the side of crime, wrongdoing, evil or sin." The Code also listed a variety of "Particular Applications," many of which applied to sexuality : no nudity, no sexual perversion, no adultery, and no miscegenation. "Scenes of Passion" were to be avoided along with any other treatments that might "stimulate the lower and baser element."[106] One taboo element of pre-Code movies involves characters who are covertly homosexual. When such a role needed to be filled, that's when a select group of actors would hear from their agents. Other, more masculine actors were unwilling to play anything but strong silent types, lest they damage their image. Eddie had no such reputation to uphold.

---

104 Tim Wu, "The Future of Free Speech," *The Chronicle of Higher Education* 57 (13), 2010.

105 With the decline of the major studios in the 1960s, filmmakers openly defied the Code. It was officially withdrawn in 1968 and replaced with the rating system, which remains in effect in 2024.

106 The Motion Picture Production Code (extract), c. 1930.

"I have my own little kingdom," he said. "I do the scavenger parts no one else wants and I get well paid for it."[107]

Historian Jordan R. Young addressed the issue of portraying stereotypical gay characters with the German-American actor Fritz Feld, who was known for slapping his mouth with the palm of his hand to create a "pop" sound. "I learned a lot from Edward Everett Horton," he said. "I imitated him many times, in my way of acting. I like the way he does things. Franklin Pangborn, Horton, and I were the only actors in Hollywood that producers could trust—we never went overboard … it's different today; they play gays too grotesque. At that time you had to be careful."[108]

Careful, indeed.

In 21st century America, two individuals of the same gender can live openly together, legally marry, and adopt children. During Eddie's lifetime, this was hardly the case. In addition to being frowned upon, particularly by religious institutions, homosexuality—even in the liberal state of California—was not legalized until 1976. Author Dan Callahan, who writes perceptively on gay themes in vintage movies, observes :

> There was always a genuine sense of panic underneath his [Horton's] technique because it was the panic of someone who is afraid of being somehow found out, for Horton was obviously not a masculine guy but he was masculine enough to pass, unlike his colleague Franklin Pangborn.[109]

---

107 "Edward Everett Horton Is Dead; Comic Character Actor Was 83 (sic). Star of Stage, Film and TV Played 'Befuddled' Role in a 60-Year Career," *New York Times*, October 1, 1970.

108 Quoted in Anthony Slide, *Eccentrics of Comedy*. (Chapter on Edward Everett Horton, pp. 57–73.) (Lanham, MD : The Scarecrow Press, 1998), pp. 62–63.

109 Dan Callahan, "Double-Takes," https ://stolenholiday.substack.com/ June 2, 2024.

Franklin Pangborn (1889–1958) was a native of Newark, New Jersey. During World War I, he served for fourteen months with the U.S. Army 312th Infantry Regiment in Europe; he was gassed and wounded in the Battle of Argonne. Following his recovery, he resumed his acting career with a successful run on Broadway. Pangborn broke into the movies in the mid-twenties, and soon found himself typecast as prissy, harassed, officious professionals, such as desk clerks, maître d's, and floorwalkers. Despite that, he was offended—and more than willing to use his fists—if any man dared question his masculinity.

Beloved by fans of screwball comedy, Pangborn's performances were often sidesplittingly hilarious. Consider the all-star pre-Code feature *International House* (1933), which is set in Wuhu, China, at a luxury hotel. A formally dressed group of guests and staff are partying on the roof when something called an autogiro lands unexpectedly in their midst. The sole passenger, a bombastic beer-drinker named Professor Henry R. Quail (W.C. Fields), yells out to no one in particular, "Hey! *Where* am I?"

A spirited woman loudly answers, "Wuuu-Huuu!"

Taking this seeming non-sequitur as flirtation, Quail says, "Woo-Hoo to you, sweetheart!" Turning his attention to the tuxedo-clad manager, Franklin Pangborn, Quail tries again : "Hey, Charlie! *Where am I?*"

"WU-HU!" Pangborn yells in a high-pitched voice.

Quail, a disgusted look on his face, removes the boutonniere from his lapel and tosses it aside, saying, "Don't let the posy fool ya!"[110]

---

110 *International House* screenplay by Francis Martin and Walter DeLeon.

Both W.C. Fields (left) and Franklin Pangborn appear to be on their best behavior in Never Give a Sucker an Even Break *(1941). Doctor Macro*

It isn't difficult to imagine Eddie in the role of the hotel manager. The biggest difference is that he would likely punctuate the scene with his signature double-take.

Eddie was, in the words of historian Anthony Slide, "the archetypal screen fusspot. … He thrived on eccentricity, nurturing it like a rare orchid."[111]

Isn't that a glorious sentence? Tony Slide, the author of more than a hundred books on film history, regularly conjectures about vintage screen actors who are either known to be gay or those he suspects of being so. Concerning Eddie, he writes :

> Edward Everett Horton never suggestively played a homosexual in any of the more than 120 films he appeared in from 1922 to 1970. Thomas Mitchell might jokingly call him "Sister" in *Lost Horizon* (1937), but that was because Horton portrayed feminine traits, not because he showed interest in other men. Horton was the quintessential sidekick, reliable as a friend or a valet, whose happiness came from worrying about and organizing the lives of his friends and employers.
>
> The closest that Horton ever came to a gay scene on screen was in the decidedly risqué 1931 feature *Reaching for the Moon*, starring Douglas Fairbanks and Bebe Daniels and directed by Edmund Goulding, a homosexual. As Fairbanks's manservant, Horton gives his master a lesson in how to make love, with Fairbanks in the female role. The two are spotted by a workman, whom Horton imperiously calls "my man," and to whom he hastens to explain what he had just witnessed. The workman responds, "I am *not* your man, and I know *what's what.*"

---

111 Slide, p. 58.

There was always something lovable about Edward Everett Horton's temper tantrums on screen, as he stamped his feet and looked suitably irritable, displaying all the mannerisms of a frustrated lover. …

Horton became known as "Hollywood's most celebrated bachelor." Asked in 1939 why he had never married, he explained, "I arouse nothing but respect, and very little of that, in the opposite sex. It is one of the crosses I bear that I never seem to inspire the cooperation on the part of designing females."[112]

Eddie played the same role, that of Nick Potter, in both the 1930 and 1938 cinematic adaptations of Philip Barry's play *Holiday*. In 1938, the *New York Times* headlined its piece on Eddie as "Hailing a New Horton."

Douglas Fairbanks Sr. (left) and Eddie in a publicity still for Reaching for the Moon, *a 1931 sound feature named for the Irving Berlin song.*
Doctor Macro

112 Ibid., pp. 59–60.

The actor developed a certain muliebrity of manner which has caused certain of the more captious among filmgoers to accuse him of effeminacy... Suddenly a new Horton is hatched, a Horton without a double-take-em to his name, without grimaces or mock shudders, a Horton with authentic dignity and, crowning wonder, a Horton married to a wife who respects his manly feelings.[113]

Comparing the films regarding Eddie's performances, Dan Callahan writes :

Horton has his guard down in the 1930 *Holiday* in the long sequence in the playroom, and he is very winning, but Cukor builds up his part in the 1938 version and lets us see many sides of his Nick Potter, professor and free spirit. He is married to Hedda Hopper in the 1930 version, which doesn't feel right, but in the 1938 version he is wed to Jean Dixon's Susan, who also works as a lecturer, and this feels like a precious glimpse of what looks like a bohemian marriage of equals where sexuality might be allowed to bend on both sides. Hepburn makes it clear that her Linda Seton is drawn strongly to Susan rather than Nick, for Susan is the dominant partner in the couple and the more politically engaged.[114]

In 1922, movie actress Patsy Ruth Miller co-starred with Eddie in a vaudeville playlet called "The Real Thing" at the Los Angeles Philharmonic Auditorium. Jeffrey L. Carrier, a writer who collaborated with the retired actress on her memoirs, told us :

As you know, Miss Miller worked with Edward Everett Horton in six films: *The Hottentot*, *The Sap*, *The Aviator* (all 1929), *Wide Open* (1930), *Lonely Wives*, and *The Great Junction Hotel* (both 1931). She liked him very much and

---

113 "Hailing a New Horton."
114 Callahan.

Hedda Hopper, a secondary player, would eventually make a name for herself as a powerful Hollywood gossip columnist. She and Eddie play a married couple in the first motion picture adaptation of Philip Barry's play Holiday *(1930).* Doctor Macro

Jean Dixon, Eddie, and Katharine Hepburn in the remake of Holiday *(1938).* Doctor Macro

Eddie and Patsy Ruth Miller in The Aviator *(1929). Jeffrey L. Carrier*

said they got along exceedingly well, although she got a little tired of being cast so often as his leading lady or foil. She said at the time they were appearing in films together, he was on a Shakespeare kick, reading the plays and looking for clues that Shakespeare was not the actual author. She also inferred that Eddie was a homosexual. "We didn't use the word *gay* in those days," she said. "So let's just say he was 'a mama's boy.'"[115]

That he was. Everyone in the movie capital knew about his utter devotion to his mother, Isabella, just as everyone knew about another stage and screen fussbudget, Clifton Webb, and his allegiance to *his* mother, Mabelle. Eddie was completely secretive,

---

115 Email from Jeffrey L. Carrier to Lon Davis, August 13, 2024. Patsy Ruth Miller (1904–1995) is known primarily for her role as the compassionate Gypsy girl Esmeralda in the Lon Chaney silent epic *The Hunchback of Notre Dame* (1923). The title of her memoir (written in collaboration with Jeffrey L. Carrier) is *My Hollywood: When Both of Us Were Young* (1988). Richard Brody of *The New Yorker* called it "a brilliant, unknown memoir about classic Hollywood."

however, concerning his alleged partner, Fred Gavin Gordon, a good-looking actor fifteen years his junior. Born in Chicora, Wayne County, Alabama, on April 7, 1901, Gordon found work at Fox and Paramount in small supporting parts beginning in 1927. He won the coveted role as Garbo's leading man in *Romance* (1930), an opportunity that was nearly thwarted by injuries he received in a serious automobile accident on the first scheduled day of shooting. Hospitalized for two weeks, he would have lost the role had not Garbo intervened on his behalf.[116] He gave a more memorable performance as the trillingly affected Lord Byron in the inventive prologue to James Whale's *The Bride of Frankenstein* (1935). Also in the realm of vintage horror is his role as Lt. Andy Anderson in the oft-played, public domain creaker *The Bat* (1959), directed by Crane Wilbur and starring Vincent Price and Agnes Moorehead. (*Spoiler alert* : At the movie's climax, it is revealed that the murderous "Bat" is, in fact, the lieutenant.) He also made numerous appearances on radio and in television dramas before retiring in the 1960s. Gordon and Eddie were in the same cast in a 1931 stage production of *Private Lives*; they are also both in the Frank Capra film *Pocketful of Miracles* (1961), although in separate scenes.

Documentary evidence of the Horton-Gordon relationship is difficult, if not impossible, to come by. To protect his reputation, Eddie spent the remaining years of his long life keeping his lifestyle a secret. That secrecy even extends to the present day. His

---

116 https://en.wikipedia.org/wiki/Gavin_Gordon_(actor).

*Gavin Gordon, early
in his acting career, c.
1930.*

boxes of personal papers offer not a single mention, or even a snapshot, of Gavin Gordon.[117]

Scene 5 : Dancing With Fred and Ginger

Among Eddie's most frequently revived films of the 1930s are three of the celebrated Fred Astaire–Ginger Rogers revelries made at RKO, directed by Mark Sandrich and choreographed by Pandro S. Berman. The first of these is *The Gay Divorcee* (1934). During its production, journalist Marie Canel arranged to meet with Eddie for an on-set interview. She seems somewhat enamored of the actor, rapturously describing him as "vital and warm" and "the most nonchalant, easy-going man you ever saw." So it was something of a shock, she writes, "to find the usually jovial Mr.

---

117 Fred Gavin Gordon died the day before his eighty-second birthday of undisclosed causes in Canoga Park, California, on April 6, 1983. His body was cremated at Live Oak Memorial Park in Monrovia, California, and his ashes were buried in Magnolia Cemetery in Mobile, Alabama. Shortly before his death, Gordon donated a horse sculpture to the Mobile Museum of Art in Mobile, Alabama. It was later determined to be from the Tang Dynasty (618–907 ce).

Horton in a most fretful frame of mind. His expressive eyebrows had a despondent droop to them and that famous smirk of his had somehow turned into a frown that presaged not much of an interview."[118]

Eddie confided to the fannish reporter that he was "simply heartsick," having just been informed that he was expected to both sing *and* dance in this picture. He then invited his visitor to join him away from the set. Finding an inconspicuous corner of the vast sound stage, he complained, "Here I spent all these years learning to do calisthenics with my face, such as it is, and now I'm called upon to produce a pair of feet and some vocal cords."[119]

He need not have worried. "Let's K-nock K-nees," is more of a comedy set piece than a musical number, with Eddie essentially "talking" the lyrics and doing a few hilariously awkward steps with a gorgeous twenty-year-old newcomer named Betty Grable.[120] The sequence is delightful; it's also somewhat surprising to see what the usually modest Eddie is wearing, or perhaps more accurately, what he *isn't* wearing. He has on a black tank top and short pants, exposing his long legs. (*Spoiler alert* : Betty's gams are far more aesthetic than Eddie's.)

Although Fred Astaire and Ginger Rogers are always a pleasure to watch, our favorite scenes in their films involve Eddie and

---

118 Canel.

119 Ibid.

120 Betty Grable (1916–1973) was a singing and dancing star of the 1930s and '40s. Wearing a bathing suit and high heels, she was photographed with her back to the camera, looking over her right shoulder at the viewer with a seductive (yet somehow wholesome) smile. This iconic photo became the most popular pin-up for the American soldiers in World War II.

Eddie and Betty in The Gay Divorcee *(1934).*

Eddie and Freddie in Top Hat *(1935). Doctor Macro*

Eric Blore.[121] In *Top Hat* and *Shall We Dance*, the scenes featuring these accomplished funnymen are fueled by slight misunderstandings that only escalate as they attempt to resolve them. Even after multiple viewings, it is all but impossible not to be amused by their delivery, timing, and exaggerated facial expressions. The following is a portion of one exchange in *Top Hat*. Incidentally, Eddie plays Horace Hardwick, the producer of a revue starring his best friend, Jerry Travers (Fred Astaire); Eric Blore is Bates, a butler.

> **Horace.** (*Panic-stricken*) Mister Travers is in trouble! He has practically put his foot right into a hornets' nest!

> **Bates.** (*Missing the metaphor*) : But hornets' nests grow on *trees*, sir.

> **Horace.** (*Exasperated*) Never mind that. We have *got* to do something.

> **Bates.** (*Helpfully*) What about rubbing it with *butter*, sir?

> **Horace.** (*Growing angrier*) You blasted fool, you *can't* rub a *girl* with butter!

> **Bates.** (*Defensively*) My SISTER got into a hornets' nest, and we rubbed HER with butter, sir!

> **Horace.** (*Explosively*) That's the *wrong* treatment; you should've used *mud—NEVER MIND THAT!*[122]

For an actor, Eddie put little stock in his appearance. One female reporter commented on the ensemble worn by her subject during a planned interview : "He had on a green tie, a brown shirt,

---

121　Eric Blore (1887–1959) was an English stage actor who appeared in more than eighty films. Usually cast as a butler or waiter, he is always precise and, at times, a tad prickly. One of his most memorable roles was as the voice of J. Thaddeus Toad in the Walt Disney animated anthology film, *The Adventures of Ichabod and Mr. Toad* (1949).

122　*Top Hat* screenplay by Alan Scott and Dwight Taylor.

Eddie and Eric Blore in Shall We Dance *(1937). Doctor Macro*

a blue suit and red wool socks—upon which at least one moth had feasted."[123] He had other ways of discouraging female interest in him, if that was indeed his intention. When publicly discussing his status as a confirmed bachelor, he would say that he was much too busy to make time for a relationship. His "only sweetheart,"[124] he added, was the theatre, to which he gave all of his energy. One rumor concerning Eddie was that his contracts included the stipulation that he would not play the part of a husband or father. For that matter, he allegedly turned down any part requiring him to kiss a woman on the lips. He denied these allegations, but the rumor persists even today, at least among seven or eight film buffs. It should be noted that he *did* play husbands in both versions of *Holiday*, and in *Design for Living* (1933). Of course, these were by

123 Irwin.
124 Canel.

Apparently, Esther Dale had not read the codicil in Eddie's contract regarding kissing scenes. Wild Money *(1937). Doctor Macro*

no means romantic roles, any more than Eddie was even remotely considered a romantic actor.

Scene 6 : *Springtime for Henry*

Most successful American movie actors have devoted fans in countries other than their own. In Eddie's case, he had a large following in the United Kingdom. This is understandable : British moviegoers thought Edward Everett Horton was one of them. Once sound became the industry standard, "It wasn't very long before I had an invitation to make a picture in London for United Artists, I did that for Gainsborough. It was called *Soldiers of the King*.[125] They offered me one thousand pounds to come and play the part of the stage manager in a story about the theatre, and I

---

125 *Soldiers of the King* was released in the U.S. as *Woman in Command.*

made friends there I have today. Just a few months ago I was in London. I saw Cicely Courtneidge [the star of *Soldiers of the King*] and we had a grand reunion. And I saw Alastair Sim. I remember he gave one of the most brilliant performances in a British film I did called *The Man in the Mirror*. I liked that film. When I say I like a movie, it usually means also that I had a very good time while I was working in it. That was a fantasy about a mean man—me— whose mirror reflection comes to life and helps him to reform, and Alastair was the interpreter of a bogus Indian prince who was try- ing to cheat me. When I saw him this year in London I told him what a fine job he had done then."[126]

In *The Private Secretary*, another British production, Eddie por- trayed the Reverend Robert Spalding, a character introduced to the stage by Sir Herbert Beerbohm Tree.[127] One reviewer gave a colorful description of the curate, as played by "the ineffable Hor- ton" : He "is fortune's fool to the life, a grave-faced, pompous, painfully precise nincompoop born to be the butt of unscrupulous persons."[128] That summation could easily apply to the majority of Eddie's depictions. Incidentally, he emerged from that particu- lar shoot with a few bruises, having refused a stunt double to roll down an embankment.

Eddie spent the majority of his career portraying one British character in particular : Henry Dewlip, the anti-hero of English playwright Benn W. Levy's three-act farce *Springtime for Henry*.

---

126 Stein, p. 37.
127 Herbert Beerbohm Tree (1852–1917) was a renowned English actor and theatre manager.
128 Ibid.

In the *New York Times* review of a rare off-Broadway revival of the play in the mid-1980s, the critic Mel Gussow noted that his use of the adjective *rare* would likely have discomfited the late Mr. Levy. "The rarity may be true in modern times," Gussow continued. "But, in its day, stretching from 1931 to well past the midcentury, 'Springtime for Henry' was the bread and butter for both Mr. Levy and the actor Edward Everett Horton. Touring the farce eternally, Mr. Horton treated it as his own personal 'Count of Monte Cristo.'"[129]

The show, starring Leslie Banks in the title role, made its Broadway debut at the Bijou Theatre on December 9, 1931. The three supporting players were Nigel Bruce as Johnny Jelliwell, Frieda Inescort as Julia Jelliwell, and Helen Chandler as Angela Smith. The play had a several-month run on the Great White Way and in London's West End.

The plot : Bachelor Henry Dewlip is the heir to his late father's prosperous automobile plant. With no interest in the business, he delegates the running of it to the employees. Meanwhile, he pursues a carefree life of hedonism. There is always at least one woman he is stringing along, the latest being Julia Jelliwell, the tempestuous wife of his longtime best friend, Johnny. There is also Henry's straitlaced secretary, Miss Smith, who secretly harbors a crush. There are plenty of comical mix-ups, moments of intrigue, and misunderstandings galore, all the ingredients necessary to create a successful farce.

---

129 Mel Gussow, "Stage: Levy's 'Springtime for Henry,'" *New York Times*, August 2, 1985.

Eddie took over the role of Henry in the play's West Coast debut in 1933, at the Hollywood Playhouse. The raucous laughter inspired by the combination of Levy's risqué dialogue and Eddie's sublime delivery was so encouraging to the star that he knew he would be doing it again—for a limited period of time. Hoping to tour nationally, Eddie (or, more likely, his publicist and a couple of overworked secretaries) sent eight hundred personalized letters to chambers of commerce across the country. The response was overwhelmingly positive. Before long, there were bookings for *Springtime for Henry* in each of the forty-eight states. Targeted were not only the established roadshow towns, but villages unaccustomed to hosting a theatrical company. When Eddie was told there would be enough interest to guarantee his touring for three years, he laughed off the idea by saying, "I couldn't remember the lines that long!"[130]

What seems odd is how divergent the role of Henry Dewlip is from Eddie's Caspar Milquetoast screen image. Dewlip is rude, ill-mannered, and a flagrant philanderer, whose wanton ways are tamed by his marriage-minded secretary. This seeming reformation eventually dissipates, and he once again indulges his flirtatious ways. This casting against type was apparently cathartic for the actor. "All my life I wanted to be a roué," he told journalist Virginia Irwin. "What's more, I secretly at heart have always wanted to order women around. As the confirmed rake of the show, I'm very definitely the boss."[131]

---

130 Irwin.
131 Ibid.

Of course, not everyone was thrilled with this new Edward Everett Horton. "One woman wrote that she couldn't for the life of her see how I could bring myself to play the wicked, vacillating Henry," he said. "And another wrote that she had supposed the play was something she could bring the children to see, that the title suggested me communing with cows and chickens on a farm in the springtime. As a matter of fact, I don't think the play would have any effect on children except that they would go home and say, 'Please, Mama and Papa, don't let us grow up to be like the people on the stage who made such superb asses of themselves.'"[132]

A December 1939 newspaper ad for Springtime for Henry. *Alarmy*

Although the play has often been minimized as "light, even frivolous," *Daily Variety's* Markland Taylor stated that "it is also fun and, at its best, as when the quips are flying, it brings to mind

---

132 Ibid.

Coward and Wilde."[133] In the following exchange from Act 1, Henry brazenly states his intentions to his best friend concerning his wife, Julia, who is also present.

Dewlip. Johnny, I intend to deceive you.

Jelliwell. You intend to what?

Dewlip. I intend to wreck your married life.

Jelliwell. [*Goodnaturedly*] You know, I don't know what you're driveling about, old boy.

Dewlip. I intend to steal your wife.

Jelliwell. Who steals my wife steals trash. Who said that?

Julia. *Nobody* said that. And one day you may be sorry that *you* did.

Jelliwell. Oh, don't take offense, darling. No harm meant. The fact is you both seem to be talking such nonsense, I don't know where I am. …

Dewlip. I will make one more effort, Johnny. I want your wife to come to me.

Jelliwell. Well, I may be a fool, but I've not the least idea what you're talking about.

Dewlip. It's perfectly simple. I want your wife.

Jelliwell. But whatever for?

Julie. Henry : kindly drive me home.[134]

---

133 Irwin.

134 Benn W. Levy, *Springtime for Henry: A Farce in Three Acts* (New York, NY: Samuel French, 1931).

When *Springtime for Henry* was adapted as a feature film by Fox Pictures in 1934, the producers passed on Eddie—he wasn't "the right type," they said. For the second time, Eddie lost a role he dearly wanted to Otto Kruger, a distinguished actor hardly known for his comic chops. Still, it is quite possible that Lady Luck was in Eddie's corner. The movie not only ran afoul of the Production Code for its adulterous theme but was also a critical and commercial failure.

Meanwhile, Eddie continued to collect kudos for his live performances of the show. When the Bucks County Playhouse in New Hope, Pennsylvania, was facing demolition, a small group of artists, including Broadway playwright (and Bucks County resident) Moss Hart, formed a coalition to save that venerable theatre. On the celebratory occasion of its grand re-opening on July 1, 1939, Eddie and *Springtime for Henry* packed the place. On October 19 of that year, Eddie (along with his co-stars Marjorie Lord, Barbara Brown, and Gordon Richards) kicked off a nationwide tour with three performances at Ford's Theatre in Baltimore, Maryland. The show was an unqualified hit. A critic for the *Sun*, Donald Kirkley, paid Eddie the ultimate compliment : "His performance is not that of a film player on display, but a comedian wise in the tricks of the theatre and willing to follow the author's instructions. The celebrated Horton mannerisms are used sparingly in this new interpretation of Mr. Levy's brilliant, whimsical lines and delightful absurd situations."[135]

---

135 Donald Kirkley, "'Springtime for Henry' Returns with Edward Everett Horton," *Baltimore Sun*, October 20, 1939.

On a performance day in Baltimore, Eddie walked through the darkened Ford's Theatre and sat in the empty balcony. He was suddenly overcome by memories of being a stage-struck college student in the same seat in the same balcony of the same temple to the arts. Eddie had strong ties to Maryland. His father was born there, and the family had lived there for a time. Eddie's uncle George was the long-reigning chief of the Baltimore Fire Department. What's more, this particular run of shows represented Eddie's debut in the city of his theatrical awakening. He was grateful, even humbled, by the trajectory of his career. His eyes began to sting as tears streamed down his cheeks. It was at this intensely private moment that one of his cousins entered the balcony, looking for him. Eddie confided just how touched he was by the memories of yesterday and the realizations of today.

"My god, Ed," his cousin said, "I wouldn't cry about *that*. After all, you should be *some* place after all these years."[136]

Eddie smiled sardonically when he relayed this story to a sympathetic female reporter a year later, but it was evident that he had been wounded by his cousin's insensitivity. He said that he hoped that, in the telling, he could erase it from his mind.

Scene 7 : The Men with the Megaphones

A movie set is often a pressurized environment, with endless intervals involving lighting changes, camera setups, and multiple retakes testing everyone's already-frayed nerves. Eddie discovered an ideal antidote to this. He would find a cozy corner someplace

---

136 Irwin.

out of the way, lay his script on his lap, and drift off to sleep. At times, when he was called to the set, he was still blissfully unaware. Eddie was discovered sound asleep more than once, missing his cue. Sometimes, it took the director himself to convince Eddie that he was "sleeping away"[137] thousands of dollars, and that it was time he was back in front of the cameras. Groggy or not, Eddie always knew his lines perfectly.

Eddie was quick to tell interviewers how well *not* being a contract player at any one studio had served him. "After I'd been in films awhile I saw how unhappy those contract people were," he said. The closest he came to being one himself was when he had three-picture deals with Warners and Universal. "The agreement was that if it did not go well—if *they* were dissatisfied—or if *I* was after one or two pictures—I didn't have to make the third."[138]

Because of his freedom to go from studio to studio, he managed to work with many of the industry's most capable directors, including James Cruze, Frank Lloyd, Lewis Milestone, Gregory La Cava, Jack Conway, James Whale, Norman Taurog, George Marshall, Wesley Ruggles, William A. Seiter, and Karl Freund. But there were two names that he believed towered above the rest.

The first was Ernst Lubitsch.

A tailor's son, he was born in Berlin on January 29, 1892. Defying his father's wishes that he follow in his career footsteps, nineteen-year-old Ernst left home to join Max Reinhardt's theatre company in 1911. Two years later, he made his film debut, appearing in

---

137 Canel.
138 Stein, p. 36.

the first of approximately thirty pictures over the next seven years. In 1918, he branched out as a director, helming *Die Augen der Mumie Ma* (*The Eyes of the Mummy*), starring Pola Negri. German cinema would exert a major influence on Hollywood beginning in the twenties. Paul Leni, Fritz Lang, F.W. Murnau, and Lubitsch were

Ernst Lubitsch.

invited to make pictures in the world's movie capital. Lubitsch's urbane comedies soon gave the five-foot-seven émigré the reputation as Hollywood's most elegant and sophisticated director. Films with that signature "Lubitsch Touch" include *Trouble in Paradise* (1932), *Design for Living* (1933), *Ninotchka* (1939), *The Shop Around the Corner* (1940), and *To Be or Not to Be* (1942). He received three Academy Award nominations for Best Director—*The Patriot* (1928), *The Love Parade* (1929), and *Heaven Can Wait* (1943)—but the Oscar statuette proved elusive. Realizing their oversight, the Academy presented him with an honorary award "for his contributions to the art of the motion picture" in 1946, the year before he died at the untimely age of fifty-five.

"I did five pictures for Mister Lubitsch," Eddie proudly stated. "He *always* had the actor in his mind. In no part of any Lubitsch

Lobby card for Lubitsch's Design for Living. *Pictured left to right are
Eddie, Fredric March, and Gary Cooper.* Doctor Macro

picture did he have an actor who was not *just right*. You rehearsed
a whole week on the picture without shooting anything at all. We
rehearsed in the sets. No matter what you thought or what you
wanted to do, Mister Lubitsch had gone over it in his mind. Just as
soon as you could put yourself *en rapport* with him, you were very
happy. He knew these actors very well, and he wanted something
from them that even *they* didn't know they had. He was a genius,
you see. Just a genius. The 'Lubitsch touch' meant bits of business
that he supplied. For example, there was one scene in *Trouble in
Paradise*, I think, in which the other actor and I are photographed
behind a big glass door that looks into the bar of a fabulous hotel.
I'm saying to another actor, 'Do you want to go in?' and that sort of

thing, but you couldn't hear a word. All pantomime. Only Lubitsch could think of a scene like that."[139]

Eddie's character in *Trouble in Paradise* is the ultra-snobbish Monsieur Filiba. An insouciant jewel thief by the name of Gaston (Herbert Marshall), posing as a physician, engages Filiba in a conversation about his tonsils, of all things. This, of course, is merely a ruse so that Gaston can surreptitiously rob his wealthy prey. Near the end of the film, while in conversation with the Major (Charlie Ruggles), it finally occurs to Filiba just where he had seen Gaston. With a renewed sense of clarity, he purposefully stands and announces : "Tonsils! Posi*tive*ly tonsils!"[140]

There were two simultaneously filmed versions of *The Merry Widow* (1934). One was directed by Lubitsch for an English-speaking audience; the other was intended for France. This practice of shooting separate language versions of the same story was a temporary, expensive answer to losing the international audiences made possible by the universal language of the silent film. Based on the 1910 Franz Lehár operetta, *The Merry Widow* tells the story of Captain Danilo (Maurice Chevalier), a notorious playboy who is ordered by King Achmed of Marshovia (George Barbier) to court and marry Madame Sonia (Jeanette MacDonald), a rich widow who owns a large portion of the kingdom. The leads were the same in both versions, although Eddie appeared exclusively in the American production. In his opinion, this Lubitsch film stood out as the best musical comedy in which he ever appeared.

---

139 *The Real Tinsel,* p. 230.

140 *Trouble in Paradise* screenplay by Samson Raphaelson, Grover Jones, and Ernst Lubitsch.

"It was filmed on a gorgeous set at MGM," he recalled with enthusiasm. "Never was there a set like it, with a palace and all that sort of thing. Chevalier and Jeanette MacDonald were the leads. I played the Baron Popoff. In the Lubitsch version, there was a king, and I played the prime minister. Anything I did that the king approved of prompted him to pin a little medal on me. If something happened that he didn't approve of, he'd take the medal off. No great reaction of any kind, but very amusing. Well, when we finished the scene, we'd all retire. Chevalier and MacDonald would go off with the French actors Chevalier had brought with him, the French director, and the French dialogue director. MacDonald wasn't allowed to say a word in the script that wasn't passed; it had to be excellent French. Then we'd watch the French actors doing the scene that we did. They had a king and a prime minister, and whenever Popoff did anything that the king liked, the king would kiss him on both cheeks. Then, when he did something wrong, there was a terrible scene, and you'd think a revolution had started. Lubitsch would look at me and say, '*Why*? Why all *that*?'[141]

Another memory Eddie cherished was the one in which the director approached him one day on the set and said, "Edward, there's trouble and it's going to be three or four weeks before things are straightened out. I understand they want you at Warner Bros. Why don't you go over there and play, and you'll still be on salary here. Go over and make the picture. Let me know when you're finished."

---

141 *The Real Tinsel*, p. 231.

"So I was getting *two* salaries at once. I remember that very well—why wouldn't I?"[142]

The other director revered by Eddie was Frank Capra.

Born Francesco Rosario Capra in Bisacquino, Sicily, on May 18, 1897, Frank Capra would succeed mightily in the film industry as a producer, director, and screenwriter. His films were often idealistic stories of ordinary individuals overcoming seemingly insurmountable odds. After working as a gag writer and director for Mack Sennett in the 1920s, he signed with Columbia Pictures and soon made his breakout film, *It Happened One Night* (1934). To call that classic romantic comedy a hit would be a major understatement : no other

Frank Capra.

Columbia feature would prove as successful until the late 1980s. It was also one of the few films that won Academy Awards for Best Picture, Best Screenplay (Robert Riskin), Best Actor (Clark Gable), Best Actress (Claudette Colbert), and Best Director (Capra). This was followed by *Mr. Deeds Goes to Town* (1936), *You Can't Take It with You* (1938), *Mr. Smith Goes to Washington* (1939),

---

142 Ibid.

and his most famous film (in retrospect only), *It's a Wonderful Life* (1946). Capra took home a total of six Academy Award statuettes: three for Best Director, and three for other categories. According to Eddie, Capra hand-picked his cast of players, and he was especially partial to those actors with stage experience. Capra not only personally requested Eddie for the role of Lovett, the paleontologist in *Lost Horizon*, but he also expanded the character's presence in the script. And because of his respect for Eddie's theatrical background, he challenged him to assist in the staging of an underwritten sequence. This occurred in what Eddie described as "a fabricated room up there in the Himalayas, a great big place with wonderful Chinese embroideries, all built on that set."

"Edward," Capra began. "In this scene I want to get over a feeling, not of fear, but sort of an *eerie* feeling, a mysterious *something*. What do you think?"

"Well, Mister Capra, I don't know."

"What do you mean you don't know? You've been on the stage for fifteen, twenty, thirty-five years. What do you mean you don't know?"

Realizing his mistake, Eddie managed to cover it up quickly.

"Well, I don't know quite what you mean by *eerie*. If I were in a room like this and I happened to see that long curtain moving back and forth, I'd be a little—."

"That's *it*. You're behind the curtain."

"I *am*?"

"Yes, you're behind the curtain."

Eddie obligingly went and stood behind the curtain.

"Now," Capra continued, "sell me on the fact that you're behind the curtain. I can't feel it unless I see some sort of a form of your body. Get up closer to it."

"What am I doing?"

Capra signaled to a stagehand. "Give him a sword, one of those samurai swords." Then, back to Eddie : "Now let's see the sword come out back and forth in front of the curtain."

"What am I doing?"

"You're sharpening a pencil or something like that." A few moments passed before Capra admitted, "Ed, I'm stuck." He then said, "How do I know it's you?"

"I have no idea, Mister Capra, unless I thought I heard something, and I looked around the curtain to see what—"

"That's *it*—that's just right! Now it's nobody, so you go over to the desk."

Eddie did as he was told and, a moment after sitting down, he jumped up.

"What's the matter?" Capra asked.

"I forgot the sword," said Eddie, sheepishly.

"Oh well, go and get it," the director said, showing a bit of pique.

Eddie again sat at the desk before looking at Capra expectantly.

"Go ahead, make me laugh." (This was something Capra's former boss, Mack Sennett, routinely said just prior to being shown his directors' latest rushes.)

Eddie concentrated while silently asking himself, *What do I want to do? I mean, what can you do behind a desk?* He then noticed a Chinese lacquer box. He opened it and peered inside. As he looked up, he saw that the box had a mirror in it, with his face staring back at him. He screamed and shut the box.

Eddie emotes in the scene he and Capra staged for Lost Horizon *(1937). Doctor Macro*

Capra laughed. *"Perfect,"* he said. "That's *just* right."[143]

Although some actors might resent being put on the spot in this manner, Eddie found it invigorating. As he told an interviewer, "It was fun working with Capra because you were thinking all the time, and you tried to please him. He knew what he was after, but he wanted to see how you'd get around to it."[144]

---

143 Ibid., p. 232.
144 Ibid., p. 233.

Mr. Witherspoon (Eddie) is about to enjoy a glass of homemade elderberry wine, courtesy of the Brewster sisters, Abby (Josephine Hull, middle) and Martha (Jean Adair, right). Arsenic and Old Lace *(1944).* Steve Cox

On January 10, 1941, Joseph Kesselring's black comedy *Arsenic and Old Lace* opened at the Fulton Theatre on Broadway. Warner Bros. secured the motion picture rights, and Capra was the film's director. And, as with *Lost Horizon*, he had a part in mind for Eddie. It wasn't a big part, mind you, but it was an important one and, as usual, he made the most of it. He plays Mr. Witherspoon, the genteel owner and manager of Happy Dale Sanitarium in Brooklyn. He is summoned by Mortimer Brewster (Cary Grant) to collect his uncle Teddy Brewster (John Alexander), who believes himself to be President Theodore Roosevelt. Mr. Witherspoon dutifully pays a visit to the Brewster family's Victorian abode. As a ruse, Mortimer respectfully addresses his uncle.

"Mr. President, I have good news! Your term of office is over."

Teddy responds. "Now I can go on my hunting trip in Africa! I must go upstairs to prepare."

Mortimer then introduces Teddy to Mr. Witherspoon, saying that "he is your guide to Africa."

"Bully! Bully!" Teddy responds. "We'll start immediately. Wait here; I'll bring down my equipment." Holding an imaginary sword aloft, he yells "CHARGE!" as he storms up San Juan Hill, otherwise known as the house's staircase, and *slams* his bedroom door.

Mr. Witherspoon looks forlorn and says, "Oh, dear. And Happy Dale is *full* of staircases."

Eschewing false modesty, Eddie made the following comparison of his two favorite directors : "You know, Mr. Lubitsch engaged his casts because he knew their capabilities and eccentricities and mannerisms of acting—and he knew exactly what he wanted them to do—and I loved that because I knew I couldn't help but be good in a Lubitsch film—but I also learned I would always be at my best in a Capra film for the opposite reason."[145]

Eddie did not discriminate—whether he was working on an A-picture like *Lost Horizon*, or a B-picture like *Little Tough Guys in Society* (1938) for Universal, he always gave the best performance of which he was capable. In that latter film, a moralizing story directed by Erle C. Kenton and featuring the Dead End Kids, he dusts off his butler uniform to play in a cleverly written, flawlessly

---

145 Stein, pp. 38–39.

timed scene with Mischa Auer.[146] A very funny man, Auer plays Dr. Trenkle; Eddie is Oliver. Trenkle attempts to describe his past success with a former patient as Oliver deliberately cuts in while serving tea:

> **Dr. Trenkle.** One day his imperial highness, the Grand Duke St. Sansonevich, sent for me. He said …

> **Oliver.** Tea?

> **Dr. Trenkle.** "Trenkle," he said, "you are my only hope. My son, St. Sansonovich junior, is a …"

> **Oliver.** Lemon?

> **Dr. Trenkle.** "Sansonovich junior has lost the will to live." "I will do what I can, your highness," I said, and I …

> **Oliver.** Cookie?

> **Dr. Trenkle.** … proceeded to look him over. In examining his head, would you believe I found …?

> **Oliver.** Two lumps?

Our personal favorite among Eddie's films is the fantasy-based *Here Comes Mr. Jordan* (1941), directed by Alexander Hall. Set in both the afterlife and on earth, the story concerns Joe Pendleton (Robert Montgomery), a professional boxer who is prematurely taken to heaven by the well-meaning but incompetent Messenger 7013 (Eddie). His supervisor, Mr. Jordan (the perfectly cast Claude

---

146 Mischa Auer (1905–1967) was a Russian-born comedic actor, whose film career in Hollywood began in 1928. His performance in the 1936 screwball comedy *My Man Godfrey* earned him an Academy Award nomination for Best Supporting Actor. He continued to be a familiar presence in both American-made films, as well as those made in Europe, for the next thirty years.

Rains), is called in to help rectify the situation. *Here Comes Mr. Jordan* was such a hit that a Technicolor musical semi-sequel was made six years later, with Eddie reprising his celestial role.

Down to Earth (1947) has Messenger 7013 assigned to look after Terpsichore, muse of the dance, on her earthly journey. The goddess was played by a Hollywood goddess, Rita Hayworth. "That was a film I really loved," Eddie said, "because of the congenial atmosphere on the set." When he was asked about playing opposite the gorgeous actress, he responded : "Why, in 1932, when I was traveling in Agua Caliente, Mexico, I saw Rita Hayworth dancing in a nightclub. You know she came from a family of generations of dancers, and she was her father's partner when she was just fourteen. Anyway, I saw her and her father and her uncle in their act and I realized how talented and pretty she was. And then in 1946 she was with me in *Down to Earth*. I told her I had seen her work when she was a child. She was so sweet and hard-working. She asked me to watch her work out her dance routines and go over her lines with her. I said to her, 'You should ask the director,' and she said, 'No, please, I want *you* to help me!' Here she was, the star of the picture, and she asked *me*! Well, I did watch her work—*so* hard—and I'd tell her little things, and she'd whisper, 'Don't tell the director, *please*.' She was so modest and affectionate."[147]

Modest? Not according to the Breen Office she wasn't. The file on *Down to Earth* at the MPAA/PCA Collection at the AMPAS Library reveals that the ever-intrusive Breen Office, after view-

____

147 Stein, pp. 37–38.

ing the completed film in January 1947, declared the picture "unacceptable" under the Production Code. Specifically, the office objected to three skimpy costumes worn by Rita Hayworth and some "offensively suggestive dance movements in the early part of the picture." According to the memo, Columbia executive Harry Cohn took "violent exception" to Joseph Breen's viewpoint and refused to make *any* changes in the film. The memo further noted that Cohn complained that the PCA had approved pictures, such as the 1946 Selznick film *Duel in the Sun*, that, in his judgment, were "unacceptable." Subsequent memos indicate that Breen approved *Down to Earth* after Columbia ordered minor cuts and changes in the film, including the use of longer shots to replace close-ups of Hayworth's dresses.[148]

Eddie was typically cordial but businesslike when he was working, which was essentially always. He must have seemed like he was from another time in that he consistently referred to his directors, co-stars, and everyone else as Mister or Miss. This may have been his way of keeping his distance, personally. Occasionally he did make friends of his co-stars, particularly actresses like Lois Wilson, Florence Eldridge, and Laura La Plante. He also got along famously with British actors. Eric Blore and he shared a sense of the ridiculous that kept moments on the set light and cheerful. One routine they did was strictly for their own amusement : "We

---

148 *The AFI Catalog of Feature Films*, 1941–1950.

(Left to right) Robert Montgomery, Eddie, and Claude Rains in Here Comes Mr. Jordan *(1941).* Doctor Macro

The goddess Terpsichore (Rita Hayworth) shares a serious moment with Messenger 7013 (Eddie) in Down to Earth *(1947).* Author's collection

kept bumping into each other and saying, '*Excuse* me'—'No, *you* excuse *me*' and bowing to each other and clicking heels."[149]

Arthur Treacher was another British actor who made a career of playing butlers. He, Charlie Ruggles, and Eddie were all cast in support of Marion Davies in *Hearts Divided* (1936). Said Eddie: "They thought if they had three comedians it would be three times as funny. It wasn't."[150] About *Hearts Divided*, he recalled, "Charlie Ruggles fell out of the apple tree in that picture, and it was the only time I worked with Arthur Treacher—we'd been good friends for years—still are."[151] Among Eddie's few negative memories concerned Spencer Tracy, his co-star in *Six Cylinder Love* (1931). The troubled actor was experiencing some personal problems when they made that film, although Eddie, ever the gentleman, did not divulge any details. He simply intimated that the film was a comedy and there was nothing funny about Tracy's behavior. He argued with both the director, Thornton Freeland, and Eddie throughout the entire shoot.[152]

"Oh, I don't think I ever had trouble with any director," Eddie said; "some of them just made me have more of a good time than others."[153] A good time was not to be had on *The Devil is a Woman* (1935), directed by Josef von Sternberg. Eddie portrayed the goatee-wearing mayor of Barcelona, who is intrigued by the story's

---

149 Stein, p. 37.

150 Ibid.

151 Ibid. In addition to *Hearts Divided*, Eddie and Arthur Treacher (1894–1975) are in the same casts of *Going Highbrow* (1935) and *Forever and a Day* (1943). They also appeared together four times on television, when Eddie was a guest on *The Merv Griffin Show*. Treacher was Merv's announcer and sidekick in the 1960s.

152 Ibid., p. 36.

153 Stein, p. 38.

femme fatale, played by Marlene Dietrich. "Von Sternberg had a reputation for being difficult," Eddie said. "And the one film I did for him dissatisfied me. I thought I was miscast—but not hopeless, and I suggested that my accent was inappropriate for Spain, but Von Sternberg gave me a long talk on the history of Spain and how it had been settled by people from all over, including England, and that my accent fitted well enough. But the film disappointed me."[154]

The type of directors Eddie found the most irksome were the ones known as company men, strictly by-the-book technicians who were under the absolute thumb of the producer. As Eddie explained, "The play has been gone over; it has a wonderful writer. It's all been timed. The movement is here. The close-up is here. You come to the close-up. It's all in the book and this is the way it's got to be shot. And it's done in a certain amount of time. There's very little leeway for anything the actor might do that is very funny. So the run-of-the-mill comment is, 'No, keep it this way. Incidentally, you said *and* instead of *if*, Edward.' 'Oh, *did* I? So sorry.' Take it again please.'

"Everything like that is watched," Eddie recalled, shaking his head. "I'd improvise anyway. They'd take it that way and then they'd take it the way it should have been. Sometimes my way was better."[155]

Those directors who gave Eddie room to do a scene his way would often get the best possible performance from him.

---

154 Ibid.
155 *The Real Tinsel*, p. 233.

"A director would say, 'Now, Eddie, we know how good you are. Just ad-lib. The part isn't really written yet, and we would like you to see how you feel about it.'"[156]

Making movies could be fun, provided all the right elements were in place. "At the same time it was grinding work," said Eddie. "I had to get up at six o'clock in the morning. I had dogs to feed and chores to do around the house, then I'd get in my automobile and drive to whichever studio, which was about forty-five minutes away. You get into the make-up chair; when that was done, you'd go on the scene. The director would come up to me and say, 'Do you know your lines, Mister Horton?' Well, I would have about three lines. 'Yes,' I would say; 'I know my lines.' The director would say excitedly, 'Did you hear that? *He knows his lines!*' Well, after all, I had been learning a hundred and twenty-five pages for every play for years, so one page was no effort.

"Lots of times, you'd do a scene, a long scene, and you'd do it over and over again. Film meant nothing in those days. And you often wondered '*Why?* Why do we do this thing *so* many times?' No comment of any kind. Actually, the director hoped that one of the actors would do something that might change the scene and make it a little better. He wouldn't know what he wanted, but maybe the actor would do or say something accidentally. Finally, he would say, 'Well, all right, we'll keep the last one.'"[157] Even when a director liked a take, the most he would do is signal "O.K.," a spiritless reaction that left Eddie cold. Perhaps to spare himself

---

156 Ibid.
157 Ibid., p. 230.

the disquieting quiet following a take, he became known as One-Take Horton. "I did it right the first time," he said proudly. "How lovely. I didn't have to do it again."[158]

Eddie was rather cut-and-dried when it came to the subject of movies. The standard two questions he asked when offered a part in a film were : "How long will it take and how much does it pay?" Nor was he fussy about the often-sensitive topic of billing. "I would say, 'You don't even have to use my name. I'll just play the part and take the money.' So that's what happened, with picture after picture. I didn't give a rap about the billing. I had no ambition at all … I couldn't take movies seriously."[159] Nor did he like watching himself on the screen. "It's so discouraging," he explained. "On stage, we live by what our friends tell us. After a performance, they say, 'Ed, you were wonderful,' and that's all we need to know. But in a movie, you see yourself and go, 'Oh, *no!*'"[160]

One odd exception is the 1947 comedy, *Her Husband's Affairs*, co-starring Lucille Ball and Franchot Tone. Eddie was cast as an advertising executive who is convinced that a new brand of shaving cream would be a marketing sensation. To prove his point, he tries it himself, only to find that it causes baldness. As Eddie told journalist Jeanie Stein, "I had a plastic head-piece that was scalloped and pasted on each day so I would look bald. But it also tightened my face muscles and people who saw me on the set or in my dressing room before I removed my make-up would tell

---

158 Ibid.
159 Ibid., p. 229.
160 "Edward Everett Horton is 79 and as Roaring Chicken is One Active Bird," *TV Guide*, October 16, 1966.

me I looked so well—younger than I had in years. After all, I was sixty-one. You know, even *I* looked in the mirror and thought how healthy and young I must be. Then I would remove the make-up—and the whole face would collapse!"[161]

When questioned beyond a superficial level, Eddie would admit that he was largely dissatisfied with the lightweight film roles he was offered. If one were to generalize which was the most common of his characters' occupations, the safe bet would be on butlers, right? Wrong. Just as Charlie Chaplin played an actual tramp in fewer of his films than one might expect, Eddie racked up numerous onscreen professions : "I have played only six butlers in my one hundred pictures," Eddie said. "But I have been, on and off, thirty-five 'best friends,' twenty-two timid clerks, and thirty-seven 'frustrated leading men.'"[162]

"Only once did I feel I was really playing myself—that is, *really acting*," he said candidly. "It was in *Summer Storm*, with Linda Darnell and George Sanders, taken from Chekhov's *The Shooting Party*. I played a Russian nobleman in it. Oh, so very stuffed shirt. Delightful. Has billions of dollars, and then the revolution comes and he's picking up cigarette butts. It was like a stage play. I was

---

161 Stein, p. 39.
162 Brooklyn online article, n.d. Regarding the number of times Eddie portrayed a butler or a valet on screen, he is quite close when he claims to have done so in six films. While compiling his filmography, we counted nine such roles: *Ruggles of Red Gap*, *Reaching for the Moon*, *The Singing Kid*, *Angel*, *Take the Heir*, *Paris Honeymoon*, *The Ghost Goes Wild*, *Springtime in the Rockies*, and *Pocketful of Miracles*. On television, he played a butler on *December Bride*, "The Butler Show" (December 16, 1957) and *Our Man Higgins*, "Who's on First?" (May 8, 1963).

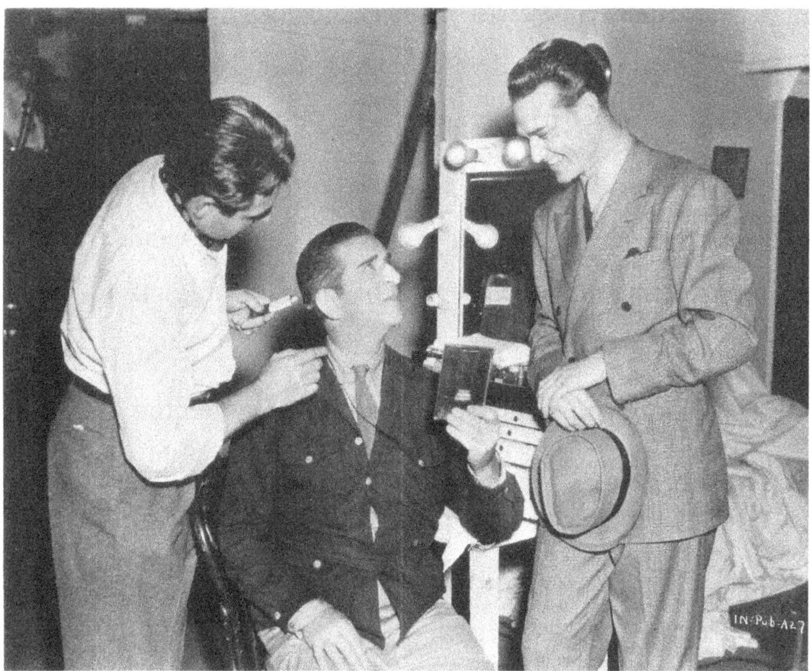

Twenty-five-year-old Red Skelton, then preparing for his motion picture debut, visits with Eddie on the set of Hitting a New High *(1937). The original caption for this publicity photo reads : "Edward Everett Horton painfully demonstrates what Richard Skelton will have to go through to be made up for the movies." Jordan R. Young*

really playing a new type. That's what I like to do. It was a part that Lionel Barrymore could have played, though not as well as I did of course."[163] Eddie had faith in the exceptional director Douglas Sirk, whom he later described as "delightful and ambitious and so well-informed."[164] Sirk knew the best way to work with Eddie was to give him the leeway he had earned. And it worked.

"In one scene," Eddie recalled with a smile, "they brought in a huge wedding cake, and I couldn't resist ad-libbing my own line. I said, 'This is an old Volsky family recipe made with three hundred

---

163 *The Real Tinsel*, p. 231.
164 Stein, p. 40.

eggs,' and Mister Sirk laughed and said he wouldn't dream of cutting it. I got along so well with Douglas Sirk. Never was a fellow so pleased with my [performance]."[165]

It seemed all but certain that *Summer Storm* would turn out to be an exceptional film, one that Eddie believed would "change my career—this would be the end of all the double-takes. Now I would be a *real* actor."[166]

One can only imagine his disappointment when the 1944 film crashed and burned with critics and moviegoers alike. It meant that he had no recourse but to continue doing double-takes for a long, long time to come.

In Eddie's all-time favorite role, that of Count "Piggy" Volsky, in Summer Storm *(1944), his old-world courtliness fails to impress Olga Kuzminichna Urbenin (Linda Darnell).* Doctor Macro

---

165 Ibid.
166 Ibid.

ACT III

Scene 1 : Television

I n 1946, there were television sets in an estimated six thousand American households; by 1952, there were 22 million.[167] Eddie, who never met a medium he didn't like, was in on the ground floor of the 20th century's latest technological sensation. He made his small screen debut on December 13, 1948, on the NBC network's *The Chevrolet Tele-Theatre*. He also made the rounds of embryonic game shows, panel shows, and talk shows, and was always dependably articulate, charming, and witty. Eddie also held his own as one of Milton Berle's on-air guests, and made several appearances on *The Red Skelton Hour*, sharing the stage with that legendary clown's Freddie the Freeloader character. He was even the substitute host on CBS's *Toast of the Town*, the Sunday night variety hour that gained almost mythic status as *The Ed Sullivan Show*.

---

167 1950s: TV and Radio | Encyclopedia.com.

On Monday nights beginning in 1951, millions of viewers tuned in to CBS at nine-thirty (E.S.T.) to watch *I Love Lucy*. Eddie paid this venerable sitcom the ultimate compliment : He said that *I Love Lucy* was the one sitcom on which he wished to be a regular cast member; specifically in the role of Fred Mertz, the character portrayed by William Frawley. Eddie's sole appearance on the series was the January 21, 1952, episode, "Lucy Plays Cupid." Eddie portrays Mr. Ritter, a rough-hewn grocer, who has recently become the fixation of a doddering spinster named Miss Lewis (Bea Benaderet). Miss Lewis is too shy to ask her crush to dinner, so her neighbor Lucy Ricardo (Lucille Ball), a hopeless romantic, offers to arrange the date, despite having been forbidden to do so by her husband, Ricky (Desi Arnaz). Mr. Ritter misreads Lucy's intentions: he thinks that it is she who is inviting him to dinner. With a knowing wink, he says: "I like you, too. You're just my type, Red." To fend off his potential advances, Lucy prepares for the evening by cooking an unappetizing meal, messing up her apartment, dressing sloppily, and (because Mr. Ritter had made it clear that he doesn't like children) corralling twenty-five kids to pass off as her own. Predictably, Lucy's guest is horrified. At that moment, in walks Miss Lewis, giving Mr. Ritter the over-the-top "come-hither" look taught to her by Lucy. Eddie's participation in the show meant a great deal to the co-producers at Desilu, Ball and Arnaz. At the episode's end, an announcer's voice could be heard identifying the guest actors over the crawl. Eddie's appearance is treated as something of an event: "We'd like

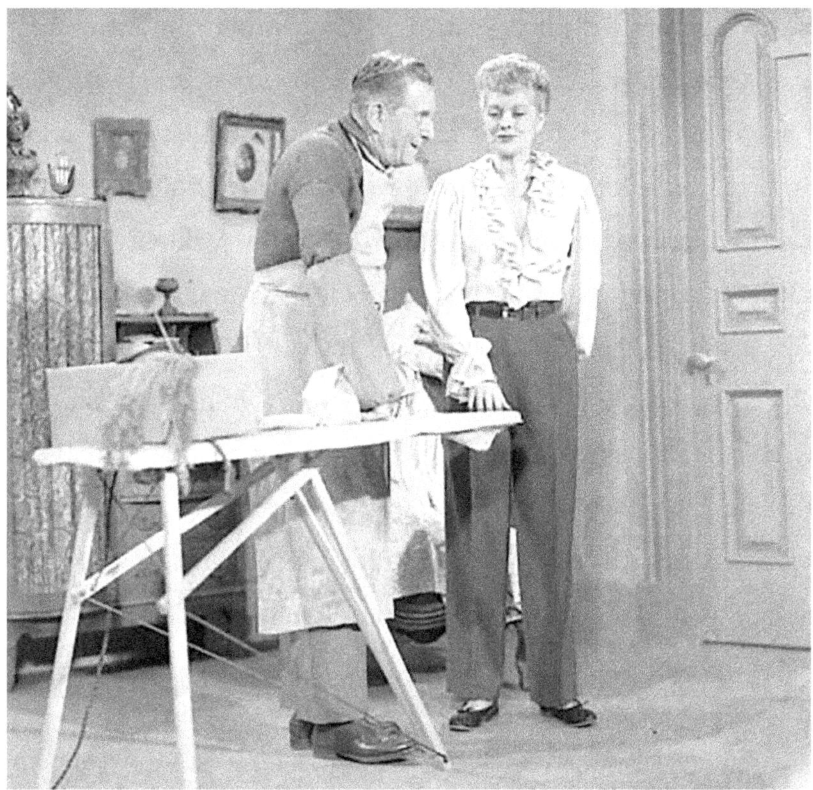

This rare production shot shows Eddie and Lucille Ball rehearsing a scene for the I Love Lucy *episode, "Lucy Plays Cupid." The show aired on the CBS network on January 21, 1952. Authors' collection*

to give our special thanks to Mister Edward Everett Horton for appearing with us tonight."[168]

Lending prestige to the evolving television landscape were the numerous, highly acclaimed anthology shows, such as *Studio One* and *Playhouse 90*. Eddie participated in several live telecasts of abridged Broadway plays, including the Kaufman–Hart comedy *The Man Who Came to Dinner* (how perfectly cast Eddie must have been as the crotchety Sheridan Whiteside, the part originated by Monty Woolley on Broadway). He effectively headed an ensemble

---

168 *I Love Lucy*, episode no. 7, "Lucy Plays Cupid," Paramount DVD, 2007.

cast portraying the manipulative newspaper editor Walter Burns in *The Front Page*. In "The Bartlett Desk," by Louis Pelletier, Eddie plays a charmingly eccentric antiques dealer, who has been trying unsuccessfully for five years to buy a valuable old desk from an equally charming but obdurate lady, played by Mildred Natwick. Little does either party realize that the supposed heirloom is a fake. Eddie also reprised his role as Mr. Witherspoon, the owner of Happy Dale Sanitarium, in *Arsenic and Old Lace*, co-starring Orson Bean, Helen Hayes, Billie Burke, Peter Lorre, and Boris Karloff. Essentially legitimate theatre's contribution to the new medium, these powerful offerings gave Mr. and Mrs. America one more excuse to stay home on a Saturday night.

Animation producer and voice artist Bill Scott had the inspired idea of hiring Eddie as the offscreen narrator of a cartoon. Entitled "The Unenchanted Princess," the three-minute fairy tale was based on a story by Theodor Geisel, better known as Dr. Seuss. It was but one of the planned segments on the December 16, 1956, telecast of CBS-TV's *The Gerald McBoing-Boing Show*. Although the results were somewhat tame, they would lead to something far more potent within a few short years. That "something" was *Rocky and His Friends*, later known as *The Rocky and Bullwinkle Show*, a half-hour cartoon program that was on CBS from 1959 to 1961, and on NBC from 1961 to 1964. The primary storyline takes place in the make-believe city of Frostbite Falls, Minnesota, the home of a pair of anthropomorphic animals, specifically a dumb but lovable moose named Bullwinkle, and his smarter friend Rocket J. Squirrel. Together, they do their best to defend themselves and their

Eddie reprises his role as Mr. Witherspoon in a televised adaptation of Arsenic and Old Lace *in 1955. This time, the doting Brewster sisters are played by two legends of the American Theatre, Billie Burke (left) and Helen Hayes.* Steve Cox.

country against two Russian spies, the black-clad Boris Badenov and Natasha Fatale. In all, there were 163 episodes and 815 segments, ninety-one of which are "Fractured Fairy Tales," narrated by Eddie. Each five-minute cartoon takes a famous story, like "Sleeping Beauty," "Tom Thumb," and "The Ugly Duckling," and turns them on their ears. The appeal of the show is not the animation, which is extremely under-animated, not to mention inconsistent. Jay Ward himself noted that his cartoons worked like old-time radio : you could follow them without seeing the pictures. Chuck Jones, the former Warner Bros. cartoon director, agreed, calling Ward's TV shows an example of "illustrated radio."[169]

The pun-filled scripts were written on two levels, allowing the show's humor to be appreciated by children and adults alike. Bringing the witty scripts to life was a talented cast of voice actors, namely Daws Butler, Paul Frees, June Foray, and the aforementioned Bill Scott. Each had his or her own library of characters, with many of them patterned vocally after some of the most memorable radio and film stars. Adult viewers at the time were no doubt amused to hear the familiar tones of Ed Wynn, Marjorie Main, Charles Butterworth, and Ronald Colman, among many others. Of course, more than a soundalike, Eddie was the real deal: a bona fide movie star from Hollywood's golden age.

Writing about the show during its initial run, television critic Dave Stringer believed that Jay Ward and company had created something unique.

> The newest and in many ways the most promising entrants in the TV cartoon field are Jay Ward and Bill Scott (a graduate of "Mr. Magoo") and their "Rocky and His Friends" series. They proceed in a barrage of puns the kiddies may or may not catch. By all odds the best things the Rocky show does are its "Fractured Fairy Tales."

---

169 In an email to Lon Davis, dated July 3, 2024, author / voice actor Keith Scott stated that animation director Chuck Jones coined the term "illustrated radio" during a 1972 interview.

Narrated by Edward Everett Horton, they are perhaps as funny as any animated works you've ever seen.[170]

In his definitive history of the Bullwinkle enterprise, *The Moose That Roared*, author and voice actor Keith Scott explains what made the choice of Edward Everett Horton as narrator one of the all-time great casting decisions.

> Horton's restrained and wry delivery of these sly little tales was a delight. He was also clever enough to send up his own screen image of the dithering, nervous characters he had played in the 1930s and '40s. His patented giggle was often heard echoing the audience's groans at the outrageous pun endings of these tales : "The bee stings in life are free" was just one painful example.[171]

June Foray's most vivid memory of Eddie involved his chauffeur picking him up and taking him to tennis matches after a recording session. She added that he was something of a cheapskate. "He was really quite penurious," she said. "One evening he was wearing a really thick sweater; I mean it was so big it wouldn't quit. I remember it was winter, and I asked him where he'd bought such a magnificent garment. And he pulled that famous prissy face, and said, very proudly, 'Why, this is my high school sweater!'"[172]

In the Edward Everett Horton Collection at the American Heritage Center are innumerable scripts from every facet of the actor's career. We have selected two of the actual scripts from the "Fractured Fairy Tales" series, "Rapunzel" and "Cinderella," by George Atkins, along with senior editor Bill Scott. The cross-outs

---

170 Keith Scott, *The Moose That Roared* (New York, NY: Thomas Dunne, 2001), p. 164.
171 Ibid., p. 117.
172 Ibid., p. 345.

and scribbled notes are in Eddie's own hand. (For a complete listing of all ninety-one "Fractured Fairy Tales" episodes, please see the entry in this book's Annotated Radio and Television Shows.)

RAPUNZEL

PAGE 1

NARRATOR: IT ALL STARTED OUT WITH A PLANT, A VARIETY OF EUROPEAN BELLFLOWER USED IN THE MAKING OF SALADS. THE PLANT IS CALLED RAMPION. THIS PLANT GREW IN A BEAUTIFUL GARDEN BELONGING TO A MEAN WITCH WHOM EVERYBODY FEARED.

UNFORTUNATELY THE RAMPION COULD BE SEEN FROM A LITTLE HUT BELONGING TO A PEASANT AND HIS WIFE. EVERY DAY THE WIFE, WHO WAS TO HAVE A BABY, WOULD SIT BY THE WINDOW AND GAZE AT THE RAMPION.

PEASANT: DEAR, WHY DO YOU SIT ALL DAY GAZING AT THE GARDEN OF THE WITCH WHOM EVERYBODY FEARS?

WIFE: DARLING...I KNOW THIS SOUNDS FANTASTIC AND UTTERLY ABSURD, BUT I HAVE THIS UNCONTROLLABLE DESIRE TO HAVE A SALAD MADE FROM THAT EUROPEAN BELLFLOWER. YOU KNOW, RAMPION!

PEASANT: YOU MEAN THOSE WEEDS THERE?

WIFE: RAMPION, DEAR, AND I FEAR I MUST HAVE SOME OR I SHALL SURELY DIE.

PEASANT: ALL RIGHT, DEAR, IF IT'S RAMPION YOU WANT, RAMPION YOU SHALL HAVE!!

NARRATOR: AND SO THE HUSBAND SNEAKED TO THE GARDEN WALL, PEERED OVER THE TOP AND LEAPED INTO THE GARDEN OF THE WITCH WHOM EVERYONE FEARED.

PEASANT: RAMPION, SHMAMPION..IT STILL LOOKS LIKE WEEDS TO ME. ...OOOOPS! YOU DON'T HAVE TO TELL ME, YOU ARE THE WITCH, RIGHT? AND I AM IN YOUR GARDEN AND I HAVE STOLEN YOUR RAMPION AND I AM <u>PUTTING BACK</u> THE RAMPION AND I AM LEAVING YOUR GARDEN AND...

WITCH: HALT! YOU CANNOT MOVE!!

PEASANT: YOU KNOW, YOU'RE RIGHT?

WITCH: YOU HAVE COME INTO MY GARDEN LIKE A THIEF, THEREFORE LIKE A THIEF, YOU MUST PAY THE SUPREME PENALTY!

PEASANT: ALAS, BE MERCIFUL. I AM ONLY HERE BECAUSE MY WIFE SEES YOUR RAMPION...

WITCH: (INTERRUPTING) I THINK I'LL TURN YOU INTO A TOAD!!

PEASANT: AND, AND HAS SUCH A LONGING FOR IT THAT SHE WOULD DIE IF SHE COULD GET NO RAMPION...

(HE CHANGES INTO TOAD BUT GOES ON SPEAKING)

<u>RAPUNZEL</u>

PAGE 2

WITCH:
THAT'S TRUE! YOU CAN TAKE AWAY AS MUCH RAMPION AS
YOU LIKE...BUT ON <u>ONE</u> CONDITION. YOU MUST GIVE ME THE
CHILD WHICH YOUR WIFE IS ABOUT TO BRING INTO THE WORLD.
~~I WILL CARE FOR IT LIKE A MOTHER AND ALL WILL BE WELL~~
~~WITH IT.~~

NARRATOR:
IN HIS FEAR THE HUSBAND CONSENTED TO EVERYTHING. AND WHEN
THE BABY WAS BORN THE WITCH APPEARED, GAVE IT THE NAME
RAPUNZEL (WHICH IS SHORT FOR RAMPION) AND TOOK IT AWAY
WITH HER.

WITCH:
HEH, HEH, HEE, HEE, HEE!

WIFE:
ALAS, NOT ONLY DOES THE WITCH TAKE OUR CHILD, BUT WHO EVER
HEARD OF A BABY NAMED AFTER A SALAD...BOO, HOO, HOO!

PEASANT:
I'LL ALWAYS THINK OF HER AS OUR EUROPEAN BELLFLOWER.

NARRATOR:
RAPUNZEL GREW INTO A BEAUTIFUL CHILD. SHE PLAYED IN THE
WOODS AND WAS VERY CAREFUL OF HER LONG HAIR WHICH SHE
WOULD COMB DAY AFTER DAY.

WHEN SHE WAS TWELVE YEARS OLD, THE WITCH SHUT HER UP IN
A TOWER. IT HAD NEITHER STAIRCASE OR DOOR...ONLY A SMALL
WINDOW. MATTER OF FACT THERE WAS ONLY ONE WAY TO CLIMB
UP THE TOWER...

WITCH:
RAPUNZEL, RAPUNZEL, LET DOWN YOUR HAIR, THAT I MAY CLIMB
THE GOLDEN STAIR.

NARRATOR:
AND <u>THAT</u> WAS THE WAY. WELL, A COUPLE OF YEARS LATER THE
KING'S SON WAS WALKING IN THE FOREST AND HE CHANCED TO HEAR
A SONG SO LOVELY...THAT HE STOPPED TO LISTEN.

THE LOVELY VOICE CAME FROM RAPUNZEL'S TOWER. THEN, AS THE
PRINCE WATCHED FROM THE BUSHES...

WITCH:
RAPUNZEL, RAPUNZEL, LET DOWN YOUR HAIR, THAT I MAY CLIMB
THE GOLDEN STAIR.

NARRATOR:
THE PRINCE WAS AMAZED INDEED, AND AS SOON AS THE WITCH HAD
GONE HE APPROACHED THE TOWER.

PRINCE:
AHEM...AHEM...RAPUNZEL, RAPUNZEL, LET DOWN YOUR HAIR...
HOO!...THAT I MAY CLIMB THE GOLDEN STAIR. WOW!
RAPUNZEL, I HAVE SEARCHED FAR AND WIDE BUT NEVER HAS MY
HEART BEEN SO TOUCHED BY SONG OR BEAUTY SUCH AS YOURS.

<u>RAPUNZEL</u>

PAGE 3

RAPUNZEL: I LIKE YOU TOO.

PRINCE: WILL YOU BE MY WIFE AND LIVE WITH ME IN MY KINGDOM?

RAPUNZEL: YES, I WILL GLADLY GO WITH YOU BECAUSE ACTUALLY THERE
DOESN'T SEEM TO BE ANY FUTURE HERE. I MEAN, RAPUNZEL,
LET DOWN YOUR HAIR...LET UP YOU HAIR. I'M SICK OF USING
MY HAIR AS A LADDER. GIVES ME A HEADACHE, I'LL TELL YOU!

PRINCE: THEN IT'S SETTLED. WE'LL BE MARRIED RIGHT AWAY. JUST
LET DOWN YOUR HAIR AND WE'LL BE OFF.

RAPUNZEL: AREN'T YOU FORGETTING SOMETHING?

PRINCE: NO...WHAT?

RAPUNZEL: ME! IF I LET DOWN <u>MY</u> HAIR HOW AM <u>I</u> TO GET DOWN?

PRINCE: OH, ER, UH, LET'S SEE. FIRST I CLIMB DOWN AND..THEN...
NO, FIRST <u>YOU</u> CLIMB...HM...RAPUNZEL, HOW LONG DO YOU
THINK IT WILL TAKE FOR <u>MY</u> HAIR TO GROW.

RAPUNZEL: I RATHER DOUBT IF YOU WILL BE ABLE TO GROW ENOUGH HAIR IN
TIME. I THINK YOU HAD BETTER GO NOW. THE WITCH WILL SOON
RETURN.

PRINCE: DON'T WORRY, RAPUNZEL. I'LL THINK OF <u>SOMETHING</u>! OOOPS!

WITCH: AH, YOU HAVE COME TO FETCH YOUR LADY LOVE. WELL, YOU GOOFED.
~~RAPUNZEL IS LOST TO YOU FOREVER.~~ YOU WILL NEVER SEE HER AGAIN.
HEH, HEH, HEE, HEE, HEE!

NARRATOR: AND SO THE POOR PRINCE WANDERED, UNABLE TO SEE A THING -
EATING ROOTS AND BERRIES. MEANWHILE, BACK AT THE TOWER...

WITCH: OH, YOU WICKED CHILD, I THOUGHT I SEPARATED YOU FROM THE
WORLD-YET YOU DECEIVED ME. JUST FOR THAT...

RAPUNZEL: WELL, NOW YOU'VE DONE IT! WE'RE <u>BOTH</u> STUCK HERE NOW.

WITCH: AREN'T YOU FORGETTING?

(ZIT!)

NARRATOR: AND SO POOR RAPUNZAL WAS LEFT TO LIVE IN THE TOWER ALL ALONE
AND IN GREAT POVERTY. THE POOR PRINCE WANDERED ABOUT IN THE
FOREST FOR TWO YEARS. THEN ONE DAY...

PRINCE: ...OOOH! IT'S...IT'S HAIR!

RAPUNZEL

PAGE 4

NARRATOR: YES, HAIR IT WAS.. FOR IN TWO YEARS RAPUNZEL'S TRESSES
              HAD GROWN TO THEIR FULL LENGTH AGAIN.

PRINCE: RAPUNZEL, I CANNOT SEE YOU, BUT I KNOW YOU'RE THERE!
              I TOLD YOU I'D THINK OF SOMETHING AND I HAVE! ONLY I
              CAN'T SEE!

RAPUNZEL: WHY DON'T YOU TAKE OFF YOUR HAT?

PRINCE: HM? ...I CAN SEE!! NOW I'LL CLIMB DOWN YOUR HAIR AND WHEN
              I GET TO THE BOTTOM I'LL EXPLAIN MY PLAN!

RAPUNZEL: WHAT'S YOUR PLAN?

PRINCE: JUMP!

RAPUNZEL: JUMP? THAT'S YOUR PLAN?

PRINCE: YES!

RAPUNZEL: SOME PLAN!

              (FAP!)

NARRATOR: AFTER THREE DAYS IN THE BARBER SHOP RAPUNZEL AND THE PRINCE
              WERE MARRIED AND LIVED HAPPILY EVER AFTER. THAT IS UNTIL ONE
              DAY...

RAPUNZEL: DARLING I KNOW THIS SOUNDS FANTASTIC AND UTTERLY ABSURD, BUT
              I HAVE THIS UNCONTROLLABLE DESIRE TO HAVE A SALAD MADE FROM
              THAT VARIETY OF EUROPEAN BELLFLOWER.

PRINCE: RAMPION?

RAPUNZEL: YES, DEAR, RAMPION.

WITCH: WELL, HERE WE GO AGAIN! HEH, HEH, HEE, HEE, HEE!

CINDERELLA   (FOURTEEN)

PAGE ONE

NARRATOR: ONCE UPON A TIME THERE WAS A GIRL NAMED CINDERELLA WHO
              LIVED WITH HER TWO SISTERS. EVERY NIGHT THE TWO SISTERS
              WOULD DRESS UP AND GO INTO TOWN WHERE THEY WERE POPULAR
              AND SOUGHT AFTER SCRUB WOMEN. NIGHT AFTER NIGHT, CINDERELLA
              WOULD STAY HOME DOING THE CHORES.

CINDERELLA: IT'S WORK, WORK, WORK...ALLA TIME, WORK.

NARRATOR: THEN ONE DAY SHE HEARD A STRANGE LITTLE VOICE.

FAIRYY   CINDERELLA...CINDERELLA...

CINDERELLA: WHO LEFT THAT SCREEN OPEN AGAIN? (SWAT, SWAT)

FAIRY: HEY, WATCH IT! HOLD IT! I'M YOUR FAIRY GODMOTHER.

CINDERELLA: OH BOY! ALL RIGHT, CHANGE ME.

FAIRY: HMMM?

CINDERELLA: DO ME OVER, YOU KNOW...THE GOWN...JEWELS...CARRIAGE...
               GLASS SLIPPERS...AND LIKE THAT.

FAIRY: OH, YOU MEAN THIS MODEL?

CINDERELLA: THAT'S IT! THAT'S IT!!

FAIRY: OF COURSE MY DEAR. JUST SIGN HERE.

CINDERELLA: SIGN WHAT?

FAIRY: IT'S OUR CONTRACT. I'LL GIVE YOU <u>ALL</u> THESE THINGS

CINDERELLA: I'LL SIGN....THERE YOU ARE.

FAIRY: FINE.   THERE <u>YOU</u> ARE. (RING!)

CINDERELLA: OOH!

FAIRY: AND IN RETURN YOU SELL ALL THIS WONDERFUL METAL COOKING
               WARE BY MIDNIGHT TONIGHT. JUST $39.95 A SET.

CINDERELLA: I'VE GOT TO SELL ALL THESE POTS AND PANS?

FAIRY: BY MIDNIGHT...IF YOU WANT TO KEEP ALL THESE GOODIES.
               EVEN WE FAIRY GODMOTHERS HAVE TO MAKE A LIVING, YOU KNOW.

                        <u>CINDERELLA</u>   (FOURTEEN)

                        <u>PAGE TWO</u>

CINDERELLA: BUT THERE'S ONLY ONE MAN IN THE KINGDOM RICH ENOUGH TO
               BUY THIS STUFF.

FAIRY: THAT'S RIGHT, HONEY. PRINCE FASCINATO HIMSELF.

NARRATOR: BUT CINDERELLA'S FAIRY GODMOTHER DIDN'T KNOW MUCH ABOUT
               ROYAL FINANCE, FOR THE PRINCE WAS AT THAT MOMENT SAYING
               TO HIS PRIME MINISTER...

PRINCE: THIS BALANCE CAN'T BE RIGHT, FROBISHER. MY FORTUNE RUNS
               INTO SIX FIGURES.

MINISTER: YES, YOUR HIGHNESS...BUT THEY ARE ALL ZEROES.

PRINCE: BUT WHAT ABOUT THE ROYAL SOCK?

MINISTER: THE ROYAL SOCK IS EMPTY SIRE. AND HARK...THE CREDITORS
               ARE POUNDING ON THE CASTLE DOOR.

PRINCE: YOU MEAN...?

MINISTER: YES, YOU HAVE UNTIL MIDNIGHT TO RAISE SOME MONEY...<u>LOTS</u>
               OF MONEY.

PRINCE: BUT MY DEAR FROBISHER...HOW?

MINISTER: HOW ELSE? YOU MUST MARRY A RICH HEIRESS.

PRINCE: BY MIDNIGHT?

MINISTER: THERE'S A BALL AT THE CASTLE TONIGHT...DO YOUR BEST.

NARRATOR: SO THAT NIGHT THE PRINCE LOOKED HIS GUESTS OVER VERY
               CAREFULLY.

PRINCE: OH, OH.

PRINCE: OH, OH.

MINISTER: SOMETHING, YOUR HIGHNESS?

PRINCE: I THINK I'VE GOT A LIVE ONE, FROBISHER.

NARRATOR: AND SO THE PRINCE AND CINDERELLA DANCED FOR HOURS.

PRINCE: YOU ARE THE LOVELIEST GIRL IN MY KINGDOM. YOUR EYES...
                YOUR DIAMONDS.

CINDERELLA: THOSE WERE SURE TERRIBLE BEANS WE HAD FOR DINNER

PRINCE: BEANS?

                    CINDERELLA   (FOURTEEN)
                    ‾‾‾‾‾‾‾‾‾‾
                    PAGE THREE

CINDERELLA: NOW WITH THIS SKILLET YOU CAN COOK THE WATERLESS WAY...

PRINCE: YOUR TEETH ARE LIKE PEARLS...YOUR PEARLS LIKE TEETH.

CINDERELLA: THE PRICE INCLUDES THIS OATMEAL STEAMER.

PRINCE: LET US GO WHERE WE CAN BE ALONE, DARLING.

NARRATOR: SO THE PRINCE AND CINDERELLA SOUGHT OUT A MOONLIT SEAT
                IN THE GARDEN.

PRINCE: OH...HOW LONG I'VE SEARCHED FOR A GIRL JUST LIKE YOU..
                SINCE THIS AFTERNOON, AS A MATTER OF FACT.

CINDERELLA: AND I KNOW YOU'RE MY KIND OF A GUY...A REAL SPENDER.

MINISTER: PSSST. HURRY!

PRINCE: WHAT ABOUT THE CREDITORS?

MINISTER: CAN'T HOLD THEM OFF PAST MIDNIGHT.

FAIRY: PSSST. HOWSIT GOING DEARIE?

CINDERELLA: I'M JUST ABOUT TO CLOSE THE SALE.

FAIRY: TELL HIM ABOUT OUR LAYAWAY PLAN...YOU'VE ONLY GOT AN HOUR
                LEFT.

PRINCE: DARLING, LET ME TAKE YOU AND YOUR MONEY AWAY FROM ALL
                THIS...HERE IN MY CASTLE.

CINDERELLA: REMEMBER, NO CASTLE IS COMPLETE WITHOUT KLOPMEYERS
                KOOKWARE.

NARRATOR: SO THE PRINCE AND CINDERELLA CONTINUED TO SPEAK OF LOVE
                AND SAUCEPANS UNTIL ALMOST MIDNIGHT.

PRINCE: SUCH GRACE, SUCH BEAUTY, SUCH REAL CASH VALUE...WILL
                YOU BE MINE?

CINDERELLA: THERE'S NO VITAMIN WASTE, SEE? AND THEY SCOUR CLEAN
                IN A JIFFY.

FAIRY: YOU'VE GOT JUST TWO MINUTES.

MINISTER: YOU HAVE JUST TWO MINUTES.

<u>CINDERELLA</u>   (FOURTEEN)

<u>PAGE FOUR</u>

prince;   say yes, my love.

CINDERELLA: WHAT'S 39.95 TO A SPORT LIKE YOU?

FAIRY: SHOW HIM THE EGG POACHERS, DEARIE. ONLY 70¢ EXTRA.

MINISTER: GIVE HER THE BENDED KNEE BIT. IT'S ALMOST MIDNIGHT.

NARRATOR: OF COURSE IN SUCH CLOSE QUARTERS, THE PRIME MINISTER AND
                   THE FAIR GODMOTHER WERE BOUND TO MEET SOONER OR LATER.

MINISTER: YOUR SERVANT, MADAM.

FAIRY: YOU'RE CUTE, HONEY...DO YOU DO YOUR OWN COOKING?

PRINCE: LET US SEAL OUR LOVE WITH A KISS.

CINDERELLA: JUST $5.00 DOWN AND PENNIES A WEEK.

PRINCE: (SMACK)

MINISTER: MARRY HER, QUICK!". I'VE GOT TO PAY CASH FOR THESE POTS.

NARRATOR: UNFORTUNATELY IT WAS ALREADY A LITTLE TOO LATE...FIRST
                   CINDERELLA LOST HER PERMANENT...THEN HER JEWELS...THEN
                   HER GOWN.

PRINCE: MY, YOU HEIRESSES CERTAINLY DEPRECIATE FAST.

NARRATOR: EMBARRASSED, CINDERELLA RAN FROM THE CASTLE...LOSING ONE
                   OF HER SLIPPERS AS SHE DID SO. THE PRINCE, OF COURSE,
                   WAS FINALLY CORNERED BY HIS CREDITORS.

                   SOUND: (YOWLS)

PRINCE: FROBISHER!

FAIRY: HE'S NOT HERE, HONEY, BUT MAYBE I CAN BE OF SOME
                   ASSISTANCE.

NARRATOR: SO CINDERELLA RETURNED TO HER OLD HOME AND HER OLD JOB.

CINDERELLA: WORK, WORK, WORK. ALLA TIME WORK.

                   SOUND:(KNOCK, KNOCK, KNOCK.)

                   ...WHO'S THERE?

<pre>
                CINDERELLA   (FOURTEEN)
                PAGE FIVE

PRINCE: HOW DO YOU DO, MISS. I AM....

CINDERELLA: I KNOW WHO YOU ARE. YOU'RE THE PRINCE.

NARRATOR: YES, IT WAS THE PRINCE. REAL LOVE HAD TRIUMPHED AT LAST..
                THE WORLD BECAME ALIVE...TO THE TEMPO OF ROMANCE...THE
                BIRDS AND BEES SANG OUT ...A THOUSAND STARS FELL ON THE
                LOVELY YOUNG GIRL AND THE HANDSOME PRINCE.

PRINCE: YOUNG LADE, I HAVE HERE...

CINDERELLA: I KNOW, I KNOW...YOU HAVE MY SLIPPER.

PRINCE: NO, AS A MATTER OF FACT, IT'S BRUSHES.

CINDERELLA: BRUSHES?

PRINCE: YES, SOME OLD LADY HAS ME SELLING THEM DOOR TO DOOR.

FAIRY: I TOLD YOU, HONEY...I'VE GOT TO MAKE A LIVING SOMEHOW.
</pre>

Another Ward & Scott production is *Fractured Flickers*. This 1963–1964 syndicated half-hour program has the novel premise of showing clips from classic silent film dramas to which crazy dialogue, music, and sound effects have been added. The vocal talents of Bullwinkle fame gave voice to the disrespected actors of the past. The show had its fans—Johnny Carson plugged it on *The Tonight Show*—but there were even more detractors. Lon Chaney Jr. tried unsuccessfully to sue Jay Ward for making a farce of his famous father's 1923 epic *The Hunchback of Notre Dame* by turning the tragic Quasimodo character into "Dinky Dunstan, Boy Cheerleader."

The comically disgruntled host of *Fractured Flickers* is Hans Conried.[173] It is his solemn duty to introduce the clips and interview whatever celebrities Ward and Scott could convince to be on the show. Eddie was the only such guest who had actually starred in silent films. Conried stepped out of character long enough to conduct a highly respectful interview. The two men are seated next to each other, rather awkwardly, due to the fact that the low-budget program had only one camera to shoot the interview segments. Conried addresses that one camera and begins a long, florid—but sincere—introduction of his esteemed guest. Although these two consummate actors do their best to make the interview seem spontaneous, it is rather obvious they are both reading from cue cards. Adding a cheesy element to the whole thing is a laugh track that was then the norm for single-camera situation comedies.

> **Hans.** Ladies and gentlemen, tonight we are indeed privileged to have with us a gentleman whose long career has embraced both silent and talking pictures, as well as television, and of course, the legitimate theatre. From his first starring role in the silent version of *Ruggles of Red Gap*, to his current busy schedule of motion picture and television work, he has for a (*addressing Eddie*)—may I candidly say half-a-century?
>
> **Eddie.** Oh, make it *fifty*—it seems easier.
>
> **Hans.** (*Re-addressing the camera*) For fifty years he has brought joy to literally hundreds of millions of theatregoers.

173 Hans Georg Conried Jr. (1917–1982) was a Maryland-born, New York City–raised actor and comedian. He is perhaps best remembered for providing the voices of George Darling and Captain Hook in Walt Disney's *Peter Pan* (1953), Snidely Whiplash in Jay Ward's *Dudley Do-Right* cartoons, and Professor Waldo P. Wigglesworth in Ward's *Hoppity Hooper* cartoons. He was also active in radio, playing Professor Kropotkin on *My Friend Irma,* and in television as the Lebanese Uncle Tonoose on the Danny Thomas sitcom *Make Room for Daddy.*

One of the grand gentlemen of the American theatre, Mister Edward Everett Horton.

Eddie. (*Smiling broadly*) Thank you, thank you, Hans, you are so right! You know, for a while there I wasn't sure if you were introducing me or one of the *lesser* saints.

Hans. Mister Horton, your roles in pictures have often portrayed you as a prime minister, a valet, uh, a confidant, one of the European noblemen, you know, for many years quite frankly, I thought of you as an English actor.

Eddie. Oh, *really?* I played them all with the same face. Well, as a matter of fact, I am what is known as a rock-ribbed American—well, maybe not *rock*.

Hans. How few can say that? I've been there. May I be so bold as to inquire where you were born?

Eddie. Oh, it's not bold at all—I think it's nice; you're showing interest. As a matter of fact, it was in Brooklyn, New York.

(*A gruff male voice off camera exclaims, "Yayyyy!" Eddie and Hans affect pained expressions.*)

Hans. (*Disdainfully*) *Please.*

Eddie. Why, *why that*, do you suppose? Why do they cheer about *that?*

Hans. It does them credit, you know. It's that warm consanguinity—

Eddie. I *love* that word; I haven't heard it in years. *Consanguinity.*

Hans. Of course, I can't write it, but I do say it on occasion. You should, then, have a vast number of films from which you could pick your favorite "flicker," Mister Horton. May I ask what it is?

Eddie. (*Chuckling wryly, as if to say, "Oh, no, you don't"*)
Well, knowing what your production [crew] does to old
pictures, I am surely not going to pick one of my own!
Oh, no, no, no. I remember seeing a marvelous picture
back in seventeen-, back in eighteen-, nineteen- . . .

Hans. *Nineteen.*

Eddie. *Nineteen twenty-six.* Yes, my mother carried me
into the theatre.

Hans. Oh, that goes without saying!

Eddie. Well, it was one of those frothy films about an
imaginary country and an American girl who becomes
a duchess or something. It's typical of many pictures
they've been making ever since. . . .

Hans. Oh, yes, of course, you must mean the picture,
from nineteen twenty-six, *Young April.*

Eddie. Oh, you guessed it!

Hans. I didn't guess it; we're really prepared to show it.[174]

The deference shown to Eddie was indicative of the regard
in which he was held by Ward and Scott. Bill Scott, in particular, viewed the aging character actor with a sense of awe. As he
recalled, "One time I asked him, 'Edward Everett, to what do you
attribute your energy at an age when most people are retired?' and
he said, 'Well, Bill, do you know where I'm going after this recording? I'm going to my mother's [one-hundredth] birthday party!'"[175]

Eddie had no objection to assuming the role of mother's boy,
even well into his maturity. When he called Isabella to let her

---

174 *Fractured Flickers,* episode no. 6, with guest Edward Everett Horton (September 5,
     1963), VCI Video, 2004.
175 Ibid., pp. 344–345.

know he was going to a cast party, she cautioned her seventy-three-year-old son, "That's fine, Edward, but remember : don't eat too much and don't talk about yourself."[176]

Despite the life of leisure Eddie's celebrity had made possible for her, she never really approved of his being an actor. "Edward," she would say, "I do wish you would give up this line of work you're pursuing and settle down and make a difference in the community."[177]

His response?

"I would say, 'Isabella …'—Isabella was her name—'Isabella, *this* [Belleigh Acres] is the community. Twenty-two acres I've got here. All I need is a post office. I'm the boss.'"[178] And he was. For example, it was he who set the rules regarding the extent of Isabella's travel plans. No matter how much she begged, he refused to subject a woman of her advanced years to the rigors of traveling from town to town, doing one-nighters. "She threatens every day to go on the stage," he told an interviewer in 1940," and she has never been able to understand why I can't get her a part in pictures."[179] He looked out for her comfort during their various European excursions, with England being an especially favored destination. Eddie loved touring London's many antique shops,

---

176 Slide, p. 60. Eddie's mother would not have been pleased with her seventy-nine-year-old son's admission regarding his television appearances: "I've been on television for years, telling everything I know. There's nothing left to tell. This week I was on 'Today' with Douglas Fairbanks Jr. to reminisce about his father. Well, we started out that way, but we ended up reminiscing about me." ("Edward Everett Horton Makes TV Series Debut," *Portland Press Herald* [Maine], September 16, 1965.)
177 *The Real Tinsel*, p. 235.
178 Ibid.
179 Irwin.

always looking for the best deals. "You see," he told a reporter, "I am quite a collector of glass, pictures, furniture, and china. I collect what I *think* are antiques, but Mother says that *anybody* could sell me *anything* that looks old and is cheap."

When her son got that certain antique gleam in his eye, Isabella would say, "Oh, Edward, *where* are you going to put it?"

Eddie and Isabella during one of their many trips together.
Edward Everett Horton Collection

He was defiant. "Don't ask me where I am going to put it," he said emphatically. "*I don't know*. I just *want* it, that's *all*."[180]

Eddie ended up storing innumerable pieces; he even built rooms onto his home to accommodate his latest purchases.

Isabella Stephen Diack Horton passed away on August 28, 1961, just two months shy of her 102nd birthday. She was laid to rest in the Horton family plot in the Whispering Pines section of Forest Lawn Memorial Park in Glendale. Her marker reads : "Beloved Mother."[181]

"There are two things I like about television," Eddie told a newspaper reporter. "If I'm working with a good director and he is pleased with my performance, that's satisfying. I don't need a big audience. The other thing is they pay you so well. There's no applause, but they keep asking you to come back for more money."[182]

On a little-remembered mid-sixties ABC sitcom called *Valentine's Day*, Eddie had two guest starring roles. The first was that of Charles Marx, a lonely English professor who hasn't had a decent night's sleep in fifty years. The other was Chief Wampum, an ancient Native American. Although this might seem like an odd

---

180 *The Real Tinsel*, p. 235.

181 Eddie purchased lot 994 in the Whispering Pines section of Forest Lawn Memorial Park in Glendale, California. It is there, in space 2, that Isabella rests. Eddie occupies space 3 (his plain marker has only his name and birth and death dates). His sister, Hannabelle Horton Grant, died in 1992 at the age of 101, the same age as Isabella at the time of her passing. Eddie's brother George Diack Horton, who died at eighty-four in 1971, is in Forest Lawn's Vale of Memory section, Map 1, lot 474, space 1.

182 McManus.

casting choice for the Caucasian actor, Eddie played it for all it was worth. The executives at ABC must have approved as the same basic character, now bearing the title Chief Roaring Chicken, appeared in six episodes of the network's half-hour Western spoof, *F Troop*, which aired Tuesday nights at nine. Politically correct it was not, but the character was (and still is) undeniably funny. He even showed up in episodes 47 and 48 of the enormously popular camp action hero series *Batman*, this time using the moniker Chief Screaming Chicken, the last of the Mohicians. Written by Stanley Ralph Ross and Edwin Self, the two-parter, "An Egg Grows in Gotham" (a play on the 1943 book title *A Tree Grows in Brooklyn*) and "The Yegg Foes in Gotham" marked the first television appearance of Egghead, a farm-fresh villain with an egg-shaped head and an endless supply of egg-related puns, e.g.g., egg-cellent; eggs-actly, egg-ceptional, egg-cettera. He is played with a side order of ham by the incomparable Vincent Price. Chief Screaming Chicken (Eddie) is an unassuming character who earns an honest living selling blankets, souvenirs, tacos, pizza, and blintzes at his roadside teepee. Egghead steals the city's charter and finds a loophole wherein he could take possession of Gotham City if the settlers' descendants fail to pay the chief nine racoon pelts, although given the rate of inflation, the chief ups the ante to twelve pelts. At one point, he says : "Indian poor businessman, my cousin, ooh . . . he sell Manhattan for twenty-four dollars, could have got thirty-five!"[183]

---

183 IMDb.

Egghead (Vincent Price, left) and Chief Screaming Chicken (Eddie) pose for a publicity still for ABC's Batman *in 1966. Steve Cox*

"I don't watch much television," Eddie candidly told an interviewer. "I mean, if you have the thing on, you have to get up from your comfortable chair to turn it off. A nuisance."[184]

---

184 McManus.

Like many actors from Hollywood's golden age, he also felt that the constant rerunning of his old movies on television should be generating some residuals, which they most certainly were not. They did, however, keep former stars before the public, which could result in current bookings. As for watching his own films, Eddie compared the experience to reading old love letters : "Either you're reminded of the days you wish weren't over, or you're reminded of things you would rather *not* remember, like lousy notices. There's nothing to be gained."

"But I'm going to watch *F Troop*," he added. "I'll watch it if it kills me."[185]

Scene 2 : Curtain Calls

By most accounts, Eddie was an affable fellow on and off the set. Frances Marion, the noted screenwriter, described him as "one of the most genuinely kind individuals in show business."[186] Doris Nolan, who plays Katharine Hepburn's sister in *Holiday*, recalled the making of that 1938 film as a less-than-friendly experience. As she told Tony Slide : "Lew Ayres was *very* quiet. I didn't like Cary Grant—he was always very rude to me. Hepburn was trying to steal my boyfriend, Gregory La Cava, away from me for her companion, a wealthy society woman, and whenever I came across well in a scene, she would demand retake after retake." But Edward Everett Horton, she said happily, was "a wonderful actor … a very amiable chap."[187]

---

185 Ibid.
186 http://www.elisarolle.com/queerplaces/ch-d-e/Edward%20Everett%20Horton.
    html.
187 Slide, p. 65.

Someone who bore witness to a different side of Eddie is nonagenarian Jerry Vermilye, who has worked in theatre productions since the age of nineteen. This accomplished gentleman shared with the authors his textured memories of working with Eddie seventy years earlier, in 1954. At that time, Vermilye was the stage manager for the Berkshire Playhouse in the Berkshire Hills section of Stockbridge, Massachusetts. As he recalls :

A number of well-known actors and actresses guest starred at our playhouse, appearing in whatever play they were touring with at the time. Edward Everett Horton was then starring in a 1951 British comedy entitled *The White Sheep of the Family* by Lawrence du Garde Peach and Ian Hay. The story revolves around a clan of crooks. One of the sons has opted for a law-abiding life, causing friction with his family members, including his father, played by Horton. In some cases, actors of note—Sylvia Sidney was one—would send an advance man to rehearse; most stars would only show up to do the actual performances. Horton, an old hand in the ways of the stock player, appeared a week prior to showtime to rehearse. These rehearsals took place at a ramshackle red barn, located on a dirt road about a mile from the playhouse.

During an early rehearsal, Horton turned on his leading lady, an experienced (and very pleasant) actress named Audrey Ridgewell. "You are unprofessional," Horton bluntly told her within earshot of the entire cast and crew. "You have *no business* even being on a stage." Utterly humiliated, Audrey tried to defend herself, saying that she had worked in many productions, including one with Helen Hayes. The playhouse's director, Billy Myers, a relaxed individual, did what he could to placate both actors. As for the onlookers, we were offended by the way Horton was treating our colleague.

At another rehearsal, Horton insisted that a booth be constructed offstage so that he could handle a quick change of suits at one point in the play. Large screens were erected to ensure his privacy. Unfortunately, this was not to his liking either. Once, while rehearsing the change, the actor's harsh voice rang out : "The floor in this quick-change booth is *filthy*! It is absolutely destroying my clothing!"

The show itself went off without a hitch. An audience favorite was the character of a Protestant minister, played by a talented comic actor named Stuart Germain. In fact, he got more, and bigger, laughs than the star himself, much to Horton's chagrin. At one point, he said that if he ever toured with this particular play again, he would assume the role of the minister instead of the family patriarch.

I wasn't sorry to see him go. Edward Everett Horton—*he was something else.*[188]

Attempting to explain his own appeal to audiences, Eddie ventured : "I think I hold up a mirror to domestic nature in my portrayals. A man and wife will come backstage to see me and say, 'Mister Horton, you're *just* like my husband. He can *never* pass a mirror without fixing his tie or stopping.' And the husband will listen to her and say, 'Mister Horton, nothing of the kind. You're just like her *brother*.' And then the battle starts. Certain things could happen in that family, if not with that husband, then with some other husband and wife, which will make them just boil over with rage at each other. They may even divorce. But they see me playing a situation exactly like what they battle over, and instead of being mad, they sit there and yell, 'Isn't that marvelous?' They're laughing at what they were going to scream about at home."[189]

---

188 Lon Davis telephone interview with Jerry Vermilye, June 1, 2024. (Arranged by J.L. Carrier.)

189 *The Real Tinsel,* p. 233.

Indicative of Eddie's work ethic and consistently good health, he was a fixture at the summer theatre in Canal Fulton, Ohio, from 1955 to 1969. (When asked if he followed any particular diet, he said that he favored desserts, particularly those made of chocolate.) Interestingly, it took a movie person to point out to Eddie a facet of being a touring actor. This occurred during the filming of the aforementioned early talkie *Reaching for the Moon*. Doug Fairbanks and Eddie were dining *al fresco* with Sam Goldwyn, Joseph Schenck, and another Hollywood mogul whose name Eddie could not recall. Samuel Goldwyn was known for his meticulous productions and his unusual aphorisms, better known as *Goldwynisms*. Expressions coined by the producer born in Warsaw, Poland, in 1879, such as "Include me out" and "Modern dancing is so old-fashioned," have long been a part of Hollywood lore. A previously unknown quote that may not have been as quotable, nevertheless had a significant impact on Eddie. "It was there I heard Mister Goldwyn say, 'Douglas, it's not how much they like you in this town; it's 'Are they going to like you in the *next* one?' That's been on my mind ever since; every time I'm performing in a play, and I hear the applause. I know it's Friday, and Sunday night is the last performance and then I'm going to play in Ohio. I wonder if they're going to like me there. They did *here*, but will they like me *there*? I think Robert Browning put it this way : 'A man's reach must exceed his grasp, Or what's a heaven for?'[190] Well, Mister

---

190 According to the website *The Socratic Method*, within "Robert Browning's famous quote, 'Ah, but a man's reach should exceed his grasp, Or what's a heaven for?' lies a profound message about the human pursuit of greatness. At first glance, the quote suggests that one should strive for goals and aspirations beyond their current capabilities. It implies that the act of reaching for something beyond our grasp is not

Goldwyn said it a little differently, 'It isn't how much they like you in this town'; it's, 'Are they going to like you in the *next* one?'"[191]

According to reviews and the memories of his supporting players, Eddie was *always* an audience favorite. Part of his success must be attributed to the plays he selected to perform, including Andre Roussin's French farce *Nina*, in which he portrayed a hypochondriacal husband whose wife is conducting a clandestine affair. These were not Broadway smashes, but they were ideal as touring shows, both in the United States and Australia. The action takes place in one setting, generally a living room; there are usually three or four characters, and the storylines are light and frothy so as not to tax the casual theatregoer unduly. Even when Eddie picked the occasional dud, the critics still praised *him*, and the ticketholders had a good time. According to the *Boston Globe*'s Cyrus Durgin,

> Edward Everett Horton is always fun, no matter what he appears in. But how he ever got sold on "His French Wife" will ever be a mystery to me. The only moments of fun are when Mr. Horton is giving out with his own wonderful pantomime; when he is posing as his own mother, to escape the Paris police, and when he sits down to read and everything goes wrong, from the position of the sofa pillows to the lamp that won't light. Otherwise, "His French Wife" is as dull and witless a piece as you can imagine.[192]

When a new play didn't work, Eddie would gladly return to *Springtime for Henry*. It was, after all, comfortably familiar. It had

---

only essential but also provides a purpose to our existence. By aspiring to attain the seemingly unattainable, we are propelled forward, spurred by the infinite possibilities that lie within our reach."

191 *The Real Tinsel*, p. 235.

192 Cyrus Durgin, "Summer Stock: Edward Everett Horton in 'His French Wife' at Boston Summer Theatre," *The Boston Globe*, August 29, 1950.

also been something of a gold mine for him. He proudly stated that he was able, with the money he made from that show alone, to buy his Adirondack summer home on Lake George, near Glens Falls, New York. Despite this, Eddie's usually ineffable judgment failed him when he consented to star in the play's revival at Broadway's John Golden Theatre in 1951.

The play's author, Benn W. Levy, traveled all the way from England to New York to personally supervise the rehearsals. This proved a headache for Eddie, who for so long had been in charge, not only of his interpretation of the role, but of the entire production. The opening was scheduled for the evening of March 14, exactly four days before Eddie's sixty-fifth birthday, or twenty-seven years older than his thirty-eight-year-old character. It should be noted that age was not a hindrance to Eddie's comedic abilities. Quite the opposite : the older he became, the funnier he was. The deep lines in his face were well earned, seemingly from years of mugging for the camera. Once in possession of a physique that looked good in a tuxedo or military uniform, he had become paunchy, out of shape. His posture was stooped, subtracting inches from his six-foot frame. His rapid delivery remained the same, however, and his timing was never less than impeccable. It was the incongruity of this aging actor attempting to portray a sexually viable man that must have caused murmuring among those involved in the production. Especially jarring is a line from a monologue in Act 3, when Dewlip confesses that as recently as three months ago, "I made love so promiscuously, so ubiquitously and, I may say, so successfully that I was a danger to the community."[193]

Oh, well. Perhaps the audience and the New York critics wouldn't notice either the age discrepancy of the lead and the supporting players or the dated quality of the play itself.

They noticed, they noticed.

John Chapman wrote that *Springtime for Henry* is "a hoked-up period piece—and so [is] Edward Everett Horton."[194] The theatre critic for *Time* observed that "it is more Autumn than Springtime."[195] Broadway ticket buyers must have read the reviews as the run lasted just six weeks and fifty-three performances, closing on April 28. Eddie, grimly disappointed and no doubt embarrassed, said he would never do the play again. He did not keep his word. The following season he was Henry Dewlip in a Bermuda repertory theater, in which the supporting cast members (Christopher Plummer, Marian Seldes, and Barbara Hamilton) were all more than forty years his junior. Astonishingly, he was still playing the amorous Henry when he was pushing eighty! Over a thirty-year period, he performed *Springtime for Henry* a grand total of 2,700 times.

From that point forward, Eddie was wise to steer clear of Broadway's jaded crowd and stick to summer stock, where the audiences welcomed him warmly and the local press treated his annual visits as a major event. And fortunately, there were some ideal parts for

---

193 Ibid., p. 105.
194 Stein, p. 40.
195 Ibid.

Eddie and Muriel Hutchinson in a posed moment from the Broadway revival of Springtime for Henry *in 1951. Author's collection*

which youth is not a prerequisite. At one of his favorite venues, the Canal Fulton Summer Arena Theatre in Ohio, Eddie gave an endearing interpretation of Elwood P. Dowd, whose companion is a 6 foot 3½-inch-tall, invisible rabbit named Harvey. In 1944, Eddie was offered the role of Elwood in the original Broadway production of Mary Chase's Pulitzer-Prize-winning play. Surprisingly, he turned it down. "I read the script, and I thought 'I never could play a part like this,'" he said. "'This is a character part. Besides, I *can't* be an alcoholic!"[196] Harvey must have convinced him to do it as he relented. A local critic rhapsodized that the seventy-four-year-old actor's "projection of warmth is genuinely moving. His eyes retain the devilish sparkle of a sixteen-year-old."[197]

A Funny Thing Happened on the Way to the Forum is a bawdy musical comedy, with a book by Burt Shevelove and Larry Gelbart, and music and lyrics by Stephen Sondheim. It is said to have been inspired by the farces of the Roman playwright Plautus (254–184 B.C.). Eddie had what amounted to a bit part as Erronious, an elderly man who has spent his life searching for his two children who had been abducted when very young.[198] As he told a reporter, "I'd much rather be carrying the entire responsibility of the show on my shoulders, but I'm not, and that's the way it is. One must be philosophical. I prefer to be working, than not working at all."[199]

Carousel, an especially poignant Rodgers and Hammerstein musical, afforded Eddie two small but choice parts. Described by one critic as "gently and lovably benign," Eddie portrayed the Starkeeper and the Commencement Speaker during a six-week run at the New York State Theatre, co-starring John Raitt as Billy Bigelow. *The Fantasticks* is another timeless show that offered a supporting role for Eddie as Henry, an old actor. Featuring the music of Harvey Schmidt and a book and lyrics by Tom Jones, the

---

196　The role of Elwood P. Dowd was introduced on Broadway by former vaudevillian Frank Fay. James Stewart made the part uniquely his in the 1950 Universal film adaptation of *Harvey.*

197　Stein, p. 40.

198　The role of Erronious was introduced on Broadway by Raymond Walburn. In one of his final roles, Buster Keaton played Erronious in the successful film version of the show in 1966.

199　McManus.

Eddie plays Erronious in a touring company of A Funny Thing Happened on the Way to the Forum *in 1963. Edward Everett Horton Collection*

story concerns two neighboring fathers who trick their teenaged children, Luisa and Matt, into falling in love by staging a feud. The show's original Off-Broadway production opened in 1960 and ran for a total of forty-two years (until 2002) and 17,162 performances, making it the world's longest-running musical. During a 1969 run of *The Fantasticks* with the Kenley Players summer stock theatre in Dayton, Ohio, Eddie "commanded the audience and the stage."[200] The role of the narrator, El Gallo, was played by John Gavin.[201] Eddie told interviewer Bette Rogge that he loved sitting offstage, "listening to the most gorgeous singing,"[202] including the show's signature song, the lyrical "Try to Remember."

One would think that an actor who had as many credits and as much money as Eddie would be secure in his stardom. Think again. According to his agent, Bill Alexander of the Richard Astor Agency: "He's a worrier and he shouldn't be—but he worries about every role."[203] Retirement, however, was not an option. "I'm very happy when I'm working," Eddie insisted. "The only time an actor retires is when nobody asks for him."[204] And, fortunately, they still did. Eddie was so determined to keep working that he accepted roles that required him to, God forbid, sing. In a two-week engagement of Cole Porter's *Kiss Me Kate*, a musical take on Shakespeare's comedy *The Taming of the Shrew*, at the Music

---

200 Uncredited review, 1969.
201 John Gavin (1931-2018) was a strikingly handsome but somewhat wooden actor, who appeared in such films as *Imitation of Life* (1959), *Spartacus* (1960), and *Psycho* (1960). His best performance was essentially a self-parody in *Thoroughly Modern Millie* (1967). In 1981, President Ronald Reagan appointed him the U.S. ambassador to Mexico.
202 YouTube / University of Dayton.
203 Stein, p. 41.
204 Ibid.

Theatre in Houston, Eddie played one of the two gangsters who perform a duet of "Brush Up Your Shakespeare."

Another literary-minded musical was *Dumas and Son*, a satire based on the creator of *The Three Musketeers*. Eighty-one-year-old Eddie posed as an 18th century gossip columnist, looking for some naughty tidbit to write about. At Canal Fulton, Ohio, in the summer of 1969, he was in the cast of a brand-new show, *How Now, Dow Jones*. In that one he played a Wall Street tycoon who can't remember his mistress's name, or even what she looks like.

Small parts notwithstanding, Eddie was in his element. "I like to be the show-off," he admitted. "I like the electric *'something'* that comes with playing a part in the theatre, 'live,' don't you know? The audience is with you and they're laughing at you. At the end of the show, there's enough applause for you to come on and make a little speech."[205] This is what he said :

> The older I grow in this wonderful profession of which I have an honor to be a member, the more convinced I become that you can listen to waves on the shore of a brook in the forest, the wind in the trees, or the rain on the roof, but there is no more thrilling, no more exhilarating sound in all of nature than applause, and I could never get enough of it.[206]

Whether or not Eddie had something to promote, he seemed to enjoy giving interviews. Jack Meredith of *The Windsor Star*, a paper in Michigan, was genuinely impressed by the veteran actor when he met him at a posh restaurant in November 1967. "Lunch with

205 *The Real Tinsel*, p. 229.
206 Ibid., pp. 229–230.

Edward Everett Horton," he writes, "is an experience in leisurely old world dining. Edward is an expert at wielding those map-sized menus and picking out such rare delicacies as fresh strawberries and fresh-sliced tomatoes. With all the concentration of his many character movie roles, Edward makes a very pleasant ritual of proceedings, while he starts off with a Bloody Mary. A martini, very dry, is optional for the guest."[207] Once the exchange of thoughts takes flight, Eddie seems to have an opinion on numerous topics, to wit :

- "I agree that San Francisco is one of the fine cities of the world, even though Los Angeles is where one must work. I settled in California in 1924, so I feel like one of the original settlers."
- "I resent the fact that no Oscars have been given to freelance actors, those not contracted to a major studio."
- "Actors should concentrate on acting and leave the intricacies of politics to the politicians."[208]

Other interviewers seemed surprised that someone of Eddie's advanced age would continue to tour so relentlessly. The reason was straightforward. "I never tire of acting," he said. "I've never wished to do anything else. If you have your moment on the stage, you step forward and take your bows, you can go back to the loneliest, dreariest hotel room, and you still feel the day had been worth something."[209] In truth, Eddie had to endure boredom and loneliness in the long daytime hours prior to the evening's show. He therefore devised a system by which he could mitigate loneli-

207 Jack Meredith, "Edward Everett Horton … Sage, Actor, Raconteur," *The Windsor Star*, November 18, 1967.
208 Ibid.
209 McManus.

ness and contribute to his physical fitness at the same time. With each new city on the tour, he would contact a local tennis pro and meet with him each morning at eight o'clock for a practice session. "We play with *my* rules," he explained. "I call them 'The King of Sweden' rules, which have very little to do with the game of tennis. I want absolutely nothing at the net : no backhands, and the ball has to come directly to me. I don't run. The object for the pro is to make it look as if I am playing. That's in case anybody comes to watch. I like them to think that the old boy is in there trying."[210]

Scene 3 : The Lord of Belleigh Acres

When not on the road or on a sound stage, Eddie enjoyed Belleigh Acres and his "baronial lifestyle."[211] That sanctum sanctorum was threatened in the late 1950s when a contingent of the City of Los Angeles approached him with their plan to turn the majority of his immensely valuable twenty-two acre estate into the Ventura Freeway. A cash settlement for the property was negotiated by Eddie's niece, an attorney, the exact amount of which was never fully revealed to the owner. This was at his request.

"I told her I didn't want to know what they gave me for it," he said, "I want to feel that I have to go on working."[212]

---

210 Ibid.

211 Stein, p. 30.

212 *TV Guide*, October 16, 1966. Eddie's attorney niece was Isabella Horton Grant, his sister Hannabelle's daughter, who would later become a Superior Court judge in San Francisco, specializing in probate and family law. She died at the age of eighty-seven in March 2011 and is buried in the Horton family plot at Forest Lawn-Glendale.

Construction promptly began on expanding the freeway, which would be passing just below his home—and which swept away the tennis courts and the guest house where F. Scott Fitzgerald lived prior to his untimely passing in 1940.[213] What remained was a short stump of Amestoy Avenue, south of Burbank Boulevard. This ultimately became known as Edward Everett Horton Lane. (Another lasting honor is his star on the Walk of Fame, located at 6427 Hollywood Boulevard.) The Horton family members were nothing if not adaptable : they continued living on what remained of the now-two-acre estate. Eddie and his widowed sister, Hannabelle, shared the big house, while younger brother George lived next door.

According to a visiting reporter :

> A flagpole stands above the freeway, and the flag flies day and night, a spotlight on it after dark. "If people don't see the flag, I get letters," says Horton. … His pride in his home is evident, but even here he can't be entirely serious. After telling the history of a pair of columns on the lawn which came from an old San Francisco theatre that had been torn down, he adds, "I think they give the place a Forest Lawn touch."[214]

Movie roles had become few and far between for Eddie. He made only one film in the fifties, and he would have been wise to

---

213 Patricia Ward Biederman, "Great Scott! Fitzgerald was a Local," *Los Angeles Times,* September 30, 1996. F. Scott Fitzgerald (1896–1940), the American writer posthumously celebrated for *The Great Gatsby* and three other novels, was in bad shape in his early forties. He felt forgotten, he was a hard drinker, and he was not always financially solvent. Fortunately, he could manage the $200 monthly rent Eddie charged him to live in his two-story guest house for a year and a half; Fitzgerald even had stationery printed bearing the address 5521 Amestoy Ave, Encino, California. At the time, he was laboring over his unfinished novel *The Last Tycoon.* He died in 1940 at the age of forty-four.

214 Ibid.

"Horton Hears a Highway" could be the accompanying title to this Associated Press photo from 1960. In fact, Eddie claimed not to be bothered by the roaring traffic's boom. "It sounds like the ocean," he insisted.

sit that one out too. We're referring to producer Irwin Allen's big-screen adaptation of Hendrik Willem van Loon's magnum opus, *The Story of Mankind.* The 1957 Warner Bros. film offers a plethora of slightly past-their-prime stars in silly vignettes as historical fig-ures. Eddie has a wordless, pointless—even undignified—cameo as Sir Walter Raleigh. He's only on the screen long enough to be doused with water.

It had been some time since he made *Lost Horizon* and *Arsenic and Old Lace* for Frank Capra, but Eddie still held that producer/director in the highest esteem. So when Capra personally asked Eddie to take a supporting role in his latest film, he could not refuse. *Pocketful of Miracles* (1961) is Capra's remake of his own 1933 comedy-drama *Lady for a Day*. The Depression-era story, with all the colorful trademarks of its author Damon Runyon, focuses on a derelict woman who ekes out a meager living selling apples on the streets of New York City, hence her sobriquet Apple Annie. One of her most dependable customers is Dave the Dude, a prosperous and benevolent bootlegger. In the original version, the leads were played by May Robson and Warren William. Casting for the remake nearly thirty years later proved all but impossible. The role of Annie—a frowsy older woman who, for one day, is transformed into a dignified society matron—was turned down by the likes of Katharine Hepburn, Jean Arthur, Shirley Booth, and Helen Hayes. Bette Davis, who had not made a film in five years, needed a job and was ultimately cast. The part of Dave the Dude was turned down by such heavyweights as Frank Sinatra, Kirk Douglas, Dean Martin, and Jackie Gleason. A far less dynamic actor, Glenn Ford, approached Capra, saying he would help finance the film if he were cast in the lead. Out of desperation, Capra accepted the offer. From day one the production was fraught with backstage drama, with the two hardheaded principals declaring war on each other. Ford insisted that his girlfriend, actress Hope Lange, be given the star's dressing room. There was also reported tension between Ford and Capra. The stress caused the director to have blinding, incapacitating headaches. When the sentimental film was released, it was considered hopelessly old-fashioned and performed disappointingly at the box office. Although he would live for another thirty years, Capra's career as a director ended with *Pocketful of Miracles*. Eddie, who avoided all on-set politics, delivers a typically polished performance as a butler who is loaned to Apple Annie to impress her long-estranged daughter (Ann-Margret, in her screen debut).

Eddie was but one of dozens of old-time comedians in the cast of Stanley Kramer's three-and-a-half-hour widescreen spectacular *It's a Mad, Mad, Mad, Mad World* (1963). In a cameo lasting but a few seconds, Eddie plays Mr. Dinkler, owner of Dinkler's Hardware Store. Standing on the sidewalk in front of his business, he observes a paint-covered man and woman (Sid Caesar and Edie Adams) emerging from an adjoining shop, with the man carrying a stolen pick and shovel. Dinkler, unable to catch them, gives voice to the withering phrase : "You *vandals!*"

Sex and the Single Girl (1964) is based on feminist Helen Gurley Brown's best-selling novel. Eddie plays a publisher in this less-than-distinguished film, which stars Natalie Wood and Tony Curtis. When asked his personal opinion of it, Eddie merely shuddered. Another uniquely sixties-era product is *The Perils of Pauline*, a far-out spoof of the 1914 silent film serial with ingénue Pamela Austin in the role made famous by Pearl White. With its campy trappings, *Perils* is, in reality, three unsold TV pilot episodes from

1965 that were edited together and passed off as a theatrical feature film in 1967. Eddie portrays Caspar Coleman, a fiendish, ninety-nine-year-old gazillionaire who sits in a wheelchair and hits with a cane anyone who displeases him. At one point, he decrees that the comely Pauline will be his grandson's bride. The only catch is that the grandson in question is a newborn baby. Caspar has a solution : freeze the young lady until the boy becomes of age. With a plan like that, what could possibly go wrong?

One of Eddie's oddest films must surely be the independently made, R-rated comedy *2000 Years Later*, which was written, produced, and directed by Bert Tenzer. During the fall of Rome, the god Mercury transforms citizen Gregorius into a ball of fire. Centuries later, Mercury, alarmed by contemporary trends on earth, dispatches the Roman to Hollywood. Horrified by American hedonism, Gregorius is unable to speak. The Roman's silence, however, does not prevent his discovery and exploitation by Goodwyn and Evermore (Eddie and Terry-Thomas), hosts of the televised *International Culture Hour*. There is even a televised Roman orgy, during which Gregorius is seduced by the Zap Pow girl, the sexy star of the show's commercials. Although the film was shot in 1966, it did not find a distributor until 1969. The handful of people who saw it were either confused, high, or not high enough, and the first week's box-office take at Los Angeles's Picwood Theatre was, according to *Daily Variety*, "a frail $7,500."[215] None of these incidentals took away from the fact that Eddie thoroughly enjoyed making the picture.

---

215 *Daily Variety*, March 25, 1969.

Octogenarian Eddie celebrates one of his late birthdays with a little help from actress Susanna Clemm. Scott H. Reboul

It was also during 1969 that Eddie accepted what would be the final film role of his career, that of a muted, crotchety, flatulent, wheelchair-bound tobacco tycoon, Hiram C. Grayson, in *Cold Turkey*. Norman Lear, then in the development phase of his groundbreaking CBS-TV series *All in the Family*, wrote, produced, and directed this dark (and occasionally hilarious) satire of the then-thriving cigarette industry. Reflecting the new permissiveness then taking hold of the movie industry, the GP-rated comedy contains profanity and implied sexual situations. United Artists let *Cold Turkey* thaw on the shelf for two years before it was finally released to theatres and airlines in early 1971.

Eddie never stopped looking ahead. "Well, I have some ideas for the future," he would inform his visitors. "I want to build a great big tower out here, about sixty-five feet high with a deck around the top. Then I want to put on the top of it a very ornate water tank that will work electrically. Then, when I press a button, all over the grounds, a marvelous fountain system, fed by this thingamajig way up on top of the tower, will flow. Like Versailles. About one hundred and seventy-five thousand dollars and I can do it. Life begins at eighty-two."[216]

During interviews, he made a point of saying that he remained open to the possibility of wedded bliss. "I never married," he would say cheerfully. "However, I have not given up hope. This is Leap Year, you know. I have a nice disposition, a lot of antique furniture, and I *still* have two acres of ground."[217] What he didn't have, sadly, was more time. While at his summer home in Glens Falls, he was diagnosed with terminal cancer. Eddie and a registered nurse, Beatrice Ducharme, left New York for Los Angeles, where Eddie was briefly hospitalized. He then went to Belleigh Acres, where he would spend his few remaining days. In a reflective mood, he said, "You know, even though I have said I am only interested in

---

216 *The Real Tinsel*, p. 235.
217 Ibid., p. 228.

'how much money and how long a time' when I'm offered a film, I do remember the really good ones. I must have been lucky! Altogether I've had a grand time!"[218]

Edward Everett Horton Jr. died at the age of eighty-four on September 29, 1970.

---

218 Stein, p. 41.

EPILOGUE

More than a half-century has passed since Eddie shuffled off this mortal coil. The joyous memories inspired by his thousands of live performances have faded away along with their innumerable audience members. Thankfully, the 146 films—some silent but mostly sound, some lost but mostly extant, some shorts but mostly features, some in glorious Technicolor but most in stunning black and white—are on DVD, Blu-ray, streaming services, and Turner Classic Movies (TCM). Thanks to the miracle of digital restoration, these films look better than they did when they were new. The ninety-one "Fractured Fairy Tales"—arguably his most fondly remembered television work—have also been digitally restored and are just a click away on YouTube.

In short, he is not forgotten.

Six years after his passing, there was a retrospective held in New York City of the sparkling Fred Astaire–Ginger Rogers RKO musicals, three of which prominently feature Eddie. Some critic (who shall remain nameless) offended one of his readers, the Pulitzer Prize–winning theatre critic Walter Kerr by insinuating that the films would be better without the inclusion of Eddie, "who merely slowed down the proceedings with his fidgeting and worrying." As Kerr passionately wrote in his Sunday morning column in the *New York Times* on September 26, 1976:

Picking on Edward Everett Horton! If ever there was an uncalled-for sport, a case of wanton cruelty, a lapse of esthetic judgment, it is that. It is just possible that some of the less fortunate among you may not remember Edward Everett Horton (I don't believe it, but I must learn to adapt), a chap who seemed like a lemony mother-hen, high in the pecking order but everlastingly fearful of what might be coming over his shoulder ...

A man of infinite hauteur but limited understanding, he looked with contempt upon the double-take as though it amounted to no more than one pushup before breakfast, multiplied it six or seven times to show what a responsive reflex could really do, if it puts its shoulder to the wheel, uttered commands with imperious authority only to break down utterly if required to repeat them, approached a stammer or an unfinished sentence as though his staying power had been challenged, and he was honor-bound to get half a reel of film out of no syntax at all.

Horton was a master farceur, and Horton was funny.

Filmography
1922–1971

Due to the loss of 80 percent of the studios' output from the silent and early talkie eras, the survival status is given of all films made between 1922 and 1930, as well as those major archives in which either complete or partial prints are housed. We personally viewed as many of Eddie's films as are on YouTube, so that we could confirm those summaries we didn't write as well as those we did.

Key to Sources

AFICFF: *American Film Institute Catalog of Feature Films*
AMPAS: Academy of Motion Picture Arts & Sciences
BFI: British Film Institute
GEH: George Eastman House
IMDb: Internet Movie Database
LBAL2: *Lame Brains and Lunatics 2*
LMCMG: *Leonard Maltin's Classic Movie Guide*
LOC: Library of Congress
MOMA: Museum of Modern Art
UCLA: University of California at Los Angeles
WCFTR: Wisconsin Center for Film and Theatre Research

Too Much Business (April 9, 1922) The Vitagraph Company of America, seven reels, comedy; presumed lost. **Producer:** Albert E. Smith. **Director:** Jess Robbins. **Screenplay:** Ford Beebe. **Camera:** Irving Reis. **Cast:** Edward Everett Horton (*John Henry Jackson*); Ethel Gray Terry (*Myra Dalton*); Tully Marshall (*Amos Comby*); John Steppling (*Simon Stecker*); Carl Gerard (*Ray Gorham*); Elsa Lorimer *(Mrs. Comby)*; Helen Gilmore (*Head Nurse*); Mark Fenton (*Robert Gray*); Tom Murray (*Officer 16*). **Summary:** John Henry Jackson (Eddie) is in love with Myra Dalton, private secretary to his employer, Amos Comby. He induces her to sign a 30-day option agreeing to marry him if he doubles his salary within that time. Learning of the agreement, Comby, determined not to lose his secretary, discharges Jackson. A month later, Jackson is the proprietor of "Hotellerie des Enfants—a parking place for children of busy mothers" and ready to claim Myra. At the same time a large firm proposes a consolidation with Comby on the condition that John Henry be made general manager. Comby is refused when he offers to buy out

Jackson's business, and Gorham induces his nurses to strike, allowing the children to escape and cause wild confusion. John Henry comes to Comby in a rage and is appointed general manager of the consolidation. Myra is only too happy to have the option taken up. —AFICFF

The Ladder Jinx (August 20, 1922) The Vitagraph Company of America, six reels, romantic farce; presumed lost. **Producer:** Albert E. Smith. **Director:** Jess Robbins. **Screenplay:** Edgar Franklin, David Kirkland. **Camera:** Irving Reis. **Cast:** Edward Everett Horton (*Arthur Barnes*); Margaret Landis (*Helen Wilbur*); Wilbur Higby (*James Wilbur*); Tully Marshall (*Peter Stalton*); Otis Harlan (*Thomas Gridley*); Colin Kenny (*Richard Twing*); Tom McGuire (*Judge Brown*); Will Walling (*Officer Murphy*); Tom Murray (*Detective Smith*); Ernest Shields (*Cheyenne Harry*); Max Asher (*Sam*). **Summary:** Peter Stalton, retiring as a bank cashier, is anxious that his nephew Richard Twing will succeed him. The directors, however, appoint Arthur Barnes (Eddie), engaged to Helen Wilbur, the president's daughter. Being highly superstitious, Helen makes Arthur promise to cross back under a ladder under which he had walked earlier in the day. In doing so, he is accused of robbing a house and is pursued by the police. Passing the bank in which he works, he sees two robbers making a getaway just as the president and Helen arrive. Arthur pursues the bandits in their car, accompanied by Helen. They are arrested and accused of robbing Stalton's house and the bank, but Arthur is cleared by Sam, the janitor, who exposes Richard Twing as the culprit. Arthur is freed and is happily reunited with his fiancée. —AFICFF

A Front Page Story (December 1922) The Vitagraph Company of America, six reels, comedy; presumed lost. **Producer:** Albert E. Smith. **Director:** Jess Robbins. **Screenplay:** F.W. Beebe, Arthur F. Goodrich. **Camera:** Vernon L. Walker. **Cast:** Edward Everett Horton (*Rodney Marvin*); James Corrigan (*Matt Hayward*); W.E. Lawrence (*Don Coates*); Mathilda Brundage (*Mrs. Gorham*); Tom McGuire (*Jack Peeler*); Lloyd Ingraham (*Mayor Gorham*); Edith Roberts (*Virginia Hayward*); Buddy Messenger (*Tommy*); Lila Leslie (*Suzanne Gorham*). **Summary:** Through sheer bluff, Rodney Marvin (Eddie) gets a job on a newspaper; becomes the partner of editor Matt Hayward; and brings about a reconciliation between Hayward and his longtime enemy, Mayor Gorham. —AFICFF

Ruggles of Red Gap (August 7, 1923) Famous Players–Lasky / Paramount Pictures, poignant comedy; eight reels, presumed lost. **Producer / **Director:** James Cruze. **Screenplay:** Anthony Coldeway, Walter Woods; based on the 1915 novel *Ruggles of Red Gap* by Harry Leon Wilson. **Notes:** The story was adapted as a Broadway musical in 1915 and as a feature from Essanay in 1918. The story (under the same title) would be remade as a talkie in 1935, starring Charles Laughton in the leading role. **Camera:** Karl Brown. **Cast:** Edward Everett Horton (*Ruggles*); Ernest Torrence (*Cousin Egbert Floud*); Lois Wilson (*Kate Kenner*); Fritzi Ridgeway (*Emily Judson*); Charles Stanton Ogle (*Jeff Tuttle*); Louise Dresser (*Mrs. Effie Floud*); Anna Lehr (*Mrs. Belknap-Jackson*); William Austin (*Mr. Belknap-Jackson*); Lillian Leighton (*Ma Pettingill*); Thomas Holding (*Earl of Brinstead*); Frank Elliott (*Honorable George*); Kalla Pasha (*Herr Schwitz*); Sidney Bracey (*Sam Henshaw*); Milton Brown (*Sen. Pettingill*); Guy Oliver (*Judge Ballard*). **Summary:** Newly rich, uncouth Cousin Egbert Floud wins Ruggles (Eddie), the valet of a British gentleman, in a poker game during a sojourn in Europe with his wife, Effie, and, to his family's chagrin, introduces Ruggles to Red Gap as a colonel. The people of Red Gap treat "Colonel" Ruggles as an honored guest. Ruggles's former employer visits them and falls in love with Kate Kenner, from the wrong side of the tracks. The chap's brother is summoned to break up the match: he does so by marrying Kate. Meanwhile Ruggles has opened a successful restaurant and married Emily Judson, charming protégée of Kate Kenner. —AFICFF

To the Ladies (November 25, 1923) Famous Players–Lasky / Paramount, six reels, comedy; presumed lost. **Producers:** Adolph Zukor, Jesse L. Lasky. **Director:** James Cruze. **Screenplay:** Walter Woods; based on the 1922 Broadway play by George S. Kaufman and Marc Connelly. **Camera:** Karl Brown. **Cast:** Edward Everett Horton (*Leonard Beebe*); Theodore Roberts (*John Kincaid*); Helen Jerome Eddy (*Elsie Beebe*); Louise Dresser (*Mrs. Kincaid*); Z. Wall Covington (*Chester Mullin*); Arthur Hoyt (*Tom Baker*); Jack Gardner (*Bob Cutter*); Patricia Palmer (*Mary Mullin*); Mary Astor (*bit, uncredited*). **Summary:** Beebe (Eddie), Baker, and Mullin, three clerks in a piano-manufacturing concern, vie for the position of factory manager. Baker, aware that the president's wife, Mrs. Kincaid, makes all the important decisions, becomes first choice by currying favor. Later, however, Mrs. Kincaid, impressed with Beebe's wife's intelligence, chooses Beebe. —AFICFF

Flapper Wives (February 23, 1924) Laurence Trimble–Jane Murfin Productions / Selznick Distributing Corp., seven reels, drama; presumed lost. **Directors:** Jane Murfin, Justin H. McCloskey. **Cast:** May Allison (*Claudia Bigelow*); Rockliffe Fellowes (*Stephen Carey*); Vera Reynolds (*Sadie Callahan*); Edward Everett Horton (*Vincent Platt*); Harry Mestayer (*Charles Bigelow*); William V. Mong (*Enoch Metcalf*); Eddie Phillips (*Tony*); Tom O'Brien (*Tim Callahan*); Evelyn Selbie (*Hulda*); Robert Dudley (*Lem*); Stanley Goethals (*Jimsy*); J.C. Fowler (*Dr. Oliver Lee*). **Summary:** Stephen Carey, a broadminded rector, is ousted from his church by the vestrymen. He befriends Claudia Bigelow, a young divorcée who defended his position in the church. Claudia's carelessness in leaving a cigarette burning causes Jimsy, the son of the housekeeper, to go blind. Stephen's prayers restore the boy's sight, and a happy future is predicted for all. **Notes:** Eddie's contribution to this mawkish-sounding lost film is unknown. —AFICFF

Try and Get It (March 9, 1924) Samuel V. Grand / Producers Distributing Corp., six reels, comedy; extant: LOC. **Producer:** Samuel Bischoff. **Director:** Cullen Tate. **Screenplay:** Jules Furthman, Eugene P. Lyle Jr. **Cast:** Bryant Washburn (*Joseph Merrill*), Edward Everett Horton (*Glenn Collins*); Lionel Belmore (*Timothy Perrin*); Hazel Dean (*Telephone Operator*); Billie Dove (*Rhoda Perrin*); Joseph Kilgour (*Larry Donavan*); Rose Dione (*Madame Floris*); Carl Stockdale (*Bookkeeper*). **Summary:** Two young bill collectors, Joseph Merrill and Glenn Collins (Eddie), must collect a debt owed by Timothy Perrin, cement manufacturer and backer of a modiste's shop, or lose their jobs. —AFICFF

The Man Who Fights Alone (September 14, 1924) Famous Players-Lasky Corp. / Paramount Pictures, seven reels, melodrama, presumed lost. **Producers:** Adolph Zukor; Jesse L. Lasky. **Director:** Wallace Worsley. **Screenplay:** Jack Cunningham (based on the short story, "The Miracle of Hate," by William Blacke and Shelley Hamilton). **Camera:** L. Guy Wilky. **Cast:** William Farnum (*John Marble*); Lois Wilson (*Marion*); Edward Everett Horton (*Bob Alten*); Lionel Bellmore (*Meggs*); Barlowe Borland (*Mike O'Hara*); George Irving (*Dr. Raymond*); Anne Shirley (*Dorothy*); Rose Tapley (*Aunt Louise*); Frank Farrington (*Struthers*). **Summary:** Construction engineer John Marble is stricken by paralysis and imagines the growth of love between his wife and his best friend, Bob Alten (Eddie). Although bent on suicide, the shock of seeing his wife and child endangered on a broken bridge causes him to recover from his illness and discover that his suspicions are unfounded. **Notes:** *The Man Who Fights Alone* was filmed on location in Yosemite National Park, California. —AFICFF

Helen's Babies (October 12, 1924) Principal Pictures, eight reels, domestic comedy; extant: Cineteca Italiana (Milan), Gosfilmofond (Moscow), LOC, BFI, UCLA. **Producer:** Sol Lesser. **Director:** William A. Seiter. **Screenplay:** Louis D. Lighton, Hope Loring, based on the 1876 novel *Helen's Babies* by John Habberton. **Camera:** William H. Daniels, Glen MacWilliams. **Cast:** Edward Everett Horton (*Uncle Harry Burton*); Baby Peggy (*Toddie*); Clara Bow (*Alice Mayton*); Jeanne Carpenter (*Budge*); Claire Adams (*Helen Lawrence*); Richard Tucker (*Tom Lawrence*); George Reed (*Rastus, the coachman*); Mattie Peters (*Mandy, the housekeeper*). **Summary:** Two little girls make life rather miserable for their Uncle Harry (Eddie), a bachelor who is left in charge of the children while their parents tour abroad. —AFICFF

Marry Me (June 29, 1925) Famous Players–Lasky / Paramount, six reels, comedy; presumed lost. **Director:** James Cruze. **Screenplay:** Anne Caldwell, Anthony Coldeway, Walter Woods. **Camera:** Karl Brown. **Cast:** Florence Vidor (*Hetty Gandy*); Edward Everett Horton (*John Smith #2*); John Roche (*John Smith #1*); Helen Jerome Eddy (*Sarah Hume*); Fanny Midgely (*Granny*); Ed Brady (*Norman Fribie*); Walt Covington (*Jenkins*); Anne Schaefer (*Mrs. Hume*); Erwin Connelly (*Jackson*). **Summary:** Hetty Gandy, an attractive schoolteacher, visits a chicken farm and falls in love with John Smith, who soon proposes marriage to her. Before she can give her consent, she is called away, leaving behind an egg inscribed with the date on which she will marry John. The egg is to be given to John for his breakfast, but it goes into cold storage instead. Five years pass, and Hetty waits in vain for John to come and claim her as his bride, meanwhile turning away the proposals of Norman Frisbie, a real estate salesman. One day a wire arrives from "John Smith" telling her to be ready to go to an adjoining town with him. The entire town knows of John's coming, and a reception is arranged. When he arrives, Hetty is appalled to find that the John Smith who wired her is not her beloved, but rather a hypochondriac, who, believing himself to have become sick from the cold-storage egg on which Hetty had written years earlier, is suing the dealer from whom he purchased it. To avoid embarrassment, Hetty goes with John to a nearby town and, through a series of unlucky circumstances, is forced to spend the night with him in a hotel room. In order to protect Hetty from scandal, John marries her. They soon come to love each other, and Hetty's love cures John of his hypochondria. **Notes:** This lost film was likely a good vehicle for Eddie, playing John Smith #2, a litigious hypochondriac. —AFICFF

The Business of Love (August 7, 1925), Cosmopolitan Studios (New York City) / Astor Pictures, six reels, comedy-drama, extant. **Director:** Jess Robbins. **Screenplay:** Ford Beebe. **Camera:** Irving Reis. **Cast:** Edward Everett Horton (*Edward Burgess*); Barbara Bedford (*Barbara Richmond*); ZaSu Pitts (*Miss Wright*); Tom Picketts (*Noah Burgess*); Dorothy Wood (*Inez Scarborough*); Carl Stockdale (*James Scarborough*); Tom Murray (*Sweeney*); James Kelly (*Martin Block*); Stanley Taylor (*Willis Graves*); Newton Hall (*Bobby*). **Summary:** Young college graduate Edward Burgess (Eddie), who prefers mechanics to the law, helps James Scarborough, an old inventor, market a revolutionary new invention. Edward, who is in love with Scarborough's niece, Barbara Richmond, further helps by keeping various lawyers away. Edward's uncle Noah thinks his nephew has wasted his education, but Edward tallies up the cost of college and soon pays back the entire amount to Uncle Noah from the money he made with the invention. **Notes:** This film began production at the Vitagraph Studios in March 1923 under the title "The Crash."—AFICFF

Beggar on Horseback (August 24, 1925) Famous Players–Lasky / Paramount, seven reels, expressionistic comedy-drama; extant (incomplete print): LOC. **Director:** James Cruze. **Screenplay:** Walter Woods, whose screenplay is based on the 1924 play by Marc Connelly and George S. Kaufman. **Camera:** Karl Brown. **Music:** Hugo Riesenfeld. **Cast:** Edward Everett Horton (*Neil McRae*); Erwin Connelly (*Mr. Cady*); Esther Ralston (*Cynthia Mason*); Gertrude Short (*Gladys Cady*); Ethel Wales (*Mrs. Cady*); Theodore Kosloff (*Prince in Pantomime*); Betty Compson (*Princess in Pantomime*); James Mason (*Homer Cady*); Frederick Sullivan (*Dr. Rice*). **Summary:** Neil McRae (Eddie), an impoverished composer of serious music, is forced to orchestrate jazz scores to make a living. Although he is in love with Cynthia Mason, a lovely and equally impoverished painter, Neil succumbs to the urging of Dr. Rice and proposes to Gladys Cady, a rich girl whom he instructs in music. After she accepts, Neil is on the verge of psychological collapse and takes medication to help him sleep. He then has a nightmare in which the vulgarity of the Cady family is greatly magnified. When he awakens, the grateful Neil returns to Cynthia. —AFICFF

La Bohème (February 24, 1926) Metro-Goldwyn-Mayer, 95 minutes, tragic drama; extant. **Producer:** Irving Thalberg (uncredited). **Director:** King Vidor. **Screenplay:** Fred de Gresac; Henry Behn, Ray Doyle (continuity); William Conselman, Ruth Cummings (titles); based on

Scènes de la vie de bohème (1847–49) by Henri Murger. **Camera:** Henrik Sartov. **Editor:** Hugh Wynn. **Music:** William Axt, David Mendoza (both uncredited). **Cast:** Lillian Gish (*Mimi Brodeuse*); John Gilbert (*Rodolphe*); Renée Adorée (*Musette*); George Hassell (*Schaunard*); Roy D'Arcy (*Vicomte Paul*); Edward Everett Horton (*Colline*); Karl Dane (*Benoit, the Janitor*); Mathilde Comont (*Madame Benoit*); Gino Corrado (*Marcel*); Eugene Pouyet (*Bernard Gene Pouyet*); Frank Currier (*Theatre Manager*); David Mir (*Alexis*); Catherine Vidor (*Louise*); Valentina Zimina (*Phemie*); Harry Crocker (*uncredited*); Blanche Payson (*uncredited*). **Summary, Review, and Notes:** Colline, a bookish Bohemian (Eddie) and his friend Schaunard manage to raise enough money to keep roommates (and struggling writers) Rodolphe and Marcel from being evicted from their apartment. According to Leonard Maltin, *La Bohème* is a "charming, floridly romantic silent vehicle for Gish and Gilbert (at their very best) as the star-crossed lovers who live among the starving artists in Paris's Latin Quarter. Gilbert and director Vidor had just made *The Big Parade* together; this was a worthy follow-up. This version of *La Bohème* is based on an 1851 novel and is substantially different from Puccini's favorite opera." (***½). —LMCMG

The Nut-Cracker (March 28, 1926; released in the UK as *You Can't Trust Your Wife*), Samuel S. Hutchinson Productions (U.S.) / Associated Exhibitors (UK), six reels, presumed lost. **Director:** Lloyd Ingraham. **Screenplay:** Madge Myton, whose screenplay is based on the 1920 comic novel by Frederic S. Isham. **Camera:** Jack MacKenzie. **Cast:** Edward Everett Horton (*Horatio Slipaway*); Mae Busch (*Martha Slipaway*); Harry Myers (*Oscar Briggs*); Thomas Ricketts (*Isaac Totten*); George Kuwa (*Saki*); Katherine Lewis (*Hortense*); Albert Prisco (*Señor Gonzales*); George Periolat (*Señor Gomez*). **Summary:** Henpecked Horatio Slipaway (Eddie) is hit by a streetcar and regaining consciousness in a hospital, feigns amnesia. Playing the market with a $500 insurance settlement, Horatio makes a fortune and conveniently assumes the identity of a Peruvian millionaire. His wife, Martha, eventually learns of this "rich South American" who so closely resembles her husband and, dressing herself in finery, goes to see if it is her Horatio. Horatio finally "regains" his memory, and he and Martha are reunited. —AFICFF

Poker Faces (September 5, 1926) Universal Pictures, 80 minutes, bedroom farce; extant: GEH, LOC, UCLA. **Producer:** Carl Laemmle. **Director:** Harry H. Pollard. **Screenplay:** Melville W. Brown, based on a story by Edgar Franklin. **Camera:** Charles Stumar. **Cast:** Edward

Everett Horton (*Jimmy Whitmore*); Laura La Plante (*Betty Whitmore*); George Siegmann (*George Dixon*); Tom Ricketts (*Henry Curlew*); Tom O'Brien (*Pug*); Dorothy Revier (*Pug's Wife*); Leon Holmes (*Office Boy*). **Summary:** Jimmy Whitmore (Eddie), a struggling office worker, is constantly harassed by his wife, Betty, and her incessant reminders that they need a new rug, and by the insinuating remarks of Henry Curlew, his employer. Having been found satisfactory by Curlew, however, he is given an important assignment—that of getting a contract with George Dixon, a tough customer. When Jimmy finds that his wife has gone to work to earn extra money, he is forced to engage a prizefighter's wife as a stand-in for the evening. —AFICFF

The Whole Town's Talking (December 26, 1926) Universal Pictures, six reels, postwar domestic comedy; extant: UCLA. **Producer:** Carl Laemmle. **Director:** Edward Laemmle. **Screenplay:** Raymond Connor, based on the play by Anita Loos and John Emerson. The film was remade in 1935 as a starring vehicle for Edward G. Robinson. **Camera:** Charles J. Stumar. **Cast:** Edward Everett Horton (*Chester Binney*); Virginia Lee Corbin (*Ethel Simmons*); Trixie Friganza (*Mrs. George Simmons*); Otis Harlan (*George Simmons*); Robert Ober (*Donald Montallen*); Aileen Manning (*Mrs. Van Loon*); Hayden Stevenson (*Tom O'Brien*); Margaret Quimby (*Sadie Wise*); Dolores del Río (*Rita Renault*). Summary: Chester Binney (*Eddie*), a wounded war veteran, erroneously believes he is carrying a silver plate in his head and must avoid all excitement. —AFICFF

Taxi! Taxi! (April 24, 1927) A Universal-Jewel Production, 70 minutes, farce; extant. **Producer:** Carl Laemmle. **Director:** Melville W. Brown. **Screenplay:** Melville W. Brown, Raymond Cannon, based on the 1925 *Saturday Evening Post* serialized story by George Weston. **Camera:** Gilbert Warrenton. **Cast:** Edward Everett Horton (*Peter Whitby*); Marian Nixon (*Rose Zimmerman*); Burr McIntosh (*Grant Zimmerman*); Edward Martindel (*David Parmalee*); William V. Mong (*Nosey Ricketts*); Lucien Littlefield (*Billy Wallace*); Freeman Wood (*Jersey*), Helen Ferguson (*uncredited*). **Summary:** Peter Whitby (Eddie), a lowly draftsman in the service of a distinguished architectural firm, is sent to the railway station to meet the president's niece, Rose, and makes a very favorable impression on her. At Rose's request, Peter goes shopping with her. He then takes her to a notorious roadhouse to which her uncle, Grant Zimmerman, has forbidden her to go. There they discover Grant with wealthy contractor David Parmalee, and make a quick exit, arousing the suspicions of the house detective. Unable to find a taxi, Peter buys one, unaware that it is the notorious "white taxi" in which a robbery and murder have been committed. —AFICFF

No Publicity (August 1, 1927) Hollywood Productions / Paramount Pictures, two reels, comedy; extant: LOC. **Director:** N.T. Barrows. **Screenplay:** J.T. Crizer, James Davis. **Camera:** Walter Lundin. **Editor:** Carl Himm. **Cast:** Edward Everett Horton (*Edward Howard*); Ruth Dwyer (Sally Lawrence); Josephine Crowell (*Mrs. Van Pelt*); Aileen Manning (*Miss Delilah Blue*); the uncredited members of the cast are Lyle Tayo, Dick Gilbert, Charles Bachman, Lillian Lawrence, Lolita Lee, and Jack Underhill. **Summary:** Newspaper photographer Edward Howard (Eddie) is given the assignment of procuring a suitable photo of the wealthy Mrs. Van Pelt's niece. —LBAL2

Find the King (November 5, 1927) Hollywood Productions / Paramount Pictures, two reels, comedy; extant: LOC. **Director:** J.A. Howe. **Story:** Edward Everett Horton (uncredited). **Screenplay:** N.T. Barrows, James Davis. **Camera:** Walter Lundin. **Editor:** Carl Himm. **Cast:** Edward Everett Horton (*Edward Fairchild*); Violet Bird (*The Girl*); Jack Raymond (*Ambrose*); Richard R. Neill (*Dandy Dick*); the uncredited cast members are Jack Curtis, Emily Gerdis, Charles Meakin, Earl Mohan, Wallace Howe, Elinor Vanderveer, and Lillian Lawrence. **Summary:** Edward Fairchild (Eddie) lives a spoiled existence in his maiden aunts' mansion on the East Coast. He experiences a "coming of age" experience during a stay in a Western town, living in a saloon and dance hall. —LBAL2

Dad's Choice (January 7, 1928) Hollywood Productions / Paramount Pictures, two reels, comedy; extant: MOMA. **Director:** J.A. Howe. **Screenplay:** N.T. Barrows, T.J. Crizer. **Camera:** Walter Lundin. **Cast:** Edward Everett Horton (*Eddie*); Sharon Lynn (*The Girl*); Otis Harlan (*The Father*); James Gordon (*The Bodyguard*); Josephine Crowell (*A Bargan Hunter*); the uncredited cast members are Silas Wilcox, Elinor Vanderveer, Addie McPhail, Winnie Parks, Bernice Parks, and Gus Leonard. **Summary:** Eddie is determined to marry his girlfriend, but fate seems to be working against him. —LBAL2

Behind the Counter (March 3, 1928) Hollywood Productions / Paramount Pictures, two reels, comedy; extant: LOC, MOMA. **Director:** J.A. Howe. **Screenplay:** J.T. Crizer, N.T. Barrows, James Davis. **Camera:** Walter Lundin. **Editor:** Carl Himm. **Cast:** Edward Everett Horton (*Eddie*

Baxter); Dorothy Dwan (*Dorothy Brown*), John Steppling (*Her Father*); Nigel Barrie (*The Floorwalker*); the uncredited cast members are Oscar Smith; Silas Wilcox; Sam Lufkin; Lyle Tayo; Wallace Howe. **Summary:** Eddie Baxter (Eddie) lands a job working in a department store, with an impossible-to-please supervising floorwalker. On the bright side, he strikes up a relationship with the store owner's daughter. —LBAL2

Miss Information (April 10, 1928) Warner Bros. Pictures, 8 minutes, experimental talkie short; presumed lost. **Director:** Bryan E. Foy. **Screenplay:** F. Hugh Herbert. **Cast:** Lois Wilson (*The Public Stenographer*); Allen Sears (*The Head of the Firm*); Edward Everett Horton (*The Firm's Representative*). **Notes:** Part of Vitaphone production reel #2237. **Summary:** A businessman (Eddie) confides to a stenographer that he plans to buy an old man's invention. —IMDb

Horse Shy (May 19, 1928) Hollywood Productions / Paramount Pictures, two reels, comedy; extant: LOC. **Director:** J.A. Howe. **Screenplay:** J.T. Crizer, James Davis. **Camera:** Henry N. Kohler. **Editor:** Carl Himm. **Cast:** Edward Everett Horton (*Eddie Hamilton*); Anita Cavalier (*Jane Calhoun*); William Gillespie (*Gilroy Gibbs*); Dick Hatton (*Roger Bates*); Bruce Covington (*uncredited*); Wallace Howe (*uncredited*). **Summary:** Eddie Hamilton (Eddie) is talked into going to a country club by his buddy Dick Hatton. Once he arrives there, he learns he is expected to ride a horse, something he has clearly never done before but something he must do if he expects to impress a wealthy debutante. —LBAL2

Scrambled Weddings (June 30, 1928) Hollywood Productions; distributed by Paramount Pictures, two reels, comedy; extant: LOC. **Director:** N.T. Barrows. **Screenplay:** J.T. Crizer, James Davis. **Camera:** Henry N. Kohler. **Editor:** Carl Himm. **Cast:** Edward Everett Horton (*Eddie Howe*); Stanley Taylor (*Billie Baxter*); Ruth Dwyer (*Betty*); Josephine Crowell (*Her Mother*); Lillian Langdon (*Billie's Mother*); the uncredited cast members are Lolita Lee, Wallace Howe, and Robert O'Connor. **Summary:** Bachelor Eddie Howe (Eddie) finds the body of his best friend, Billie Baxter, on the floor of his office, a victim of suicide—at least that's what Eddie deduces. —LBAL2

The Terror (September 6, 1928, sound version; October 10, 1928, silent version) Warner Bros., 80 min. (sound); 85 minutes (silent), eerie haunted house mystery; both versions of the film are presumed lost, although the Vitaphone soundtrack discs are preserved at UCLA.

Producer: Darryl F. Zanuck. **Director:** Ray Enright. **Screenplay:** Harvey Gates, Joseph Jackson; based on the 1927 play *The Terror* by Edgar Wallace; the play itself was based on Wallace's 1926 novel, *Black Abbott*. **Camera:** Chick McGill. **Editors:** Thomas Pratt, Jack Killifer. **Cast:** May McAvoy (*Olga Redmayne*); Louise Fazenda (*Mrs. Elvery, a Spiritualist*); Edward Everett Horton (*Ferdinand Fane, a Scotland Yard Detective*); Alec B. Francis (*Dr. Redmayne*); Matthew Betz (*Joe Connors, a just-released criminal*); Otto Hoffman (*Soapy Marks*); Holmes E. Herbert (*Goodman*); Joseph Gerard (*Supt. Hallick*); John Miljan (*Alfred Katman*); Frank Austin (*Cotton*). **Summary:** The Terror, a maniacal killer whose identity is a mystery, makes his headquarters in an old English country house that has been converted into an inn. With unexplained organ recitals and strange noises, The Terror frightens the guests, including Mrs. Elvery, a spiritualist; Ferdinand Fane (Eddie), a Scotland Yard detective who is not as dumb as he looks; and Joe Connors and Soapy Marks, a couple of criminals just released from jail who have sworn vengeance on The Terror. After a night of murder and mayhem, the identity of The Terror is revealed. **Notes:** The credits in the sound version were spoken by a caped and masked Conrad Nagel. —AFICFF

Vacation Waves (September 15, 1928) Hollywood Productions; distributed by Paramount Pictures, two reels, comedy; extant: LOC. **Director:** N.T. Barrows. **Screenplay:** J.T. Crizer, James Davis. **Camera:** Robert Doran. **Editor:** Carl Himm. **Cast:** Edward Everett Horton (*Eddie Davis*); Duane Thompson (*His Wife*); Aileen Manning (*His Mother-in-Law*); Charles Force (*His Brother-in-Law*). **Summary:** "Eddie Davis was a natural born fisherman—even as a child he had worms." That title card tells us all we need to know about the protagonist's character. He's just a working stiff who is looking forward to spending a weekend fishing with his wife. The girl's mother and younger brother show up just as they're planning to depart. Naturally, they invite themselves along. Eddie registers that his peaceful trip is doomed; the remainder of the film bears that out. —LBAL2

Call Again (October 20, 1928) Hollywood Productions; distributed by Paramount Pictures, two reels, comedy; extant: LOC. **Director:** J.A. Howe. **Screenplay:** J.T. Crizer, James Davis. **Camera:** Henry N. Kohler. **Editor:** Carl Himm. **Cast:** Edward Everett Horton (*Eddie*); Duane Thompson (*Peggy*); Aileen Manning (*Mrs. Tuttle*); Kelly (*Bull Dog*); the uncredited players are Wallace Howe and Lillian Lawrence. **Summary:** Eddie's girlfriend Peggy is a student at Mrs. Tuttle's Boarding School, a strict institution that forbids the presence of men. Eddie's objective is to sneak Peggy out for a day on the town. Complications arise—and how. —LBAL2

Ask Dad (February 17, 1929) Coronet Talking Comedies / Educational Film Corporation of America, two reels, comedy; extant. **Director:** Hugh Faulcon. **Screenplay:** Joseph Jackson. **Camera:** William Hyers. **Cast:** Edward Everett Horton (*Dad*); Ruth Renick (*Miss Grace Wilson, his secretary*); Winston Miller (*Tommy, his son*). **Summary:** Tommy, a college student, pays a visit to his father (Eddie) at his workplace to propose to his secretary, Miss Grace Wilson. She turns him down, saying that she is already engaged. When Tommy asks, "To whom?" she answers, "Ask Dad." —Educational-Coronet publicity materials

Sonny Boy (April 18, 1929) Warner Bros. Pictures, 70 minutes, sentimental comedy; extant. **Screenplay:** Charles Graham Baker and James A. Starr; based on a story by "Leon Zuardo," the pseudonym for Jack L. Warner. **Camera:** Ben F. Reynolds. **Editor:** Owen Marks. **Music:** Louis Silvers. **Cast:** Davey Lee (*Sonny Boy*); Betty Bronson (*Aunt Winigred Canfield*); Edward Everett Horton (*Crandall Thorpe*); Gertrude Olmstead (*Mary*); John T. Murray (*Hamilton*); Tom Dugan (*Mulcahy*); Lucy Beaumont (*Mother Thorpe*); Edmund Breese (Thorpe); Jed Prouty (*Phil*). **Summary:** Mary and Hamilton, Sonny Boy's parents, quarrel, and Hamilton plans to take the boy to Europe while Mary telegraphs her sister, Winifred, to help her retain custody of the child. **Notes:** The film's title is derived from the popular 1928 song "Sonny Boy," which was written by Ray Henderson, Buddy De Sylva, and Lew Brown; it was introduced by Al Jolson in the 1928 part-talkie *The Singing Fool*. Eddie portrays Crandall Thorpe, an attorney whose apartment is used as a hideout for Sonny Boy and his aunt. —AFICFF

The Eligible Mr. Bangs (June 13, 1929); Coronet Talking Comedies / Educational Film Corporation of America, one reel, romantic comedy; extant: GEH. **Producer:** Al Christie. **Director:** Hugh Faulcon. **Screenplay:** Robert Housum. **Camera:** William Hyer. **Cast:** Edward Everett Horton (*Mr. Bangs*); Florence Eldridge (*Lucille Morgan*); Johnny Arthur (*Tom*); Mabel Forrest (*Jane Foster*). **Summary:** Jane has invited Lucille and a certain Mr. Bangs (Eddie) to spend a weekend with Tom and herself. Lucille is mortified when she learns of the mystery guest's identity. He is Mr. Bangs, a man with whom she was in love the previous year, although her feelings for him were unrequited. **Notes:** *The Eligible Mr.*

Bangs appears to be one of the rare surviving examples of Eddie's early sound work. The eminent British film historian William K. Everson screened what was likely his own 16mm print of the film in 1960 for the Theodore Huff Society and made the following observations:

> Considering the static, stagey quality of so many early talkie shorts, it's really quite amazing how well these early Horton comedies stand up based as all of them were on one-act stage plays and making no bones about it. The fact that they were good one-acters, old reliables like vaudeville routines that had been practiced to perfection, helped a great deal no doubt; but it is mainly the Horton personality that puts them over so expertly. His playing and timing are fine; and in terms of photography and sound recording they are of a high standard, so that it is really only the costuming of the women that makes one realise with a start that these shorts are now some thirty-two years old!"

Trusting Wives (June 23, 1929) Coronet Talking Comedies / Educational Film Corporation of America, two reels, romantic comedy; extant. **Director:** Leslie Pearce. **Screenplay:** Florence Ryerson. **Cast:** Edward Everett Horton (*Wilfort Wendall*); Natalie Moorhead (*Jane, his wife*); Helen Ferguson (Azalia, his new sweetheart); Shep Camp (*her husband*). **Summary:** Wilfort Wendall (Eddie), a poet, is always falling in love with other women, much to the amusement of Jane, his wife. Very much unamused is his current sweetheart's husband. In fact, he loads his pistol and goes to Wilfort's home to end the dalliance … permanently. —Educational-Coronet publicity materials

The Hottentot (August 10, 1929) Warner Bros. Pictures, 79 minutes, farce; presumed lost. **Director:** Roy Del Ruth. **Screenplay:** Harvey Thew; based on the 1920 Broadway play *The Hottentot* by William Collier Sr. and Victor Mapes. **Camera:** Barney McGill. **Editor:** Owen Marks. **Music:** Cecil Copping, Alois Reiser. **Cast:** Edward Everett Horton (*Sam Harrington*); Patsy Ruth Miller (*Peggy Fairfax*); Douglas Gerrard (*Swift*); Edward Earle (*Larry Crawford*); Stanley Taylor (*Alec Fairfax*); Gladys Brockwell (*Mrs. Chadwick*); Maude Turner Gordon (*May Gilford*); Otto Hoffman (*Perkins*); Edmund Breese (*Ollie*). **Summary:** Peggy Fairfax, whose family is devoted to horses and everything associated with them, mistakes Sam Harrington (Eddie) for a famous steeplechase rider and enthusiastically asks him to ride her horse, Hottentot, in an important race. Because Sam is in love with Peggy, he tries to oblige her but is thrown by the high-spirited horse. **Notes:** This was a remake of a 1922 Thomas Ince–directed silent feature starring Raymond Hatton. It is also the first of six films Eddie made with Patsy Ruth Miller. —AFICFF

Prince Gabby (September 15, 1929). Coronet Talking Comedies / Educational Film Corporation of America, two reels, romantic comedy; presumed lost. **Director:** Leslie Pearce. **Screenplay:** Jane Martin; based on a short story by Edgar Wallace. **Cast:** Edward Everett Horton (*Prince Gabriel, a.k.a. Prince Gabby*); Rita Carewe (*Millicent Canton*); Gordon De Main (*Mr. Canton, her husband*). **Summary:** Known to the police as "Prince Gabriel" and to his intimates as "Prince Gabby," the intruder in the mansion of Mr. Canton is more than a burglar. He is a gentleman and connoisseur of art, music, and the drama. He is in the Canton home because he has learned that both Canton and his wife, Millicent, are to be away over the weekend. He does not know that they have suddenly changed plans and returned home. **Notes:** Eddie was widely praised for his depiction of the suave Prince Gabriel. —Educational-Coronet publicity materials

The Right Bed (October 15, 1929) Coronet Talking Comedies / Educational Film Corp. of America, two reels, comedy, bedroom farce; presumed lost. **Director:** Hugh Falcon. **Screenplay:** Wilson Collison. **Cast:** Edward Everett Horton (*Bobby Kent*); Wilson Benge (*Vickers*); Helen Kent (*Mabel Forrest*); Betty Boyd (*Patricia*). **Summary:** Bobby Kent (Eddie) is depressed that his wife, Patricia, has left him and is considering divorce. Returning home late one night from an uninspiring date, Bobby finds Vickers, his valet, terribly upset. Earlier that evening, he had entered his master's bedroom only to find a strange woman in Bobby's bed. This coincides with the news that Patricia has decided to end the separation and is coming home shortly. —Educational-Coronet publicity materials

The Sap (November 9, 1929) Warner Bros. Pictures, 75 minutes, small town domestic comedy; presumed lost. **Director:** Archie Mayo. **Screenplay:** De Leon Anthony, Robert Lord, whose screenplay was based on the 1924 play *The Aviator* by William A. Grew. **Camera:** Devereau Jennings. **Editor:** Desmond O'Brien. **Cast:** Edward Everett Horton (*The Sap, Bill Small*); Alan Hale (*Jim Belden*); Patsy Ruth Miller (*Betty, Bill's wife*); Russell Simpson (*The Banker*); Jerry Mandy (*The Wop*); Edna Murphy (*Jane*); Louise Carver (*Mrs. Sprague*); Franklin Pangborn (*Ed Mason, Bill's brother-in-law*). **Summary:** Bill Small (Eddie), a day-dreaming inventor in South Dakota, is full of impractical ideas and generally seen by the town folks as a ne'er-do-well and clown. His wife, Betty, spends much of her time defending him against her sister Jane and brother-in-law Ed Mason, with (and upon) whom they live. When Ed, a bank clerk, confesses that he has been using the bank's funds for speculation, Bill, acting on a hunch, discovers that another cashier, Jim Belden, has been doing the same thing. Bill offers Ed and Jim a plan: If they give him $50,000 and a week's head start, he will leave town and take the blame for robbing the bank. **Notes:** This was the last part-talking film released by Warner Bros., the studio that stood at the forefront of sound films, including the seminal 1927 part-talkie *The Jazz Singer.* —AFICFF

Good Medicine (December 8, 1929); Coronet Talking Comedies / Educational Film Corp. of America, one reel, comedy; presumed lost. **Director:** Leslie Pearce. **Screenplay:** Edwin Burke and Jack Arnold. **Cast:** Edward Everett Horton (*doctor*); Enid Bennett (*wealthy woman*); Olive Tell (*nurse*). **Summary:** An unpopular young doctor is about to become a grocery clerk when a patient, a wealthy woman, enters the office. She claims every illness, but Horton, honest to the last, refuses the opportunity to make a meal ticket of the case, tells her the truth, loses a patient but finds a patron—the woman is seeking an honest doctor to head the staff at a hospital she has built. **Notes:** According to *Motion Picture News* magazine, *Good Medicine* has "cleverly constructed plotting [and is] very cleverly played. A good number for a high classic program." —AFICFF

The Aviator (December 14, 1929) Warner Bros. Pictures, 75 minutes, farce; presumed lost. **Producer:** Irving Asher. **Director:** Roy Del Ruth. **Screenplay:** Anthony Caeser, Robert Lord (screenplay); De Leon Anthony (titles). **Camera:** Barney "Chick" McGill. **Editor:** William Holmes. **Cast:** Edward Everett Horton (*Robert Street*); Patsy Ruth Miller (*Grace Douglas*); Johnny Arthur (*Hobart*); William Norton Bailey (*Brooks*); Armand Kaliz (*Major Jules Gaillard*); Edward Martindel (*Gordon*); Lee Moran (*Brown*); Kewpie Morgan (*Sam Robinson*); Phillips Smalley (*John Douglas*). **Summary:** Wishing to assure the success of an anonymously written wartime memoir, Brooks, a publisher, and Brown, his publicist, scheme to attribute the book to famous author Robert Street (Eddie). He detests aviation, knows nothing about the book in question, and finds the situation socially embarrassing. —AFICFF

Take the Heir (January 13, 1930) Screen Story Syndicate / Big 4 Film Corp., 64 minutes, comedy; presumed lost. **Producer:** John R. Freuler. **Director:** Lloyd Ingraham. **Screenplay:** Beatrice Van. **Camera:** Alden G. Siegler. **Cast:** Edward Everett Horton (*Smithers*); Dorothy Devore (*Susan*); Frank Elliot (*Lord Tweedham*); Edythe Chapman (*Lady Tweedham*); Kay Delsys *(Muriel Walker)*; Margaret Campbell (*Mrs. Bellingham*). **Summary:** Lord Tweedham, a tipsy Englishman, falls heir to his deceased uncle's estate in the U.S. Upon his arrival there, his valet, Smithers (Eddie), is forced to impersonate Tweedham because of his master's drunken state. At the home of the uncle's executor, John Walker, Smithers falls in love with the maid, Susan, though he is pursued by the executor's less attractive daughter, Muriel. After numerous complications, Smithers admits his identity and marries Susan, while Lord Tweedham falls victim to the wiles of Muriel. **Notes:** *Take the Heir* was released in both silent and sound formats; the sound version featured synchronized music and sound effects, but no dialogue. —AFICFF

Wide Open (February 1, 1930) Warner Bros. Pictures, 67 minutes, business comedy; extant: LOC, WCFTR. **Director:** Archie Mayo. **Screenplay:** Edwin Bateman Morris, James A. Starr (screenplay); based on the novel by Arthur Caser. **Camera:** Ben F. Reynolds. **Music:** Louis Silvers. **Cast:** Edward Everett Horton (*Simon Haldane*); Patsy Ruth Miller (*Julia Faulkner*, a.k.a. "*Doris*"); Louise Fazenda (*Agatha Hathaway*); Vera Lewis (*Agatha's Mother*); T. Roy Barnes (*Bob Wyeth*); E.J. Ratcliffe (*Trundle*); Louise Beavers (*Easter*); Edna Murphy (*Nell Martin*); Frank Beal *(Faulkner)*; Vince Barnett (*Dvorak*); Lloyd Ingraham (*Doctor*); Bobby Gordon (*Office Boy*); Fred Kelsey (*Detective*); Robert Dudley (*Office Worker*). **Summary:** Simon Haldane, a timid bachelor, lives alone with his cat and works as bookkeeper for the Faulkner Phonograph Co., and though he offers many improvements, everyone—from Easter, his maid, to Bob Wyeth, the star salesman—treats him shabbily. He resents the attentions of women, particularly those of Agatha, a stenographer with an eye for romance whose marriage proposal is accidentally recorded. But Doris, a stranger, finds his address and comes with her mother to demand that he marry her. **Notes:** *Wide Open* is a remake of the silent film *The Narrow Street* (1925). —AFICFF

Holiday (July 3, 1930) Pathé Exchange, 98 minutes, society comedy; extant. **Director:** Edward H. Griffith. **Screenplay:** Horace Jackson; adapted from the 1928 play *Holiday* by Philip Barry. **Camera:** Norbert Brodine. **Editor:** Daniel Mandell. **Music:** Josiah Zuro. **Cast:** Ann Harding (*Linda Seton*); Mary Astor (*Julia Seton*); Edward Everett Horton (*Nick Potter*); Robert Ames (*Johnny Case*); Hedda Hopper (*Susan Potter*); Monroe Owsley (*Ned Seton*); William Holden (*Edward Seton*); Elizabeth Forrester (*Laura*); Mabel Forrest (*Mary Jessup*); Creighton Hale (*Pete Hedges*); Hallam Cooley (*Seton Cram*); Mary Forbes (*Pritchard Ames*). **Summary:** Wealthy Julia Seton meets Johnny Case at Lake Placid and takes him home, introducing him to her family as her future husband. A poor, struggling young lawyer, Johnny is greeted with kindly tolerance by old Seton and his children, Linda and Ned. Seton finally agrees to Julia's plans and arranges an engagement party; but Linda gives a party of her own at which Nick (Eddie) and Susan Potter are the honored guests. Johnny reveals that he has invested in the stock market and plans to quit work after marriage. When Seton learns of this announcement, he is furious, but Linda, who is taken with Johnny, supports him. Johnny and Julia separate, and he plans to go to Europe with Nick and Susan, but he changes his mind and agrees to work for three years before going on holiday. However, he revolts at the idea of Seton's planning his life, and Linda, pleased by his assertion of personal freedom, joins him aboard the steamer. —AFICFF. **Notes:** *Holiday* was nominated for Academy Awards for Best Actress in a Leading Role (Ann Harding) and Best Writing, Adaptation. Eddie plays the same character, Professor Nick Potter, in the remake of *Holiday*. He is the only actor to appear in both versions.

Once a Gentleman (September 1, 1930); James Cruze Production / Sono Art–World Wide Pictures, 85 minutes, farce; presumed lost. **Director:** James Cruze. **Camera: Screenplay:** George F. Worts (story); Walter Woods (screenplay); Maud Fulton (dialogue); **Sound recording engineers:** Fred J. Lau, W.C. Smith. **Cast:** Edward Everett Horton (*Oliver*); Lois Wilson (*Mrs. Mallin*); Francis X. Bushman (*Bannister*); King Baggot (*Van Werner*); Emerson Treacy (*Junior*); Frederick Sullivan (*Wadsworth*); Estelle Bradley (*Gwen*); Cyril Chadwick (*Jarvis*); Drew Demarest (*Timson*); Charles Coleman (*Wuggins*); George Fawcett (*Colonel Breen*); Gertrude Short (*Dolly*); William J. Holmes (*Oglethorpe*); Evelyn Pierce (*Natalie*); Willis H. O'Brien (*Reeves*). **Summary:** As a reward for his perfection as a valet, Oliver (Eddie) receives from Mr. Van Warner, his employer, a month's paid vacation, a complete wardrobe, and an admonition to enjoy himself as a gentleman. Before Oliver leaves, however, Warner asks him to call on his friend Colonel Breen at the Gotham Club. The colonel is away, but Oliver is assumed to be a close friend and is introduced as just having arrived from India, a fact strengthened by his knowledge of the recipe of the colonel's favorite drink, Bombay Bombshell. Mr. Bannister insists that Oliver be his guest, and another member presents him with 5,000 shares of American Tin. At the Bannister home he falls in love with Mrs. Mallin, the housekeeper, and is helpful with Junior, the wayward son. When, to his dismay, he loses his money in a market crash, Oliver is branded an imposter by Colonel Breen; but he is reinstated by Van Warner and wins the love of Mrs. Mallin. —AFICFF

Reaching for the Moon (December 29, 1930) Feature Productions / United Artists, 91 minutes (contemporary prints run from 62 to 72 minutes), comedy with music. **Producers:** Joseph Schenck, Douglas Fairbanks Sr. **Director:** Edmund Goulding. **Screenplay:** Edmund Goulding, based on a story by Irving Berlin. **Camera:** Ray June, Robert H. Planck. **Editors:** Hal C. Kern, Lloyd Nosler. **Music:** Alfred Newman. **Cast:** Douglas Fairbanks Sr. (*Larry Day*); Bebe Daniels (*Vivien Benton*); Edward Everett Horton (*Roger*); Claud Allister (Sir Horace Partington Chelmsford); Jack Mulhall (*Jimmy Carrington*); Walter Walker (*Benton*); June MacCloy (*Kitty*); Helen Jerome Eddy (*Larry's Secretary*); Bing Crosby (*Bing*); Larry Steers (*Flier, uncredited*). **Summary:** Larry Day knows everything there is to know about making money in the stock market, but he is clueless in the ways of love. His valet, Roger (Eddie), does his best to coach him on making love to a girl. Following Vivian Benton onto an ocean liner, he laces her cocktail with a "love potion." **Notes:** Originally conceived as a musical, only one song was sung in the final cut: "When the Folks High Up Do the Mean Low Down," written by Irving Berlin and introduced by newcomer Bing Crosby. An instrumental version of Berlin's title song, "Reaching for the Moon," can be heard over the opening and closing credits. —IMDb

Lonely Wives (February 22, 1931) Pathé Exchange / RKO Radio Pictures, 85 minutes, double identity comedy. **Producer:** E.B. Derr. **Director:** Russell Mack. **Screenplay:** Walter DeLeon, based on a 1912 German vaudeville sketch called *Tanzanwaltz* by Pordes Milo, Walter Shütt, and Eric Urban; the sketch was adapted as a 1922 play. **Camera:** Edward Snyder. **Editor:** Joseph Kane. **Music:** Francis Gromon. **Cast:** Edward Everett Horton (*Richard "Dickie" Smith, and Felix, the Great Zero*); Esther Ralston (*Madeline Smith*); Laura La Plante (*Diane O'Dare*); Patsy Ruth Miller (*Kitty "Minty" Minter*); Spencer Charters (*Andrews, the Butler*); Maude Eburne (*Mrs. Mantel*); Maurice Black (*Taxi Driver*). **Summary:** With his wife away for an indeterminate period of time, the respectable defense attorney Richard "Dickie" Smith (Eddie) turns into a philandering Don Juan when the clock strikes 8 o'clock. **Notes:** Mordaunt Hall, the movie critic for the *New York Times*, praised the film, particularly concerning Eddie's performance. Hall states that Horton "delivers a wonderfully clever dual impersonation ..." and "is wonderfully amusing."—AFICFF

Kiss Me Again (February 21, 1931; released in the UK as *The Toast of the Legion*). First National (a subsidiary of Warner Bros. Pictures), 76 minutes, Parisian comedy with music. **Director:** William A. Seiter. **Screenplay:** Julien Josephson and Paul Perez; based on the 1905 operetta *Mlle. Modiste* by Victor Herbert and Henry Martyn Blossom. **Camera:** Lee Garmes. **Technicolor Supervisor:** Alfred Gilks. **Cast:** Bernice Claire (*Mademoiselle Fifi*); Edward Everett Horton (*René*); Walter Pidgeon (*Paul de St. Cyr*); June Collyer (*Marie*); Frank McHugh (*Francois*); Claude Gillingwater (*Count de St. Cyr*); Judith Vosselli (*Mademoiselle Cecile*); Albert Gran (*General de Villafranche*). **Summary:** At Madame Cecile's Paris dress shop, Marie and her father, General de Villafranche, shop for her trousseau. Her father wants her to marry soldier Paul de St. Cyr, but she is in love with René (Eddie), another soldier in her father's Foreign Legion regiment. —AFICFF

The Front Page (April 4, 1931) Caddo / United Artists, 101 minutes, newspaper melodrama. **Producer:** Lewis Milestone, Howard Hughes. **Director:** Lewis Milestone. **Screenplay:** Bartlett Comack and Charles Lederer; based on the 1928 Broadway play *The Front Page* by Ben Hecht and Charles MacArthur. **Camera:** Glen MacWilliams. **Editor:** W. Duncan Mansfield. **Cast:** Adolphe Menjou (*Walter Burns*); Pat O'Brien (*Hildebrand "Hildy" Johnson*); Mary Brian (*Peggy Grant*); Edward Everett Horton (*Roy V. Bensinger*); Walter Catlett (*Jimmy Murphy*); George E. Stone (*Earl Williams*); Mae Clarke (*Molly Malloy*); Slim Summerville (*Irving Pincus*); Matt Moore (*Ernie Kruger*); Frank McHugh (*"Mac" McCue*); Clarence Wilson (*Sheriff Peter B. "Pinky" Hartman*); Fred Howard (*Schwartz*); Phil Tead (*Wilson*); Eugene Strong (*Endicott*); Spencer Charters (*Woodenshoes*); Maurice Black (*Diamond Louie*); Effie Ellsler (*Mrs. Grant*); Dorothea Wolbert (*Jenny*); James Gordon (*Fred, the Mayor*); Richard Alexander (*Jacobi, uncredited*). **Summary:** Walter J. Burns, the manipulative editor of a prominent Chicago paper, does everything in his power to prevent his ace reporter, Hildy Johnson, from getting married and abandoning the hectic, 24/7 life of a newspaperman. **Notes:** *The Front Page* was remade by Howard Hawks in 1940 as

His Girl Friday, starring Cary Grant and Rosalind Russell. It was made again in 1973 by Billy Wilder as a vehicle for Walter Matthau and Jack Lemmon. In 2010, the 1931 version of *The Front Page* was selected for the United States National Film Registry by the Library of Congress as being «culturally, historically, or aesthetically significant." The film is in the public domain. Two versions exist, each made up of different takes, one for the international market and director Lewis Milestone's preferred version for its original U.S. domestic release. Eddie stands out in a fine cast as Bensinger, a fussy, hypochondriacal poet who must share a grimy newsroom with hard-bitten reporters. —AFICFF

Six Cylinder Love (May 10, 1931) Fox Film Corporation, 71 minutes, romantic comedy. **Producers:** William Fox, John W. Considine Jr. **Director:** Thornton Freeland. **Screenplay:** William Conselman and Norman Houston; based on the 1921 Broadway play *Six Cylinder Love* by William Anthony McGuire. **Camera:** Ernest Palmer. **Editor:** J. Edwin Robbins. **Cast:** Spencer Tracy (*William Donroy*); Edward Everett Horton (*Monty Winston*); Sidney Fox (*Marilyn Sterling*); Lorin Raker (*Gilbert Sterling*); William Collier Sr. (*Richard Burton*); Una Merkel (*Margaret Rogers*); William Holden (*Stapleton*); Bert Roach (*Harold Rogers*); Ruth Warren (*Mrs. Burton*); El Brendel (*Axel*). **Summary:** Newlyweds Gilbert and Marilyn Sterling tease each other and talk baby talk one Sunday morning in their suburban home, while their older neighbors, the Burtons, start the day off with an argument. At the breakfast table, Richard Burton confesses to his wife that he's broke and that his troubles began when she insisted that they buy an expensive car to impress her friends, Monty Winston and the Rogerses, whom Burton calls "sponges." After the Rogerses and Winston show up for breakfast, Donroy, an auto salesman whom Burton has called, arrives. Burton tells Donroy that he wants to sell the Lincoln, which, he says, has led to an expensive night life. **Notes:** This 1931 talkie was a remake of the 1923 silent original. It was remade again in 1939 as *The Honeymoon's Over*. —AFICFF

Smart Woman (September 12, 1931) RKO Radio Pictures, 68 minutes, comedy. **Producer:** William LeBaron. **Director:** Gregory La Cava. **Screenplay:** Salisbury Field; based on the 1930 play *Nancy's Private Affair* by Myron Coureval Fagan. **Camera:** Nick Musuraca. **Editor:** Ann McNight. **Cast:** Mary Astor (*Mrs. Nancy Gibson*); Robert Ames (*Donald Gibson*); John Halliday (*Sir Guy Harrington*); Edward Everett Horton (*Billy Ross*); Ruth Weston (*Mrs. Sally Gibson Ross*); Noel Francis (*Peggy Preston*); Gladys Gale (*Mrs. Preston*); Alfred Cross (*Brooks, the Butler*); Lillian Harmer (*Mrs. Windleweaver*); Bill Elliott (*Reporter on ship*); Harold Miller (*Deck Lounger*); Dennis O'Keefe *(Passenger Departing Ship)*; Pearl Varvalle (*Gibson's maid, Helen, uncredited*). **Summary:** After an extended visit with her sick mother in Paris, well-to-do Nancy Gibson sails home to New York, eager to see her home and her husband, Donald. However, when she finally arrives at her estate, she is told by her sister-in-law, Sally Ross, and Sally's husband Billy (Eddie), Donald's business partner, that Donald has fallen in love with a gold digger named Peggy Preston. In shock, Nancy, who had bragged about her marriage to her fellow passenger, Sir Guy Harrington, declares that she will never grant Donald a divorce. The wiser Sally, however, counsels her to be a smart woman and play hard-to-get around Donald. —AFICFF

The Great Junction Hotel (October 1931) RKO / Pathé, 21 minutes, farce comedy, extant, LOC. **Producer:** The Masquers of Hollywood. **Director:** William Beaudine. **Story:** Lew Lipton. **Adaptation:** Ralph Ceder. **Production Manager:** Edmund Earle. **Camera:** Dwight Warren. **Film Editor:** Jack Ogilvie. **Cast:** Edward Everett Horton, Patsy Ruth Miller, Harry Gribbon, Richard Carle, Lionel Bellmore, Frank McHugh, Lucien Littlefield, Tommy Dugan, Hank Mann, Richard Carlyle (The Masque), Harry Stubbs, Armand Kaliz, Bobby Vernon, Louis Aberni, Mack Swain, Maurice Black, Tom Wilson, George Chandler, Glenn Tryon, and Eighty Masquer Players. **Summary:** Eddie and Patsy Ruth Miller are a newly married couple who register at a hotel late one night, and become the fixation of everyone present, particularly the woefully incompetent hotel detective, played by Harry Gribbon. A high-pitched scream emanates from the couple's room, alarming everyone. That scream belonged to Eddie. It seems his bride is missing. While being interrogated by other detectives that had been called to the scene, Eddie sees his wife on the second floor, a somnambulant figure in a white negligee, wandering aimlessly. Once she is awakened, the two, still in their bedclothes, walk out of the hotel, arm in arm. **Notes:** Unusual talkie short has some energetic performances, especially by Eddie as the frantic groom. A creepy guy in a clown outfit, known as The Masque, introduces the film and makes it clear that those involved in making this silly two-reel comedy were not compensated for their time. Judging by the results, no major injustice was committed. —The authors viewed this short in September 2024 on YouTube.

The Age for Love (October 17, 1931) Caddo / United Artists, 81 minutes, comedy-drama. **Producer:** Frank Lloyd. **Director:** Frank Lloyd. **Screenplay:** Ernest Pascal and Frank Lloyd, based on the 1930 novel *The Age for Love* by Ernest Pascal. **Camera:** Harry Fishbeck, John F. Seitz. **Editor:** W. Duncan Mansfield. **Music:** Alfred Newman. **Cast:** Billie Dove (*Jean Hurd*); Charles Starrett (*Dudley Crome*); Lois Wilson (*Sylvia Pearson*); Edward Everett Horton (*Horace Keats*); Mary Duncan (*Nina Donnet*); Adrian Morris (*Jeff Aldrich*); Betty Ross Clarke (*Dot Aldrich*); Vivien Oakland (*Grace*); George Beranger (*The Poet*); Jed Prouty (*Floyd Evans*); Joan Standing (*Eleanor*); Alice Moe (*Annie*); Charles Sellon (*Mr. Pearson*); Pierre de Ramey (*Jules*); Cecil Cunningham (*Pamela*); Edna Heard (*Singer*). **Summary:** Jean Hurd, who works in the office of literary agent Horace Keats (Eddie), meets poet Dudley Crome at a party. Although they are attracted to each other, their views on marriage are totally opposed, as Jean believes that married women should not be subordinate to their husbands. Dudley takes Jean to visit his married friends, Dot and Jeff Aldrich, and their baby. Dot, who is pregnant with their second child, is completely submissive to Jeff, who doesn't consider her needs at all. Put off by this marriage, Jean insists that if she and Dudley marry, Dudley must agree that she will not have a baby until she wants one. Dudley persuades Jean to marry him and give his vision of married life a chance. —AFICFF

But the Flesh is Weak (April 9, 1932) Metro-Goldwyn-Mayer, 77 minutes, comedy. **Director:** Jack Conway. **Screenplay:** Ivor Novello; based on his 1928 play *The Truth Game*. *But the Flesh is Weak* was remade as *Free and Easy* in 1941. **Camera:** Oliver T. Marsh. **Editor:** Tom Held. **Cast:** Robert Montgomery (*Max Clement*); Nora Gregor (*Mrs. Rosine Brown*); Heather Thatcher (*Lady Joan Culver*); Edward Everett Horton (*Sir George Kelvin*); C. Aubrey Smith (*Florian Clement*); Nils Asther (*Prince Paul*); Frederick Kerr (*Duke of Hampshire*); Eva Moore (*Lady Florence Ridgway*); Forrester Harvey (*Gooch*); Desmond Roberts (*Findley*). **Summary:** Londoner Max Clement and his father Florian are impoverished, but handsome and charming, enabling them to eke out a paltry living off rich women. Florian tries to convince Max to make a good marriage with a rich woman to ensure his future, but Max always cancels at the last minute to romance prettier but poorer women. When he meets the wealthy Lady Joan Culver, who is plain, but very kind, she takes him to a party at her home, where he meets the beautiful Mrs. Rosine Brown, a Viennese widow, with whom he falls immediately in love. The next day, at Ascot, he tells her he loves her and later, at her London house, proposes. When she finds out that he is poor, she refuses to marry him, preferring the dull but wealthy Sir George Kelvin (Eddie). —AFICFF

Roar of the Dragon (July 8, 1932) RKO Radio Pictures, 69 minutes, adventure melodrama set in the Orient. **Producer:** William LeBaron. **Director:** Wesley Ruggles. **Screenplay:** Howard Estabrook; story by Merian C. Cooper and John Bigelow; based on the novel *A Passage to Hong Kong* by George Kibbe Turner. **Camera:** Edward Cronjager. **Editor:** William Hamilton. **Cast:** Richard Dix (*Chauncey Carson*); Gwili Andre (*Natascha*); Edward Everett Horton (*Busby*); Arline Judge (*Hortense O'Dare*); ZaSu Pitts (*Gabby Woman*); Dudley Digges (*Johnson*); C. Henry Gordon (*Voronsky*); William Orlamond (*Dr. Pransnitz*); Arthur Stone (*Sholem*); Toshia Mori (*Chinese Proprietor's Daughter*); Will Stanton (*Sailor Sam*). **Summary:** From their remote inland hideout, Voronsky and his savage gang of Tartar bandits plan a raid on a Mandarin coast town, where Natascha, a Russian beauty whom Voronsky desires, is hiding. Warned of the bandits' arrival, Chauncey Carson, the alcoholic captain of a commercial steamboat, hurries to ready his boat for departure, pushed by Johnson, his cowardly employer, and other anxious white people who are staying at the town's hotel. There, Carson meets Natascha, a former captive and sexual slave of Voronsky's, who begs him to take her on his boat. Sure that she is a spy, the hard-boiled Carson demands sex from Natascha in exchange for her passage, and she is about to comply when Voronsky's men attack the hotel. Carson, who in a previous encounter with Voronsky had chopped off his ear, hastily sets up a machine gun and turns back the attackers. Although safe inside, the hotel's occupants, who include Helen, a young American entertainer, her admirer Busby (Eddie), an engineer, and a group of Chinese orphans, discover they are surrounded by the bandits and have a limited supply of food. After Busby and Helen find a goat in a nearby stable and milk it to provide nourishment for the children, Carson catches a Voronsky spy sneaking around the hotel, then notices a group of bandits sawing the hotel's water pipes. Unknown to Carson, another Voronsky spy has sent a message to his boss informing him of Natascha's apparent interest in the captain. Furious at his men's inability to take the hotel, Voronsky sets off for town, while Natascha, who had threatened Johnson with a gun because he wanted to kill the goat for its meat, is accepted by Carson. Just before Voronsky's arrival, Helen is shot and killed by a bandit while passing in front of a window. Then, Sholem, a Jewish butcher, is caught and burned at the stake by Voronsky as he tries to run from the hotel to his shop. By creating a diversion at the hotel's gate, Voronsky is able to penetrate the building and locate Natascha. As Voronsky is leaving with Natascha, however, Carson knocks his gun away and exposes the rest of the bandits to the machine gun, which is manned by a revenge-hungry Busby. Temporarily reprieved, Carson orders the group to flee to the boat while he fights Voronsky. Made brave by his desire for vengeance, Busby remains behind with Carson but is stabbed by Voronsky. Incensed, Carson kills Voronsky, then risks his life to carry the wounded Busby to the boat. Once safely on board, Carson holds a dying Busby in his arms and is comforted by Natascha. —AFICFF

Trouble in Paradise (October 30, 1932) Paramount Pictures, 83 minutes, sophisticated Parisian comedy. **Producer:** Ernst Lubitsch. **Director:** Ernst Lubitsch. **Screenplay:** Samson Raphaelson; Grover Jones (adaptation); Ernst Lubitsch (uncredited), based on the 1931 play *The Honest Finder* (*A Becsületes Megtaláló*) by László Aladár. **Camera:** Victor Milner. **Music:** W. Frankie Harling; Leo Robin (lyrics). **Cast:** Miriam Hopkins (*Lily*); Kay Francis (*Madame Colet*); Herbert Marshall (*Gaston Monescu*); Charles Ruggles (*The Major*); Edward Everett Horton (*François Filiba*); C. Aubrey Smith (*Adolph J. Giron*); Robert Greig (*Jacques, the Butler*). **Summary:** In Venice, Lily (Miriam Hopkins), a pickpocket posing as a countess, meets and falls for the internationally famous thief Gaston Monescu (Herbert Marshall), who is posing as a baron. Posing as a doctor, Gaston robs aristocrat François Fileba (Eddie), of rooms 253, 5, 7, and 9, but escapes with Lily before he is found out. Nearly a year later, in Paris, Gaston and Lily are still very much in love when, at the opera, Gaston steals a diamond-studded purse from widow Mariette Colet, owner of Paris's reputable perfumery, Colet and Co. Posing as Monsieur LuValle, a member of the "nouveau poor," Gaston returns the bag and, after receiving a 20,000 franc reward from Mariette, charms her into hiring him as her secretary. Although she is known all over Paris, Mariette believes marriage is a beautiful mistake and has turned down proposals made by ardent suitors Fileba and the Major (Charles Ruggles), who continually bicker as they compete for Mariette's attention. When Gaston learns that Mariette keeps 100,000 francs in her house safe, he is determined to steal it and embezzle money from the company. Meanwhile, Lily, wearing eye glasses and assuming an officious manner, works as Gaston's assistant under the name Mlle. Votier. She pretends to be devoted to Mariette even though she is jealous of her attentions toward Gaston and advises him to stay a crook and not become a gigolo. After a few weeks, Mariette introduces Gaston to her social set, and Fileba, who is sure he has seen Gaston somewhere before. —AFICFF

Soldiers of the King (March 1933; released in the United States as *Woman in Charge*; reissued in 1939) Gaumont-British, Gainsborough / Woolf & Freedman Film Service, 80 minutes, romantic comedy. **Producer:** Michael Balcon. **Director:** Maurice Elvey. **Screenplay:** Douglas Furber, Jack Hulbert, W.P. Lipscomb, J.O.C. Orton. **Art Director:** Alex Vetchinsky. **Music:** Louis Levy. **Camera:** Percy Strong, Leslie Rowson. **Editors:** R.E. Dearing, Ian Dalrymple. **Cast:** Cicely Courtneidge (*Jenny Marvello / Maisie Marvello*); Edward Everett Horton (*Sebastian Marvello*); Anthony Bushell (*Lieutenant Ronald Jamieson*); Dorothy Hyson (*Judy Marvello*); Frank Cellier (*Colonel Philip Markham*); Leslie Sarony (*Wally*); Bransby Williams (*Dan Marvello*); Albert Rebla (*Albert Marvello*); Herschel Henlere (*Mozart Marvello*); Ivor McLaren (*Harry Marvello*); Olive Sloane (*Sarah Marvello*); Arty Ash (*Doug*); O.B. Clarence (*Tom*); David Deveen (*Frank Marvello*); André Rolet (*Marvello Adagio Troupe member*); Betty Semsey (*Marvello Adagio Troupe member*); William Pardue (*Marvello Adagio Troupe member*); Ian Wilson (*Customer at Coffee Stall*). **Summary:** After her mother's retirement, Maisie Marvello takes over as the head of her travelling vaudevillian family. When her sister Judie falls in love with Ronald Jamieson, a member of the King's guard, Maisie goes to his commanding officer to seek permission for the young couple to marry. The commanding officer is Maisie's old sweetheart, Colonel Philip Markham, who failed fifteen years earlier to marry her in a similar situation. **Notes:** According to a review in the *Sydney Morning Herald* (August 14, 1933), "Told more deftly and succinctly, the story of the *Marvellos* might have had a serious as well as a farcical interest, but at present this just misses fire. Edward Everett Horton, fresh from triumphs in Hollywood, provides invaluable support for Miss Courtneidge in his inimitable way."

A Bedtime Story (April 21, 1933) Paramount Pictures, 87 minutes, comedy. **Producer:** Ernest Cohen. **Director:** Norman Taurog. **Screenplay:** Benjamin Glazer, Nunnally Johnson, Waldemar Young; based on the novel *Bellamy the Magnificent*. **Music:** Karl Hajos, John Leipold, Ralph Rainger (all uncredited). **Camera:** Charles Lang. **Editor:** Otho Lovering. **Cast:** Maurice Chevalier (*Monsieur Rene*); Helen Twelvetrees (*Sally*); Edward Everett Horton (*Victor Dubois*); Adrienne Ames (*Paulette*); Baby LeRoy (*Monsieur "Baby"*); Earle Foxe (*Max de l'Enclos*); Leah Ray (*Mademoiselle Gabrielle*); Betty Lorraine (*Suzanne Dubois*); Gertrude Michael (*Louise*); Ernest Wood (*Robert*); Reginald Mason (*General Louse's father*); Henry Kolker (*Agent de Police*); George MacQuarrie (*Henry Joudain*); Paul Panzer (*Concierge*); Frank Reicher

(*Aristide*); George Barbier (*Toy Seller*); Florence Roberts (*Flower Shop Customer*). **Summary:** Rene, the Vicomte de St. Denis, returns to Paris from a hunting trip in Africa before his fiancée Louise expects him and makes dates with Paulette de l'Enclos at 10, Suzanne at 12, and Gabrielle at 1 a.m. He forgets all three, however, when he finds an abandoned baby in his car. —AFICFF. **Notes:** On September 3, 2015, author Cliff Aliperti posted a review titled, "'A Bedtime Story' (1933), Starring Maurice Chevalier and Helen Twelvetrees," on https://immortalephemera. com. He mentions that the adults in the film are upstaged by the debut of one-year-old Baby LeRoy; he amends this by writing: "While the baby stole the movie from Chevalier back in 1933, he's not the pervasive force you might expect. He and Chevalier come across as equals in terms of screen presence, and once Twelvetrees arrives Baby LeRoy doesn't do much more than lie still being adored. You could make just as big a case for Edward Everett Horton stealing the movie, as he's a major presence throughout, especially during the first hour. He also shares the funniest scene in the movie, when he prepares to shave Chevalier immediately after discovering that his wife was one of Rene's many conquests." In sum, Aliperti describes *A Bedtime Story* as a "very entertaining romantic comedy with a bit of music, from Paramount and director Norman Taurog."

The Way to Love (October 20, 1933) Paramount Pictures, 80 minutes, whimsical comedy set in Paris. **Producer:** Benjamin Glazer. **Director:** Norman Taurog. **Screenplay:** Gene Fowler, Benjamin Glazer. **Camera:** Charles Lang. **Editor:** Hugh Bennett. **Cast:** Maurice Chevalier (*François*), Edward Everett Horton (*Prof. Gaston Bibi*); Arthur Pierson (*M. Joe*); John Miljan (*Marco*); Sidney Toler (*Pierre*); George Regas (*Pedro*); Arthur Housman (*Drunk being photographed*); George Hagen (*Wladek the Mighty*); Lona Andre (*M. Prial's assistant, uncredited*); Ann Dvorak (*Madeline*); Mina Gombell (*Suzanne*); Nydia Westman (*Annette*); Blanche Friderici (*Rosalie*); Grace Bradley (*Sunburned Lady*); Douglass Dumbrille (*Agent Chapusard*); Billy Bevan (*M. Prial*); Jason Robards Sr. (*Guide*); Mischa Auer (*Songwriter at piano*). **Summary:** François, a cheerful Parisian bohemian, wants more than anything to be a tour guide in his beloved city. Presently, however, he is a walking advertisement for Professor Gaston Bibi (Eddie), who is in the business of L' amour. Bibi helps the adulterers of Paris deceive their spouses by making mock postcards of them in exotic places and administering suntans to those who are supposed to have been at the sea. While working the streets for Bibi, François meets Madeleine, who is on the wrong end of a knife-throwing act in a circus. —AFICFF

Alice in Wonderland (December 22, 1933) Paramount Pictures, 77 minutes, classic children's story. **Producer:** Louis D. Lighton (uncredited). **Director:** Norman Z. McLeod. **Screenplay:** Joeseph L. Mankiewicz, William Cameron Menzies; based on the novels *Alice's Adventures in Wonderland* (1865) and *Through the Looking Glass* (1872) by Lewis Carroll. **Camera:** Bert Glennon, Henry Sharp. **Editor:** Elsworth Hoagland (uncredited). **Cast** (in alphabetical order): Richard Arlen (*Cheshire Cat*); Roscoe Ates (*Fish Footman*); William Austin (*Gryphon*); Gary Cooper (*White Knight*); Leon Errol (*Uncle Gilbert*); Louise Fazenda (*White Queen*); W.C. Fields (*Humpty Dumpty*); Alec B. Francis (*King of Hearts*); Richard "Skeets" Gallagher (*White Rabbit*); Cary Grant (*Mock Turtle*); Lillian Harmer (*The Cook*); Raymond Hatton (*The Mouse*); Charlotte Henry (*Alice*); Sterling Holloway (*Frog Footman*); Edward Everett Horton (*The Mad Hatter*); Mae Marsh (*The Sheep*); Polly Moran (*The Dodo*); Jack Oakie (*Tweedledum*); Edna May Oliver (*Red Queen*); May Robson (*Queen of Hearts*); Charlie Ruggles (*March Hare*); Jackie Searl (*Dormouse*); Alison Skipworth (*Duchess*); Ned Sparks (*Caterpillar*); Ford Sterling (*White King*). **Notes:** Because of his belief that he resembled John Tenniel's drawings of The Mad Hatter, Eddie decided, for the first and last time, to campaign for the role. Although he was cast, he was terribly disappointed by the completed film. He disliked the heavy, concealing costuming used on the actors, himself included. **Summary:** In 19th century England, a young girl named Alice becomes bored while reading a book in the company of her cat and climbs on top of the fireplace to look into a mirror. Alice steps through the mirror and falls into an enchanted land where chess pieces come to life, among other amazements. **Notes:** Walt Disney saw this film and was inspired to make an animated version of the story, which was released in 1951. When casting the voice actor for The Mad Hatter, Ed Wynn, not Edward Everett Horton, was chosen. —AFICFF

Design for Living (December 29, 1933) Paramount Pictures, 91 minutes, sophisticated comedy. **Producer:** Ernst Lubitsch. **Director:** Ernst Lubitsch. **Screenplay:** Ben Hecht; based on the 1932 play *Design for Living* by Noël Coward. **Camera:** Victor Milner. **Editor:** Frances Marsh. **Cast:** Fredric March (*Tom Chambers*); Gary Cooper (*George Curtis*); Miriam Hopkins (*Gilda Farrell*); Edward Everett Horton (*Max Plunkett*); Franklin Pangborn (*Mr. Douglas*); Isabel Jewell; (*Max's stenog-*

rapher); Jane Darwell (*George's housekeeper*); Wyndham Standing (*Max's butler*). **Summary:** On a train bound for Paris, commercial artist Gilda Farrell meets fellow Americans George Curtis, a painter, and Thomas B. Chambers, a playwright, who share an apartment in the Bohemian section of Paris. Gilda works for prudish advertising agent Max Plunkett (Eddie), who is currently running an ad campaign for Kaplan and McGuire's non-wrinkling underwear featuring Gilda's caricature of Napoleon in his skivvies. Although Max has known Gilda for five years, he has never gotten to first base with her romantically. After he discovers Gilda's separate rendezvous with Tom and George, whom he calls "hooligans," Max warns each of them that "immorality might be fun, but not fun enough to take the place of one hundred percent virtue and three square meals a day." Tom decides the line makes a good close for the first act of his new play, and when he reads it to George, each realizes that the other is in love with Gilda. —AFICFF

Easy to Love (January 13, 1934) Warner Bros. Pictures, approx. 60 minutes, romantic comedy. **Producer:** Henry Blanke (uncredited). **Director:** William Keighley. **Screenplay:** Carl Erickson, Manuel Seff; based on the 1930 play *As Good as New* by Thompson Buchanan. **Music:** Heinz Roemheld (uncredited). **Camera:** Ernest Haller. **Editor:** William Clemens. **Cast:** Genevieve Tobin (*Carol Townshend*); Adolphe Menjou (*John Townshend*); Mary Astor (*Charlotte Hopkins*); Edward Everett Horton (*Erich Schulz*); Patricia Ellis (*Janet Townshend*); Guy Kibbee (*Justice of the Peace*); Hugh Herbert (*Detective John McTavish*), Paul Kaye (*Paul Smith*); Hobart Cavanaugh (*Hotel desk clerk*); Robert Greig (*Andrews, the butler*); Harold Waldridge (*Elevator boy*). **Summary and Review:** "While Menjou plays footsie with Astor, his wife [Tobin] pretends to fool around with Horton. Simple but pleasing marital comedy, deftly played by a good cast" (***). —LMCMG

The Poor Rich (February 26, 1934). Universal Pictures, 77 minutes, comedy. **Producer:** Carl Laemmle Jr. **Director:** Edward Sedgwick. **Screenplay:** Ebba Havez, Dale Van Every. **Camera:** George Robinson. **Editor:** Robert Carlisle. **Cast:** Edward Everett Horton (*Albert Stuyvesant Spottiswood*); Edna May Oliver (*Harriet Spottiswood*); Andy Devine (*Andy*); Leila Hyams (*Grace Hunter*); Grant Mitchell (*Tom Hopkins*); Thelma Todd (*Gwendolyn Fetherstone*); Una O'Connor (*Lady Fetherstone*); E.E. Clive (*Lord Fetherstone*); John Miljan (Prince Abdul Hamidshan); Sidney Bracey (*Arbuthnot*); Jack Rube Clifford (*Station Agent*); Henry Armetta (*Tony*); Ward Bond (*Motor Cop*). **Summary:**

Impoverished Albert Stuyvesant Spottiswood (Eddie) arrives in Old Haven, Connecticut, expecting to settle down at the family estate, Spottiswood Manor. He soon discovers, however, that the manor has been deserted and that the Spottiswood fortune has been lost. After his disappointed valet leaves him in town, Albert is rescued by Andy, a lunch wagon cook. —AFICFF

Uncertain Lady (April 3, 1934) Universal Pictures, 65 minutes, marital comedy. **Producers:** Carl Laemmle Jr., Dale Van Every. **Director:** Karl Freund. **Screenplay:** Daniel Evans, Doris Anderson, Edward A. Curtiss, George O'Neil, Don Ryan. **Music:** Edward Ward. **Camera:** Charles J. Stumar. **Editor:** Edward Curtiss. **Cast:** Edward Everett Horton (*Elliot Crane*); Genevieve Tobin (*Doris Crane*); Paul Cavanagh (*Bruce King*); Mary Nash (*Edith Hayes*); Renee Gadd (*Myra Spaulding*); Donald Reed (*Carlos Almirante*); Dorothy Peterson (*Cicily Prentiss*); George Meeker (*Dr. Alexander Garrison*); Herbert Corthell (*Harley*); Arthur Hoyt (*Superintendent*); Gay Seabrook (*Secretary*); Dick Winslow (*Office Boy*); James Durkin (*Mr. Weston*). **Summary:** Elliot Crane (Eddie) asks his wife for a divorce. She agrees, provided he finds her a replacement husband. —AFICFF

Sing and Like It (April 20, 1934) RKO Radio Pictures, 72 minutes, satire. **Producer:** Merian C. Cooper. **Associate Producer:** Howard J. Green. **Director:** William A. Seiter. **Music:** Max Steiner. **Camera:** Nicholas Musuraca. **Editor:** George Crone. **Cast:** ZaSu Pitts (*Anne Snodgrass*); Pert Kelton (*Ruby*); Edward Everett Horton (*Adam Frink*); Nat Pendleton (*T. Fenny Sylvester*); Ned Sparks (*Toots McGuire*); John Qualen (*Oswald*); Matt McHugh (*Junker*); Stanley Fields (*Butch*); William H. Griffith (*Webster, Frink's secretary*); Roy D'Arcy (*Mr. Gregory, the leading man*); Joseph Sauers (*Gunner*). **Summary:** While breaking into the Union Bank safe, gangster T. Fennimore "Fenny" Sylvester overhears bank employee Annie Snodgrass singing "Your Mother" during an upstairs amateur variety show rehearsal. Moved to tears by the sentimental tune, Fenny decides to put the tin-eared Annie in a Broadway revue and uses numerous threats to coerce theatrical producer Adam Frink (Eddie) into staging it. —AFICFF

Success at Any Price (May 3, 1934) RKO Radio Pictures, 74 minutes, bitter Depression melodrama. **Producer:** Merian C. Cooper. **Director:** J. Walter Ruben. **Screenplay:** John Howard Lawson, Howard J. Green; based on the 1932 play *Success Story* by John Howard Leslie. **Music:**

Max Steiner. **Camera:** Henry Gerrard. **Editor:** Jack Hively. **Cast:** Douglas Fairbanks, Jr. (*Joe Martin*); Genevieve Tobin (*Agnes Carter*); Frank Morgan (*Raymond Merritt*); Colleen Moore (*Sarah Griswold*); Edward Everett Horton (*Harry Fisher*); Nydia Westman (*Dinah*); Henry Kolker (*Hatfield*); Allen Vincent (*Geoffrey Halliburton*). **Summary:** Depression-era morality tale about an ambitious young man, Joe Martin (Douglas Fairbanks Jr.), who steps on everyone and everything to get the money and power he craves. When his life begins to fall apart and he realizes how shallow he has been, he attempts suicide. His former girlfriend, Sarah (Colleen Moore), stands with him through this awakening, pledging her undying support. **Notes:** Eddie portrays Fisher, an office statistician who marries his dingy secretary, Dinah (Nydia Westman). Together, they provide comic relief. —AFIFFC

It's a Boy (June 7, 1934) Gainsborough Pictures, 80 minutes, farce. **Director:** Tim Whelan. **Screenplay:** Franz Arnold, Ernst Bach, John Paddy Carstairs. **Camera:** Mutz Greenbaum. **Editor:** Harold M. Young. **Art Director:** Alex Vetchinsky. **Costume Designer:** Gordon Conway. **Sound:** Slim Hand. **Music:** Louis Levy. **Cast:** Leslie Henson (*James Skippett*); Edward Everett Horton (*Dudley Leake*); Alfred Drayton (*Eustace Bogle*); Wendy Barrie (*Mary Bogle*); Joyce Kirby (*Lillian*), Clifford Buckton (*Inspector Burns, uncredited*), Gladys Hamer (*Bride at registrar's office*); Roddy Hughes (*George, uncredited*); Albert Burdon (*Joe Piper*); Heather Thatcher (*Anita Gunn*); Robertson Hare (*Allister*); Helen Haye (*Mrs. Bogle*); J.H. Roberts (*Registrar*); Finlay Currie (*Publisher, uncredited*). **Summary:** Dudley Leake (Eddie) is engaged to Mary Bogle (Wendy Barrie). Shortly before the wedding, Dudley confesses to his best man, Jim Skippett, that twenty years earlier he had a brief affair with a certain Miss Piper, but he's never heard from her since. In a nightmare scenario, a young man with blackmail on his mind shows up on the day of the wedding, claiming to be Dudley's illegitimate son. The IMDb features an uncredited, thoughtful review by a British movie buff. The following is an extract.

> The American character actor Edward Everett Horton had the sort of precise, well-modulated diction which American audiences tend to mistake for an upper-class English accent. In "It's a Boy", Horton actually plays an Englishman. Even more amazingly, he does so in a British film (from the splendid Gainsborough Pictures) made by producers who had their pick of genuine English actors. Presumably, Horton's presence here

was intended to make this British movie more attractive to American audiences.

The movie's director (Tim Whelan, who helmed several excellent English films) is also American, although this fact was unlikely to matter to American filmgoers. "It's a Boy" is funny, but not nearly so funny as it ought to be. Part of the problem is that Joe Piper (supposedly the son of the character portrayed by Horton) is played by an actor who doesn't resemble Edward Everett Horton at all. Also, Horton's characterisation here as Dudley Leake comes very close to the fussbudget 'nelly' character he played in so many Hollywood films, which makes it somewhat implausible that Leake would be in this particular situation. There's one sequence which I found especially wince-worthy, when male actor Leslie Henson dons a makeshift bridal train and links arms with a very discomfited Horton ... as if the two men were bride and groom.

I'll rate "It's a Boy" 6 out of 10. Edward Everett Horton was never one of my favourite character actors, but he works hard here ... and he and the delightful Heather Thatcher play off each other very capably.

Kiss and Make Up (July 13, 1934) Paramount Pictures, 78 minutes, romantic comedy. **Producer:** B.P. Schulberg. **Director:** Harlan Thompson, Helen Negulesco (associate director). **Screenplay:** Harlan Thompson, George Marion Jr., Jane Hinton; based on the play *Kozmetika* by Istaván Békeffy (credited as Stephen Bekeffi). **Music:** Ralph Rainger. **Lyrics:** Leo Robin. **Camera:** Leon Shamroy. **Cast:** Cary Grant (*Dr. Maurice Lamar*); Genevieve Tobin (*Eve Caron*); Helen Mack (*Annie*); Edward Everett Horton (*Marcel Caron*); Lucien Littlefield (*Max Pascal*); Mona Maris (*Countess Rita*); Rafael Alcayde (*Rolando, credited as Rafael Storm*); Toby Wing (*Consuelo Claghorn*); Dorothy Christie (*Greta*); listed in the opening credits are "The WAMPAS Baby Stars of 1934": Judith Arlen, Betty Bryson, Jean Carmen, Helen Cohan (credited as Helene Cohan), Dorothy Drake, Jean Gale, Hazel Hayes, Ann Hovey, Lucille Lund, Lu Ann Meredith (as Lu-Anne Meredith), Gigi Parrish (as Gi-Gi Parrish), Jacqueline Wells, Katherine Williams. **Summary:** Dr. Maurice Lamar's Temple de Beauté in Paris attracts women from all over the world who wish to be made beautiful. One of Lamar's prized creations is Eve Caron, whom he has transformed into visual perfection. Eve's husband Marcel (Eddie), however, is furious with Lamar for changing his wife's appearance. When the superficial Eve comes to the realization that Marcel's naturally curly hair is, in fact, a toupee, she immediately swears her love for Lamar. —AFICFF

Ladies Should Listen (August 10, 1934) Paramount Pictures, 62 minutes, romantic comedy. **Director:** Frank Tuttle. **Screenplay:** Claude Binyon, Guy Bolton; based on a play by Alfred Savoir. **Camera:** Henry Sharp. **Cast:** Cary Grant (*Julian De Lussac*); Frances Drake (*Anna Mirelle*); Edward Everett Horton (*Paul Vernet*); Nydia Westman (*Susi Flamberg*); Rosita Moreno (*Marguerite Cintos*); Joseph North (*Butleras*); Charles Ray (*Henri, the porter*); Rafael Corio (*Ramon Cintos*); George Barbier (*Joseph Flamberg*); Charles Arnt (*Albert, the manservant*); Clara Lou Sheridan [Ann Sheridan] (*Adele*); Henrietta Burnside (*Operator*). **Summary:** Julian de Lussac, a man-about-town in Paris, is being chased by three women when he returns from South America with an option on a Chilean nitrate concession. The first woman, Marguerite, is the wife of thief Ramon Cintos, who followed Julian from Chile to steal his nitrate option. The second is Susi, the myopic daughter of millionaire Joseph Flamberg. She has little sex appeal but is adored by Julian's friend, Paul Vernet (Eddie), who claims that she is his fiancée. At Cintos's request, Marguerite makes love to Julian, and he falls for her. When Marguerite calls to tell Julian goodbye, he threatens to kill himself, after which the third woman, Anna Mirelle, the telephone operator, who has been listening in on his calls to Marguerite, rushes in to save his life. In the end, Julian advises Paul to be more aggressive in showing his ardor for Suzi. Paul accepts Julian's suggestion and passionately accosts her. —AFICFF

Smarty (September 29, 1934; released in the UK as *Hit Me Again*) Warner Bros. Pictures, 65 minutes, marital comedy. **Director:** Robert Florey. **Screenplay:** Carl Erickson; based on a play by F. Hugh Herbert. **Camera:** George Barnes. **Editor:** Jack Killifer. **Cast:** Joan Blondell (*Vicki Wallace Thorpe*); Warren William (*Tony Wallace*); Edward Everett Horton (*Vernon Thorpe*); Frank McHugh (*George Lancaster*); Claire Dodd (*Anita*); Joan Wheeler (*Mrs. Bonnie Durham*); Virginia Sale (*Vicki's Maid*); Leonard Carey (*Tony's Butler*). **Summary, Review, and Notes:** "Blondell teases husband William so relentlessly he finally hits her, prompting her to seek a divorce, but her marriage to their friend (and divorce attorney) Horton is equally doomed. This was a pre-production code film and one of the reasons for the creation of same" (**). —LMCMG

The Merry Widow (October 11, 1934) Metro-Goldwyn-Mayer / Loew's Inc., 99 minutes, operetta. **Producers:** Irving Thalberg (uncredited), Ernst Lubitsch. **Director:** Ernst Lubitsch. **Screenplay:** Victor Leon, Leo Stein (libretto); based on the 1905 operetta by Franz Lehár. **Camera:** Oliver T. Marsh. **Editor:** Frances Marsh. **Cast:** Maurice Chevalier (Captain Danilo); Jeanette MacDonald (*Madame Sonia / Fifi*); Edward Everett Horton (*Ambassador Popoff*); Una Merkel (*Queen Dolores*); George Barbier (*King Achmed*); Minna Gombell (*Marcelle*); Ruth Channing (*Lulu*); Sterling Holloway (*Mischka*); Donald Meek (*Valet*); Herman Bing (*Zizipoff*); Jason Robards Sr. (*Arresting Officer, uncredited*); Akim Tamiroff (*Maxim's Manager, uncredited*). **Summary:** In 1885, in the tiny European kingdom of Marshovia, playboy Count Danilo, the captain of the royal guard, admires the veiled rich widow Sonia during a military parade and later slips into her garden to woo her. Obeying a Marshovian edict that stipulates that widows must always wear veils in public, the surprised Sonia covers her face before Danilo sees her and, in spite of his begging, refuses to lift it. Sonia then firmly rejects Danilo's deft flirtations but, over the next few days, is filled with conflicted thoughts about him. Unable to deal with her emotions, Sonia declares her one-year Marshovian widowhood over and moves to Paris. Because Sonia owns fifty-two percent of every cow in Marshovia and therefore controls the economy, her departure alarms the king, Achmed II, who frantically confers with his wife, Queen Dolores, about possible local suitors for the widow. **Notes:** The film's elaborate sets were responsible for the picture's sole Academy Award win for Best Art Direction. Budgeted at close to $2 million (the equivalent of $47 million in 2024), it performed better in Europe than in the U.S. In fact, it took several years and a major re-release in 1949 for *The Merry Widow* to finally break even. Two versions of the film—one in English, directed by Lubitsch, and a French version with a different director and the same cast, with the exception of Eddie. —AFICFF

The Gay Divorcee (October 12, 1934) RKO Radio Pictures, 107 minutes, musical comedy. **Producer:** Pandro S. Berman. **Director:** Mark Sandrich. **Screenplay:** George Marion Jr., Dorothy Yost, Edward Kaufman; based on the 1932 stage musical *Gay Divorce* by Dwight Taylor. **Music score:** Max Steiner. **Camera:** David Abel. **Editor:** William Hamilton. **Cast:** Fred Astaire (*Guy Holden*); Ginger Rogers (*Mimi*); Alice Brady (*Hortense*); Edward Everett Horton (*Egbert*); Erik Rhodes (*Tonetti*); Eric Blore (*The Waiter*); William Austin (*Cyril Glossop*); Charles Coleman (*The Valet*); Lillian Miles (*Guest*); Betty Grable (*Guest*). **Summary:** In their first film together, Fred Astaire and Ginger Rogers portray American tourists Guy Holden and Mimie Glossop, who "meet cute" in London. Guy is traveling with his best friend and attorney, Egbert "Pinky" Fitzgerald (Eddie), and Mimi's companion is her aunt Hortense (Alice Brady), who just so happens to be Pinky's former fiancée. There is a convoluted subplot involving Mimi's need for a co-respondent to extricate herself from an unhappy marriage. There are also some funny exchanges, particularly between Pinky and a waiter, played by Eric Blore. All of this plays out in between the solid dance numbers, with "The Continental" a particular standout. **Notes:** "The Continental," with music by Con Conrad and lyrics by Herb Magidson, won the first Academy Award for Best Song. "Night and Day" was written by Cole Porter. "Let's K-nock K-nees," with music by Harry Revel and lyrics by Max Gordon, is delightfully performed by Eddie and newcomer Betty Grable. The Broadway play on which this film is based is titled *Gay Divorce*; that might have been the title of the movie if the newly invigorated Production Code hadn't objected to it. —AFICFF

Biography of a Bachelor Girl (January 4, 1935) Metro-Goldwyn-Mayer, 82 minutes, Depression comedy-drama. **Producer:** Edward H. Griffith. **Director:** Edward H. Griffith. **Screenplay:** Anita Loos, Horace Jackson; based on the 1932 play *Biography* by S.N. Behrman. **Camera:** James Wong Howe. **Editor:** William S. Gray. **Cast:** Ann Harding (*Marion Forsythe*); Robert Montgomery (*Richard "Dickie" Kur*); Edward Everett Horton (*Leander 'Bunny' Nolan*); Edward Arnold (*Mr. "Feydie" Feydak*); Una Merkel (*Slade Kinnicott*); Charles Richman (*Mr. Orrin Kinnicott*); Greta Meyer (*Minnie*); Willard Robertson (*Grigsby*); Donald Meek *(Mr. Irish)*. **Summary:** Richard Kurt, a managing editor at a large magazine, is determined to have Bohemian artist Marion Forsythe's autobiography published and takes a two thousand dollar advance to her to convince her that he is serious. In the face of destitution and the repossession of her belongings, Marion agrees to Richard's offer. When Slade, the fiancée of senatorial candidate Leander Nolan (Eddie), comes across a newspaper article announcing the arrival of Marion, Leander's childhood flame, she relates the news to Leander, but he feigns disinterest. Later, the candidate secretly visits Marion, who, at first sight, does not recognize him, to resolve a quarrel they had in Knoxville, Tennessee, their home town, many years earlier. Uninterested in such trivial matters, Marion offers to paint Leander's portrait, which she feels would be a necessary monument to his vanity and senatorial aspirations. Leander and Richard take an immediate dislike to each other, and Richard disparages

Marion's tolerance of the shifty political windbag. Fearing that Marion's book would reveal too much of his past with her, Leander desperately tries to stop the book's publication, even offering Marion money to discontinue her plans, but she insists on finishing her memoirs. Richard, appalled at the candidate's attempt at bribery, hopes that the book will ruin his chances of winning an election, and taunts Leander by pretending to have read the scandalous references to her old flame. Realizing that Marion is offered little privacy in her home, Richard decides to take her to a secluded cabin at Moose Lake, Maine, where she can write in peace. Again, Richard discounts Marion's Bohemian lifestyle, criticizing her superficial and casual manner, but soon finds that he has become enamored with her, despite her flaws. Meanwhile, Leander discovers Marion's whereabouts and seeks her out to make her realize how much unhappiness she has caused him. At the same time, the suspicious, jealous bride-to-be, Slade, follows him there and chaos ensues. In the confusion, the dejected Leander confesses that he is afraid of his fiancée and deeply in love with Marion. Leander proposes marriage to Marion, but she tells him that she has fallen in love with Richard. When Marion threatens to leave Richard forever unless he tells her that he loves her, he admits that he is uncomfortable with expressing his feelings toward her, but then admits that he is indeed in love with her. **Notes:** In June 1933, the Hays Office warned MGM producer E. J. Mannix that the story contained "one dangerous element, in the various affairs which the heroine is portrayed as having indulged in." The Hays Office reiterated its objection to the characterization of "Marion" in July 1934, stating that she is "a woman who has gained considerable notoriety through a succession of affairs with men. Such a characterization is, of course, unacceptable under the Code." Thalberg reportedly responded to the Hays Office complaints by agreeing to "add lines from Marion indicating that she regrets her loose life; a line definitely establishing that she and Kurt do not sleep together in the mountain cabin...[and] a line for an earlier scene in which she implies that gossip about her is exaggerated." At the time of the film's release, the Hays Office received a letter from the International Federation of Catholic Alumnae expressing the organization's outrage over the inclusion of the following line in the film: "Of course you were always interesting, even fornicationally." Joseph Breen of the Hays Office reacted quickly to the letter and stated: "We were astounded when we read this letter....It [the film] was witnessed by four of our staff, none of whom caught the line at all." The film was sent back for a second review to find the line in question, but no such line was found. Instead, Breen suggested that the following line spoken by Ann

Harding to Edward Everett Horton was misunderstood: "You used to be quite a nice boy—even fun occasionally."—AFICFF

The Night is Young (January 11, 1935) Metro-Goldwyn-Mayer, 81 minutes, musical comedy. **Producer:** Harry Rapf. **Director:** Dudley Murphy. **Screenplay:** Edgar Allan Woolf, Franz Schulz; based on a story by Vicki Baum. **Camera:** James Wong Howe. **Editor:** Conrad A. Nervig. **Cast:** Ramon Novarro (*Archduke Paul 'Gustl' Gustave*); Evelyn Laye (*Elizabeth Katherine Anne 'Lisl' Gluck*); Charles Butterworth (*Willy Fitch*); Una Merkel (*Fanni Kerner*); Edward Everett Horton (*Baron Szereny*); Donald Cook (*Toni Berngruber*); Henry Stephenson (*Emperor Franz Josef*); Rosalind Russell (*Countess Zarika Rafay*); Herman Bing (*Nepomuk*); Gustav von Seyffertitz (*Ambassador*). **Summary, Review, and Notes:** "Novarro, wretchedly miscast and mugging mercilessly, brings his ten-year MGM career to a pitiful end playing a Viennese archduke who spurns his royal fiancée for a fling with ballerina Laye (who bolted back to England after this disaster). Oscar Hammerstein–Sigmund Romberg score, including 'When I Grow Too Old to Dream,' is an insufficient saving grace" (BOMB). —LMCMG. This particular review seems rather harsh, but Leonard Maltin usually knows whereof he speaks. The one thing he didn't mention was Eddie's performance as Baron Szereny. Looking especially dashing in his military uniform, he adds genuine humor to this operetta by voicing his absolute revulsion to the word *doodlesack*.

All the King's Horses (February 13, 1935) Paramount Pictures, 87 minutes, musical comedy. **Director:** Frank Tuttle. **Screenplay:** Edmund H. North, Frank Tuttle, Frederick Stephani; based on the play *Carlo Rocco* by Lawrence Clarke, Max Giersberg, Frederick Herendeen, and Edward Horan. **Camera:** Henry Sharp. **Cast:** Carl Brisson (*King Rudolf XIV / Carlo Rocco*); Mary Ellis (*Elaine, Queen of Langenstein*); Edward Everett Horton (*Count Josef von Schlapstaat*); Katherine DeMille (*Miss Mimi*); Eugene Pallette (*Con Conley*); Arnold Korff (*Baron Kraemer*). **Summary and Review:** "Mediocre musical about a movie star who exchanges places with look-alike king, causing complications for both men, especially where l'amour is concerned" (**). —LMCMG. **Notes:** Calling this musical *mediocre* seems generous to us; it is turgid at best. But when the tuxedo-clad Count Josef von Schlapstaat (Eddie) appears on the screen in all his nervousness, there is cause for celebration. He is in on the scheme to pass off the leading character (the uncharismatic Carl Brisson) as the king, and even throws in a well-timed double-take.

The Devil is a Woman (March 15, 1935) Paramount Pictures, 79 minutes, satirical comedy-drama. **Producer:** Josef von Sternberg. **Director:** Josef von Sternberg. **Screenplay:** Jon dos Passos; based on the 1898 novel *The Woman and the Puppet* by Pierre Louÿs and the 1910 play by Pierre Louÿs and Pierre Frondale. **Camera:** Josef von Sternberg. **Editor:** Sam Winston. **Music score:** John Leipold, Heinz Roemheld. **Cast:** Marlene Dietrich (*Concha Pérez*); Lionel Atwill (*Captain Don Pasqual Costelar*); Edward Everett Horton (*Governor Don Paquito*); Alison Skipworth (*Señora Pérez*); Cesar Romero (*Antonio Galvan*); Don Alvarado (Morenito); Tempe Pigott (*Tuerta*); Luisa Espinel (*Gypsy Dancer, uncredited*). **Summary:** "Sumptuous-looking film about alluring but heartless woman and the men who all but ruin their lives for her, set against backdrop of 19ᵗʰ century Spanish revolution. Hypnotic, if dramatically shaky. Luis Buñuel used some of the same source material for *That Obscure Object of Desire*" (***). —LMCMG. **Notes:** Eddie's character has been described as a "despotic commander of Seville's police force, who is responsible for maintaining order during the festivities. He is susceptible to the charms of attractive women."

$10 Raise (May 4, 1935; released in the UK as *Mr. Faintheart*) Fox Film Corporation, 70 minutes, small town domestic comedy. **Producer:** Joseph W. Engel. **Director:** George Marshall. **Screenplay:** Henry Johnson, Lou Breslow; based on the novel *The Ten Dollar Raise* by Peter B. Kyne. **Camera:** Harry Jackson. **Cast:** Edward Everett Horton (*Hubert T. Wilkins*); Karen Morley (*Emily Converse*); Alan Dinehart (*Fuller*); Glen Boles (*Don Bates*); Berton Churchill *(Mr. Bates)*; Rosina Lawrence (*Dorothy Converse*); Ray Walker (*Perry*); Frank Melton (*Clark*); William "Billy" Benedict (*Jimmy*). **Summary:** Timorous Hubert T. Wilkins (Eddie), a forty-year-old bookkeeper who has worked eighteen years for the San Francisco importing and exporting firm of Bates & Co., refrains from proposing to Emily Converse, the firm's thirty-five-year-old secretary, because he does not think that they can live on his forty dollars-a-week salary. After Emily convinces Hubert to be more aggressive, he decides to ask his ill-tempered boss for a raise. —IMDb

In Caliente (May 25, 1935) Warner Bros. Pictures, 84 minutes, romantic musical comedy. **Producer:** Edward Chodorov. **Director:** Lloyd Bacon. **Screenplay:** Jerry Wald, Julius J. Epstein. **Camera:** George Barnes, Sol Polito. **Editor:** James Gibbon. **Cast:** Dolores del Río (*Rita Gomez*); Pat O'Brien (*Larry MacArthur*); Leo Carrillo (*José Gomez*); Edward Everett Horton (*Harold Brandon*); Glenda Farrell (*Clara*); Tony

De Marco (*One of The De Marcos*); Sally De Marco (*One of The De Marcos*); Phil Regan (*Peter*); Wini Shaw (*Lois*); Luis Alberni (*Magistrate*); George Humbert (*Photographer*); Harry Holman (*Biggs*); Soledad Jiménez (*Rita's Maid*); Herman Bing (*Florist*); Judy Canova (*Specialty Singer*). **Summary, Review, and Notes:** "Pedestrian comedy filmed in Agua Caliente, with fast-talking O'Brien wooing dancer Del Rio. Horton's comic relief is the saving grace, along with Busby Berkeley's production numbers for 'Muchacha' and 'The Lady in Red' (sung by Wini Shaw, with a novelty chorus by Judy Canova)" (**). —LMCMG

Going Highbrow (August 23, 1935) Warner Bros. Pictures, 67 minutes, comedy. **Producer:** Samuel Bishoff. **Director:** Robert Florey. **Screenplay:** Edward Kaufman, Sy Bartlett, Ralph Spence, Ben Markson. **Camera:** William Rees. **Editor:** Harold McLemon. **Music score:** Leo F. Forbstein. **Cast:** Guy Kibbee (*Matt Upshaw*); ZaSu Pitts (*Mrs. Cora Upshaw*); Edward Everett Horton (*Augie Winterspoon*); Ross Alexander (*Harley Marsh*); June Martel (*Sandy Long*); Gordon Westcott (*Sam Long*); Judy Canova (*Annie*); Nella Walker (*Mrs. Forrester Marsh*); Jack Norton (*Sinclair*); Arthur Treacher (*Waiter*). **Summary and Review:** "Ingratiating lunacy with Kibbee and Pitts as nouveau riches trying to crash New York society with Horton's help by throwing a lavish coming-out party for their debutante daughter … except they don't have a daughter, so they hire a waitress to pose as her. Funny showcase for trio of wonderful character actors" (**½). —LMCMG

Top Hat (August 29, 1935) RKO Radio Pictures, 101 minutes (some prints are 93 minutes), show business musical comedy. **Producer:** Pandro S. Berman. **Director:** Mark Sandrich. **Screenplay:** Allan Scott, Dwight Taylor; based on the 1911 play *A Scandal in Budapest* by Aladar Laszlo. **Music:** Irving Berlin. **Camera:** David Abel. **Editor:** Edward Hamilton. **Cast:** Fred Astaire (*Jerry Travers*); Ginger Rogers (*Dale Tremont*); Edward Everett Horton (*Horace Hardwick*); Erik Rhodes (*Alberto Beddini*); Helen Broderick (*Madge Hardwick*); Eric Blore (*Bates*). **Notes:** Eddie plays Horace Hardwick, the producer of a revue starring his friend Jerry Travers. **Summary and Review:** "What can we say? Merely a knock-out of a musical with Astaire and Rogers at their brightest doing 'Cheek to Cheek,' 'Isn't This a Lovely Day to Be Caught in the Rain,' 'Top Hat, White Tie, and Tails,' and the epic 'Piccolino,' and other Irving Berlin songs, as the duo goes through typical mistaken-identity plot. Wonderful support from rest of cast" (****). —LMCMG. **Notes:**

Eddie and Eric Blore, who had been so hilarious in their scenes together in *The Gay Divorcee*, are back and in grand form.

Little Big Shot (September 7, 1935) Warner Bros. Pictures, 78 minutes, Runyonesque-style comedy. **Producer:** Samuel Bishoff. **Director:** Michael Curtiz. **Story:** Harrison Jacobs. **Screenplay:** Jerry Wald, Julius J. Epstein, and Robert Andrews. **Music score:** Heinz Roemheld, Frank Dixon, Allie Wrubel. **Camera:** Tony Gaudio. **Editor:** Jack Killifer. **Cast:** Sybil Jason (*Gloria "Countess" Gibbs*); Glenda Farrell (*Jean*); Robert Armstrong (*Steve Craig*); Edward Everett Horton (*Mortimer Thompson*); Jack La Rue (*Jack Doré*); Arthur Vinton (*Kell "Nort" Norton*); J. Carrol Naish (*Bert*); Edgar Kennedy (*Onderdonk*); Addison Richards (*Hank Gibbs*). **Summary and Review:** "Warners' first attempt to create their own Shirley Temple stars five-year-old South African–born Jason playing a gangster's orphaned daughter who is taken in by a pair of Broadway's con men. Engaging cast and swift direction make it painless. Jason's impressions of Garbo, Mae West, and Jimmy Durante are pretty cute" (**½). —LMCMG. **Notes:** In a change-of-pace role, Eddie plays a confidence man on Broadway.

The Private Secretary (September 1935) Julius Hagen Productions, Twickenham Film Distributors, 70 minutes, country house farce. **Producer:** Julius Hagen. **Director:** Henry Edwards. **Screenplay:** George Broadhurst, Arthur Macrae, H. Fowler May; based on the stage farce *The Private Secretary* by Charles Hawfrey, and the book by Von Moser (*Der Bibliotheker*). **Music:** W.L. Trytel (uncredited). **Camera:** Sydney Blythe, William Luff. **Cast:** Edward Everett Horton (*Reverend Robert Spalding*); Barry MacKay (*Douglas Cattermole*); Judy Gunn (*Edith Marsland*); Oscar Asche (*Robert Cattermole*); Sydney Fairbrother (*Miss Ashford*); Michael Shepley (*Henry Marsland*); Alastair Sim (*Nebulae*); Aubrey Dexter (*Gibson*); O. B. Clarence (*Thomas Marsland*); Davina Craig (*Annie*). **Summary:** A timid and dim-witted clergyman (Eddie) is duped into helping a playboy avoid his creditors, inherit his uncle's fortune, and get the girl. —IMDb

His Night Out (October 1, 1935) Universal Pictures, 67 minutes, small town comedy. **Producer:** Irving Stan. **Director:** William Nigh. **Screenplay:** Harry Clork, Doris Malloy. **Camera:** Edward Snyder. **Editor:** Daniel Mandell. **Cast:** Edward Everett Horton (*Homer B. Bitts*); Irene Hervey (*Peggy Taylor*); Jack La Rue (*Joe Ferranza*); Robert McWade (*Davis*); Lola Lane (*Lola*); Willard Robertson (*J.J. Trent*);

Oscar Apfel (*Dr. Kraft*); Theodore von Eltz (*Parsons*); Clara Kimball Young (*Mrs. Davis*); Ward Bond (*Lanky*); George Cleveland (*Detective*); Jack Mulhall (*Salesman*); Jack Norton (*Dr. Singer*); Dewey Robinson (*Beef*); Bill Burrud (*Jimmie*). **Summary:** Homer B. Bitts, a bumbling hypochondriac (Eddie), is informed by a quack doctor that he has only three months to live. This earth-shattering news prompts the meek Homer to pilfer $100,000 worth of bonds from his workplace in order to fund his secretary's younger brother's hip surgery. —IMDb

Your Uncle Dudley (December 13, 1935) Fox Film Corporation, 70 minutes, dramatic comedy. **Producer:** Edward T. Lowe Jr. **Director:** Eugene Forde. **Screenplay:** Allen Birkin, Joseph Hoffman, Dore Schary. **Camera:** Harry Jackson. **Editor:** Louis R. Loeffler. **Cast:** Edward Everett Horton (*Dudley Dixon*); Lois Wilson (*Christine Saunders*); John McGuire (*Robert Kirby*); Rosina Lawrence (*Ethel Church*); Alan Dinehart (*Charlie Post*); Marjorie Gateson (*Mabel Dixon*); William "Billy" Benedict (*Cyril Church*); Florence Roberts (*Janet Dixon*); Jane Barnes (*Marjorie Baxter*). **Summary:** As his sister-in-law Mabel forces her daughter Ethel to practice for the Deepwater Music Contest, paint and varnish dealer Dudley Dixon (Eddie) receives another silver loving cup from the "Thursday Morning Club" for his efforts on behalf of their community of Fairview. Mabel is insistent that Ethel win the music contest so the two can travel to Europe on the $5,000 grand prize, the same amount of money Dudley has owed Mabel for fifteen years. The community leaders, meanwhile, are planning a big boxing event on which they hope to make money, with their "committee of one," namely Dudley, doing all the work. —IMDb

Her Master's Voice (January 17, 1936) Paramount Pictures, 75 minutes, domestic comedy. **Producer:** Walter Wanger. **Director:** Joseph Santley. **Screenplay:** Dore Shary, Harry Sauber; based on the play *Her Master's Voice* by Claire Kummer. **Art Director:** Alexander Toluboff. **Music:** Heinz Roemheld. **Camera:** James Van Trees. **Editor:** Robert Simpson. **Cast:** Edward Everett Horton (*Ned Farrar*); Peggy Conklin (*Queena Farrar*); Laura Hope Crews (*Aunt Minnie Stickney*); Elizabeth Patterson (*Mrs. Ellie Martin*); Grant Mitchell (*Horace J. Twilling*); Charles Coleman (*Craddock*); Ruth Warren (*Phoebe*); Dick Elliott (*Police Captain*); Robert Homans (*Stationmaster*); Fred Santley (*Motorcycle Cop*). **Summary:** Passive Ned Farrar (Eddie) loses his job after his wife, Queena, and mother-in-law, Ellie Martin, convince him to ask for a raise. Ned sees no cause for despair, and good-naturedly brings home champagne to "celebrate," but Queena and Ellie are distraught and disappointed. —IMDb

The Singing Kid (April 11, 1936) First National Pictures / Warner Bros. Pictures, 85 minutes, romantic musical extravaganza. **Director:** William Keighley. **Screenplay:** Warren Duff, Pat C. Flick. **Music:** Ray Heindorf, Heinz Roemheld, Harold Arlen. **Camera:** George Barnes. **Editor:** Thomas Richards. **Cast:** Al Jolson (*Al Jackson*); Sybil Jason (*Sybil Haines*); Beverly Roberts (*Ruth Haines*); Edward Everett Horton (*Davenport Rogers*); Lyle Talbot (*Robert "Bob" Carey*); Allen Jenkins (*Joe Eddy*); Claire Dodd (*Dana Lawrence*); Frank Mitchell (*Dope*); Wini Shaw (*Blackface Singer*); Joe King (*Dr. May*); William B. Davidson (*Barney Hammond*); Cab Calloway and His Cotton Club Orchestra; The Yacht Club Boys. **Summary:** Al Jackson is a musical star whose generosity is well known. His lack of interest in money and busy schedule allows his lawyer, Robert Carey, to steal millions from him. Dana Lawrence, his fiancée, has also benefitted from Al's money and plans to repay him by running off with Bob. Al learns about their betrayal when the Internal Revenue Service demands payment of back taxes. That night Al loses his voice during his performance, and his doctor recommends a long trip to the country. Accompanied by his valet, Davenport Rogers (Eddie), and his driver, Joe, Al drives to Maine where he has rented a cottage. They meet a small girl named Sybil and learn that she has been living in the house. While they are getting acquainted, Ruth Haines, the landlady, arrives. She and Sybil, her niece, had planned to move out before Al arrived, but forgetful Davenport had never sent a telegram announcing their arrival. —AFICFF

Nobody's Fool (June 1, 1936) Universal Pictures, 75 minutes, small town comedy in the manner of *Mr. Deeds*. **Producer:** Irving Starr. **Director:** Arthur G. Collins. **Screenplay:** Ralph Block, Ben Markson, Jerry Sackheim; based on a story by Frank Mitchell Dazey and Agnes Christine Johnston. **Camera:** Norbert Brodine. **Editor:** Morris Wright. **Cast:** Edward Everett Horton (*Will Wright*); Glenda Farrell (*Ruby Miller*); Cesar Romero (*Dizzy Rantz*); Frank Conroy (*Jake Cavendish*); Warren Hymer (*Sour Puss*); Clay Clement (*Fixer Belmore*); Henry Hunter (*Doc*); Florence Roberts (*Mary Jones*); Edward Gargan (*Tom*); Pierre Watkin (*George Baxter*). **Summary:** Will Wright (Eddie), a small town waiter with idealistic views, goes to New York City and becomes mixed up with real estate swindlers. According to a review in the *New York Times* (June 4, 1936): "'Nobody's Fool,' which moved into the Albee

Theatre in Brooklyn yesterday with Universal's splendid picturization of "Show Boat," makes its chief bid for fame as a harbinger of Summer doldrums in the cinema. A feeble mélange of soporific comedy and far-fetched melodrama, the new film works an unfair hardship on such talented comedians as Edward Everett Horton, Glenda Farrell and Warren Hymer—not to mention its audience. Put together with apparently more speed than inspiration, the film narrates the oft told story of a country yokel who comes to Manhattan and outsmarts a gang of real estate racketeers intent on defrauding a nice old lady of three feet of property in Fifty-third Street. That's the gist of 'Nobody's Fool,' which would probably make a compact three-reeler." —IMDb

Hearts Divided (June 20, 1936) Warner Bros. Pictures, 87 minutes, historical romantic comedy. **Producer:** Frank Borzage, Marion Davies (uncredited). **Director:** Frank Borzage. **Screenplay:** Larid Doyle, Casey Robinson; based on the 1908 play *Glorious Betsy* by Rida Johnson Young. **Music:** Eric Wolfgang Korngold. **Camera:** George J. Folsey. **Editor:** William Holmes. **Cast:** Marion Davies (*Betsy Patterson*); Dick Powell (*Captain Jerome Bonaparte*); Charles Ruggles (*Senator Henry Ruggles*); Claude Rains (*Napoleon Bonaparte*); Edward Everett Horton (*Senator John Hathaway*); Arthur Treacher (*Sir Harry*); Henry Stephenson (*Charles Patterson*); Clara Blandick (*Aunt Ellen Patterson*); John Larkin (*Isham*); Walter Kingsford (*Monsieur Pichon*); Etienne Girardot (*Monsieur Du Fresne*); Halliwell Hobbes (*Cambaceres*); George Irving (*President Thomas Jefferson*); Beulah Bondi (*Madame Letizia Bonaparte*); Philip Hurlic (*Pippin*); John Elliott (*James Monroe, uncredited*); Sam McDaniel (*Zachariah, uncredited*). **Summary:** In 1803, Napoleon Bonaparte is negotiating with the United States for the sale of the Louisiana territory. He sends his brother Jerome to America as his ambassador. Arriving incognito at the races in Baltimore, Jerome meets Betsy Patterson, the attractive daughter of Charles Patterson, one of the negotiators. Still in disguise, he applies for the job of her French tutor, and the two fall in love. —AFICFF

The Man in the Mirror (October 15, 1936) Twickenham Studios / Wardour (UK) 71 minutes, fantasy drama. **Producer:** Julius Hagen. **Director:** Maurice Elvey. **Screenplay:** Hugh Mills, F. McGrew Willis; based on the novel by William Garrett. **Camera:** Curt Courant. **Editor:** Ralph Kemplem. **Cast:** Edward Everett Horton (*Jeremy Dilke*); Genevieve Tobin (*Helen Dilke*); Ursula Jeans (*Veronica Tarkington*); Garry Marsh (*Charles Tarkington*); Aubrey Mather (*Bogus of Bokhara*); Alastair

Sim (*Bogus's interpreter*); Renee Gadd (*Miss Blake*); Viola Compton (*Mrs. Massiter*); Stafford Hillard (*Dr. Graves*); Felix Aylmer (*Earl of Wigan*); Merle Tottenham (*Mary*); Syd Crossley (*Porter*). **Summary:** Jeremy Dilke (Eddie), a withdrawn, mild-mannered man, works in the city. He is preparing an important report on nitrates, but his partner considers him too weak-willed to proceed with the deal. —AFICFF

Let's Make a Million (December 13, 1936) Warner Bros. Pictures, 61 minutes, small town farce. **Producer:** Harold Hurley. **Director:** Raymond McCarey. **Screenplay:** Manuel Seff, Robert Yost; based on a story by Thomas Ahearn and Lawrence Pohle. **Camera:** Karl Struss. **Editor:** Doane Harrison. **Cast:** Edward Everett Horton (*Harrison Gentry*); Charlotte Wynters (*Caroline*); Porter Hall (*Spencer*); J. M. Kerrigan (*Sam Smith*); Margaret Seddon (*Aunt Martha*); Margaret McWade (*Aunt Lucy*); Purnell Pratt (*Gilbert*); Irving Bacon (*Jerry*); Ivan Miller (*Peter Winton*). **Summary:** After the U.S. Senate allocates two billion dollars for veteran bonuses, Harrison Gentry (Eddie), owner of Gentry Machinery and Supply Co. in Gentry, Oklahoma, plans to use his $1,100 bonus to marry his secretary and fiancée of five years, Caroline Williams. Harrison's maiden aunts, with whom he lives, however, hope to use his bonus to erect a granite shaft in honor of their father on twenty acres they purchased eleven years before as Ezra Gentry Park. —AFICFF

Lost Horizon (February 18, 1937; re-released in 1942 as *The Lost Horizon of Shangri-La*) Columbia Pictures, 132 minutes, fantasy drama. **Producer:** Frank Capra. **Director:** Frank Capra. **Screenplay:** Robert Riskin; based on the 1933 novel *Lost Horizon* by James Hilton. **Music:** Dimitri Tiomkin. **Camera:** Joseph Walker, Elmer Dyer. **Cast:** Ronald Colman (*Robert Conway*); Jane Wyatt (*Sondra*); Edward Everett Horton (*Lovett*); John Howard (*George Conway*); Thomas Mitchell (*Barnard*); Margo (*Maria*); Isabel Jewell (*Gloria*); H.B. Warner (*Chang*); Sam Jaffe (*High Lama*); **Uncredited:** Hugh Buckler (*Lord Gainsford*); Sonny Bupp (*Boy being carried to plane*); Willie Fung (*Bandit leader at fuel stop-over*); Noble Johnson (*Leader of porters on return journey*); Richard Loo (*Shanghai airport official*); Margaret McWade (*Missionary*); Leonard Mudie (*Foreign Secretary*); David Torrence (*Prime Minister*); Victor Wong (*Bandit leader*); Chief John Big Tree (*Porter*). **Summary and Review:** "James Hilton's classic story about five people stumbling into a strange Tibetan land where health, peace, and longevity reign. A rare movie experience, with haunting finale. After being shown in edited reissue prints for years, this classic has been restored to its original length—though several scenes are still missing, and are represented by dialogue only, with stills." (****) —LMCMG. **Notes:** *Lost Horizon* went overbudget by $776,000, plunging Columbia Pictures into a financial crisis. What's more, it irrevocably damaged Capra's working relationship with both studio head Harry Cohn and screenwriter Robert Riskin. It took approximately five years to earn back its cost. Critically, however, the film was an immediate success. It was nominated for five Academy Awards, including Best Picture, winning for Best Art Direction (Stephen Goosson) and Best Editing (Gene Havlick, Gene Milford). In the ensuing decades it would be considered one of the all-time great American films. Eddie, who often cited *Lost Horizon* as his favorite film in which he took part, described his role thusly: "I'm the fellow who carries the vertebrae of a prehistoric animal around in a little box."

The King and the Chorus Girl (March 27, 1937) Warner Bros. Pictures, 94 minutes, romantic comedy. **Producer:** Mervyn LeRoy. **Director:** Mervyn LeRoy. **Screenplay:** Norman Krasna, Groucho Marx. **Music:** Werner R. Heymann. **Camera:** Tony Gaudio. **Editor:** Thomas Richards. **Cast:** Fernand Gravey (*Alfred Bruger VII*); Joan Blondell (*Miss Dorothy Ellis*); Edward Everett Horton (*Count Humbert Evel Bruger*); Alan Mowbray (*Donald Taylor*); Mary Nash (*Duchess Anna of Elberfield*); Jane Wyman (*Babette Latour*); Luis Alberni (*Gaston*); Lionel Pape (*Professor Kornisch*); Kenny Baker (*Folies Bergère Soloist*); Al Shaw and Sam Lee (*Folies Bergère Entertainers*); unbilled players include Virginia Dabney and Carole Landis. **Summary:** Former king Alfred VII drinks every night because he is so bored. His only two remaining subjects, Count Humbert (Eddie) and Duchess Anna, take him to the Folies Bergère, hoping the show will interest him. He is about to fall asleep in his seat when he notices one of the chorus girls, Dorothy Ellis, and asks Anna and Humbert to invite her to supper. —AFICFF

Oh, Doctor! (April 1, 1937) Universal Pictures, 72 minutes, small town farce. **Producer:** Edmund Grainger. **Director:** Raymond McCarey. **Screenplay:** Harry Clork, Brown Holmes; based on the 1923 novel *Oh, Doctor!* by Harry Leon Wilson. **Camera:** Milton Krasner. **Editor:** Bernard W. Burton. **Cast:** Edward Everett Horton (*Edward J. Billop*); Donrue Leighton (*Helen Frohman*); William Hall (*Rodney Cummings*); Eve Arden (*Shirley Truman*); Thurston Hall (*"Doc" Erasmus Thurston*); Catherine Doucet (*Martha Striker*); William Demarest (*Marty Short*); Edward Brophy (*Meg Smith*); Minerva Urecal (*Death Watch Mary Mackleforth*). **Summary:** In six months, hypochondriac Edward "Ned" J. Billop (Eddie), reared by maiden aunts, will inherit half a million dollars, but he is sure he will not live until then. Forced to leave the hospital in which he has been living, Ned goes by boat to California. There he meets four crooks, Shirley Truman, "Doc" Erasmus Thurber, "Marty" Short and "Meg" Smith, and agrees to sell them his legacy in exchange for $50,000 so that he might live out his last days in luxury. —AFICFF

Shall We Dance (May 7, 1937) RKO Radio Pictures, 109 minutes, romantic musical comedy. **Producer:** Pandro S. Berman. **Director:** Mark Sandrich. **Screenplay:** Allan Scott, Ernest Pagano; based on a story by Lee Loeb and Harold Buckman. **Music:** George Gershwin. **Lyrics:** Ira Gershwin. **Camera:** David Abel, Joseph R. Biroc. **Editor:** William Hamilton. **Cast:** Fred Astaire (*Peter P. "Petrov" Peters*); Ginger Rogers (*Linda Keene*); Edward Everett Horton (*Jeffrey Baird*); Eric Blore (*Cecil Flintridge*); Jerome Cowan (*Arthur Miller*); Ketti Gallian (*Lady Denise Tarrington*); William Brisbane (*Jim Montgomery*); Harriet Hoctor (*Herself*); Dudley Dickerson (*Singing Crew Member in "Slap That Bass"*); Charles Coleman (*Policeman in Central Park, uncredited*). **Summary and Review:** "Lesser Astaire-Rogers is still top musical, with Gershwin's 'Let's Call the Whole Thing Off,' 'They All Laughed,' and 'They Can't Take That Away from Me,' holding together flimsy plot about dance team pretending to be wed." (***½) —LMCMG. **Notes:** This was Eddie's third, and final, time of working in an Astaire-Rogers picture. As was the case with *The Gay Divorcee* and *Top Hat*, there is a hilariously comical exchange between Eddie and Eric Blore.

Wild Money (July 9, 1937) Paramount Pictures, 71 minutes, newspaper comedy-drama. **Producer:** Stuart Walker. **Director:** Louis King. **Screenplay:** Paul Gallico, Edward T. Lowe Jr., Marguerite Roberts, Eddie Welch. **Camera:** Henry Sharp. **Editor:** Stuart Gilmore. **Cast:** Edward Everett Horton (*P.E. Dodd*); Louise Campbell (*Judy McGowan*); Lynne Overman (*Perry Brown*); Lucien Littlefield (*Bill Hawkins*); Esther Dale (*Jenny Hawkins*); Porter Hall (*Bill Court*); Benny Baker (*Al Vogel*); Ruth Coleman (*Mrs. West*); Louis Natheaux (*Cyrus K. West*); Billy Lee (*Malcolm West*); Howard M. Mitchell (*Sheriff Jones*); William Burress (*Spreckett*); Gertrude Short (*Miss Green*). **Summary:** Newspaper reporter Perry Brown is infatuated with fellow reporter Judy McGowan, but although she flirts with him, she is not romantically inclined. The staff accountant, P.E. Dodd (Eddie), is also in love with Judy, but he is so prudish, penny-pinching, and regimented that he is unappealing. P.E. goes to the cabin belonging to his cousins, Bill and Jennie Hawkins, for a vacation in the mountains. When Cyrus K. West, the wealthiest man in the country, is kidnapped from his nearby estate, managing editor Bill Court puts P.E. in charge of the story, even though he is not a reporter. Using his efficient methods, P.E. gets control of the only phone in town and all the vehicles and commands the respect of the sheriff and townspeople. Determined to meet Mrs. West, P.E. is on his way to the estate when a tree falls across the road and he is given a ransom note. —AFICFF

Danger, Love at Work (September 30, 1937) 20th Century-Fox, 84 minutes, screwball comedy. **Producer:** Harold Wilson. **Director:** Otto Preminger. **Screenplay:** James Edward Grant, Ben Markson. **Music:** Cyril J. Mockridge. **Camera:** Virgil Miller. **Editor:** Jack Murray. **Cast:** Ann Sothern (*Toni Pemberton*); Jack Haley (*Henry MacMorrow*); Edward Everett Horton (*Howard Rogers*); Mary Boland (*Alice Pemberton*); John Carradine (*Herbert Pemberton*); Walter Catlett (*Uncle Alan*); Benny Bartlett (*Junior Pemberton*); Maurice Cass (*Uncle Goliath*); Charles Coleman (*Henry's butler*); Margaret Seddon (*Aunt Pitty*); Margaret McWade (*Aunt Patty*). **Summary and Review:** On IMDb, an astute overview of the film, entitled "Master Screwball Comedy," reads in part:

"Danger, Love at Work" is an especially effervescent and sophisticated screwball comedy. And it is a very legitimate example, based on the essential "crazy family" format. It completely ignores the social consciousness aspect of the classic screwball ("You Can't Take It With You" and "My Man Godfrey" are otherwise close relatives), and benefits perhaps from this narrow focus on plot and character. And what characters! Mary Boland, who can sometimes annoy, fits in here very nicely as Ann Sothern's mother; diminutive Etienne Girardot -- a fascinating and lively little actor (his nervous performance here, as in "Twentieth Century" is priceless) as her father (and has a charming counterpart -- equally diminutive -- in "Uncle Goliath," a "back-to-nature" type); brother John Carradine (as a "post-Surrealist" painter); Walter Catlett as a philatelist uncle -- all delightful. Miss Sothern herself is every bit as charming as Carole Lombard (and has a rather less annoying role than Lombard's) in "Godfrey," and, besides, has a lovely vocal duet with Jack Haley on the title song. She really can sing! And here we have Haley two years before "The Wizard of Oz" -- nicely done, though no Cary Grant of course. Edward Everett Horton is, as always, superb, though his straight-man adversarial role here doesn't point up his own best strengths.

The Perfect Specimen (October 23, 1937) Warner Bros. Pictures, 97 minutes, romantic comedy. **Director:** Michael Curtiz. **Screenplay:** Norman Reilly Raine, Lawrence Riley, Brewster Morse, Fritz Falkenstein; based on a novel by Samuel Hopkins Adams. **Music:** Heinz Roemheld. **Camera:** Charles Rosher. **Editor:** Terry O. Morse. **Cast:** Errol Flynn (*Gerald Beresford Wicks*); Joan Blondell (*Mona Carter*); Hugh Herbert (*Killigrew Shaw*); Edward Everett Horton (*Mr. Gratten*); Dick Foran (*Jink Carter*); Beverly Roberts (*Alicia*); May Robson (*Mrs. Leona Wicks*); Allen Jenkins (*Pinky*); Dennie Moore (*Clarabelle*); Hugh O'Connell (*Hotel clerk*); James Burke (*Snodgrass*); Granville Bates (*Hooker*). **Summary:** "Fairly amusing whimsy of super-rich Flynn, who's kept locked up and sheltered by grandmother Robson until vivacious Blondell comes crashing through his fence and they go off on a whirlwind courtship." (**½)   — LMCMG. **Notes:** The venerable (and intimidating) May Robson makes Eddie's character cower in their scenes together.

Angel (October 28, 1937) Paramount Pictures, 91 minutes, sophisticated romantic comedy. **Producer:** Ernst Lubitsch. **Director:** Ernst Lubitsch. **Screenplay:** Samson Raphaelson, Frederick Lonsdale; based on the English play adaptation (by Guy Bolton and Russell Medcalf) of the play *Angyal* by Melchoir Lengyel. **Score:** Frederick Hollander (with additional music by Gioacchino Rossini from *The Barber of Seville.*) **Camera:** Charles Lang. **Editor:** William Shay. **Cast:** Marlene Dietrich (*Maria, Lady Barker, a.k.a. Mrs. Brown, a.k.a. "Angel"*); Herbert Marshall (*Sir Frederick Barker*); Melvyn Douglas (*Anthony "Tony" Halton*); Edward Everett Horton (*Graham, Sir Frederick's valet*); Ernest Cossart (*Christopher "Chris" Wilton, the Barkers' butler*); Laura Hope Crews (*The Grand Duchess Anna Dmitrievna*); Herbert Mundin (*Mr. Greenwood*); Dennie Moore (*Emma McGillicuddy Wilton*); Lionel Pape (*Lord Davington*); Michael Visaroff (*Gregori, the Grand Duchess's Butler*); James Finlayson (*Barker's Second Butler*); Gerald Hamer (*Barker's Footman*); Gino Corrado (*Assistant Hotel Manager*); Olaf Hytten (*Consolidated Press Photographer*); Suzanne Kaaren (*Gambling woman*). **Summary:** Maria Barker, wife of foreign diplomat Sir Frederick Barker, feels neglected at home. Unknown to her husband, Maria flies to Paris to visit Grand Duchess Anna Dmitrievna, who runs a salon. While there, Maria meets Anthony Halton, who, immediately enchanted by her, invites her to dinner. Because Maria refuses to give her name, Anthony calls her

"Angel" and fervently longs to see her again. Maria refuses to maintain contact and returns home, there attempting to regain her husband's attention. Frederick, however, is completely preoccupied by his work. At the races Frederick encounters Anthony, with whom he had a brief acquaintance during the war. Anthony relates his story about "Angel," intriguing Frederick, who invites his old friend to meet his wife. **Notes:** Eddie told the film's director, Josef von Sternberg, that he was concerned his English accent would seem out of place in a film about the history of Spain. Von Sternberg insisted it would not.—AFICFF

The Great Garrick (October 30, 1937) Warner Bros. Pictures, 89 minutes, comedy-drama. **Producer:** Mervyn LeRoy. **Director:** James Whale. **Screenplay:** Ernest Vajda, Rowland Leigh (uncredited). **Music:** Adolph Deutsch. **Camera:** Ernest Haller. **Editor:** Warren Low. **Cast:** Brian Aherne (*David Garrick*); Olivia de Havilland (*Germaine*); Edward Everett Horton (*Tubby*); Melville Cooper (*M. Picard*); Lionel Atwill (*Beaumarchais*); Luis Alberni (*Basset*); Lana Turner (*Auber*); Marie Wilson (*Nicolle*); Linda Perry (*Molee*); Fritz Leiber Sr. (*Horatio*); Etienne Girardot (*Jean Cabot*); Dorothy Tree (*Mme. Moreau*); Craig Reynolds (*M. Janin*); Paul Everton (*Innkeeper of Adam and Eve*); Trevor Bardette (*M. Noverre*); Milton Owen (*Thierre*); Albert Dekker (*LeBrun*); Chester Clute (*M. Moreau*); Harry Davenport (*Innkeeper of Turk's Head, uncredited*); Fritz Lieber Jr. (*Fortinbras in the* Hamlet *play, uncredited*). **Summary:** Before David Garrick, the famous 18th century English actor, is to make a guest appearance at the *Comédie Française,* the French actors hear rumors that he has said he will teach them the art of realistic acting. Determined to teach him a lesson, they take over a roadside inn. When Garrick arrives at the Adam & Eve Inn, however, he instantly recognizes the staff and guests of the inn as actors by their conventional gestures and decides to play along to see what will happen. **Notes:** Eddie plays Gerrick's valet/companion Tubby, one of his least-flattering character names. —AFICFF

Hitting a New High (December 24, 1937) RKO Radio Pictures, 85 minutes, comedy. **Producer:** Jesse L. Lasky. **Director:** Raoul Walsh. **Screenplay:** Gertrude Purcell, John Twist. **Music:** Nathaniel Shilkret. **Camera:** J. Roy Hunt. **Editor:** Desmond Marquette. **Cast:** Lily Pons (*Suzette, a.k.a. Oogahunga, the Bird-Girl*); Jack Oakie (*Corny Davis*); John Howard (*Jimmy James*); Eric Blore (*Cedric Cosmo, a.k.a. Captain Braceridge Hemingway*); Edward Everett Horton (*Lucius B. Blynn*). **Summary:** Before millionaire opera benefactor and would-be big game hunter Lucius B. Blynn (Eddie) leaves Paris for Africa with his press agent, Corny Davis, Corny hears Suzette, an impressive French soprano, singing with a band led by her boyfriend, American Jimmy James. Corny offers Suzette a chance to audition for Blynn in Africa, and Suzette, who longs to abandon jazz in favor of opera, accepts. While hunting in an African jungle, Corny leads Blynn to "discover" Suzette, now called Oogahunga, the Bird-Girl. —AFICFF

Bluebeard's Eighth Wife (March 23, 1938) Paramount Pictures, 80 minutes, French farce. **Producer:** Ernst Lubitsch. **Director:** Ernst Lubitsch. **Screenplay:** Charles Brackett, Billy Wilder; based on the 1921 French play *La huitième femme de Barbe-Bleue* by Alfred Savoir. This 1938 talkie is a remake of the 1923 silent version directed by Sam Wood and starring Gloria Swanson. **Music:** Werner R. Heymann, Frederick Hollander. **Camera:** Leo Tover. **Editor:** William Shea. **Cast:** Claudette Colbert (*Nicole de Loiselle*); Gary Cooper (*Michael Brandon*); Edward Everett Horton (*Marquis de Loiselle*); David Niven (*Albert De Regnier*); Elizabeth Patterson (*Aunt Hedwige*); Herman Bing (*Monsieur Pepinard*); Warren Hymer (*Kid Mulligan*); Franklin Pangborn (*Assistant Hotel Manager*); Armand Cortes (*Assistant Hotel Manager*); Rolfe Sedan (*Floorwalker*); Lawrence Grant (*Professor Urganzeff*); Lionel Pape (*Monsieur Potin*); Tyler Brooke (*Clerk*); Leon Ames (*Ex-Chauffeur, uncredited*). **Summary:** Nicole De Loiselle meets American millionaire Michael Brandon while shopping in a store on the French Riviera. — AFICFF. **Notes:** A March 17, 1938, review in *Variety* reads, "Edward Everett Horton makes the most of a short role as the girl's titled but slightly zany parent."

College Swing (April 13, 1938; released in the UK as *Swing, Teacher, Swing*) Paramount Pictures, 86 minutes, college musical comedy. **Producer:** Lewis E. Gensler. **Director:** Raoul Walsh. **Music:** Burton Lane, Hoagy Carmichael, Manning Sherwin, Gordon Jenkins, John Liepold, Victor Young. **Lyrics:** Frank Loesser. **Camera:** Victor Milner. **Editor:** LeRoy Stone. **Cast:** George Burns (*George Jonas*); Gracie Allen (*Gracie Alden*); Martha Raye (*Mable*); Bob Hope (*Bud Brady*); Edward Everett Horton (*Hubert Dash*); Florence George (*Ginna Ashburn*); Ben Blue (*Ben Volt*); Betty Grable (*Betty*); Jackie Coogan (*Jackie*); John Payne (*Martin Bates*); Cecil Cunningham (*Dean Sleet*); Robert Cummings (*Radio Announcer*); Skinnay Ennis (*Prof. Yascha Koloski, uncredited*); The Slate Brothers (*Themselves*); Robert Mitchell and St. Brendan's Choristers (*Themselves*). **Summary:** In 1738 in Aldentown, Gracie

Alden fails to graduate from college for the ninth consecutive year and her grandfather, founder of the college, bequeaths the institution to the first female Alden progeny to graduate. Two hundred years later, Gracie's namesake is again about to lose her inheritance, which will be forever forfeited to the city. Bud Brady offers to tutor her for $10,000, to be paid by the Guarantee Trust Company, which controls the university's mortgage. Guarantee Trust is owned by Hubert Dash (Eddie), an Alden descendant who has a chronic fear of women and who will prepare Gracie's final exam. Hubert's secretary, George Jones, shares Hubert's fear of women. —AFICFF

Holiday (June 15, 1938; released in the UK as *Free to Live*) Columbia Pictures, 95 minutes, society comedy. **Producer:** Everett Riskin. **Director:** George Cukor. **Screenplay:** Donald Ogden Stewart, Sidney Buchman. **Camera:** Franz Planer. **Editor:** Al Clark, Otto Meyer. **Cast:** Katharine Hepburn (*Linda Seton*); Cary Grant (*Johnny Case*); Doris Nolan (*Julia Seton*); Lew Ayres (*Edward "Ned" Seton Jr.*); Henry Kolker (*Edward Seton Sr.*); Edward Everett Horton (*Professor Nick Potter*); Jean Dixon (*Susan Potter*); Binnie Barnes (*Laura Cram*); Henry Daniell (*Seton Cram*). **Summary:** Upon returning to New York from a December holiday in Lake Placid, Johnny Case drops by to see his dear friends, Nick and Susan Potter, and gleefully informs them that he has become engaged to a beautiful woman he met at the resort. When Susan questions Johnny about his bride-to-be, Julia Seton, Johnny confesses that he knows nothing about her background or family life. Later, when he shows up at Julia's Park Avenue address, he is stunned to discover that she is the daughter of Edward Seton, an extremely wealthy banker. **Notes:** Although Eddie made much over his supposed inability to sing, at one point in the film he leads a rousing singalong of Stephen Foster's 1850 ditty "Camptown Races," and has no problem staying on key.—AFICFF

Little Tough Guys in Society (November 1, 1938) Universal Studios, 63 minutes, sentimental comedy. **Producer:** Max H. Gordon. **Director:** Erle C. Kenton. **Screenplay:** Edward Eliscu, Mortimer Offner. **Camera:** George Robinson. **Editor:** Bernard W. Burton. **Cast:** Frankie Thomas (*Danny*); Harris Berger (*Sailor*); Hally Chester (*Murphy*); Charles Duncan (*Monk*); David Gorcey (*Yap*); William Benedict (*Trouble*); Mischa Auer (*Dr. Trenkle*); Mary Boland (*Mrs. Berry*); Edward Everett Horton (*Oliver*); Helen Parrish (*Penny*); Jackie Searl (*Randolf Berry*); Peggy Stewart (*Jane*); Harold Huber (*Uncle Buck*); David Oliver

(*Footman*); Stanley Blystone (*Policeman*); Eddie Hall (*Cabbie*); Samuel S. Hinds (*Judge*); Lon McCallister (*unnamed*); Sarah Padden (*Victim*); Frances Robinson (*Guest*); Dick Rush (*Jim*). **Summary:** Society woman Gussie Berry asks psychiatrist Dr. Trenkle to visit her son Randolph, who refuses to get out of bed. Trenkle recommends the companionship of underprivileged children as an antidote for Randolph's self-absorption. Gussie immediately places an ad, which is seen by Danny Burns and his gang, the "Dead End Kids," who need a place to hide out after they destroy a glassworks factory. Taking a strong dislike to the boys, Randolph tries to have them sent back to the city, but his girlfriend, Penny Brandt, convinces him to make friends with them. **Notes:** Eddie plays a butler in this Universal picture. —AFICFF

Paris Honeymoon (January 27, 1939) Paramount Pictures, 92 minutes, musical romance set in a fictitious Balkan country. **Producer:** Harlan Thompson. **Director:** Frank Tuttle. **Screenplay:** Frank Butler, Don Hartman. **Music:** Gerard Carbonara, John Liepold, Ralph Rainger, Leo Shuken (uncredited). **Camera:** Karl Struss. **Editor:** Alma Macrorie. **Cast:** Bing Crosby ("*Lucky*" *Lawton*); Franciska Gaal (*Manya*); Akim Tamiroff (*Mayor Peter Karloca*); Shirley Ross (*Barbara Wayne*); Edward Everett Horton (*Ernest Figg*); Ben Blue (*Sitska*); Rafaela Ottiano (*Fluschotska*); Gregory Gaye (*Count Georges De Remi*). **Summary:** "Lucky" Lawton, a superstitious cowboy who made fortune and fame from a gold mine, is forced to delay his marriage to steel heiress Barbara Wayne because Parisian records show she is still officially married to the Count George de Remi. While Barbara processes the divorce in Paris, Lucky stays at a castle in the Balkans that he rented for their honeymoon, which is surrounded by eighty miles of roses. Manya, the local rose queen, forcibly moves into the castle for one week as part of her honorarium. Ebullient and childlike, Manya falls in love with Lucky in spite of his indifference, thus causing havoc in the castle. —AFICFF. **Notes:** Eddie plays a traditionally outfitted butler, complete with a tailcoat.

The Gang's All Here (March 4, 1939; released in the U.S. as ***The Amazing Mr. Forrest***), Associated British Picture Corporation / Associated British Film Distributors (UK); Producers Releasing Company (U.S.A.), 71 minutes, comedy. **Producers:** John W. Gossage, Walter C. Mycroft. **Director:** Thornton Freeland. **Music:** Harry Acres (uncredited). **Camera:** Claude Fries-Greene. **Editor:** Edward B. Jarvis. **Cast:** Jack Buchanan (*John Forrest*); Googie Withers (*Alice Forrest*); Edward Everett Horton (*Treadwell*); Syd Walker (*Younce*); Otto Kruger (*Mike*

Chadwick); Jack La Rue (*Alberni*); Walter Rilla (*Prince Homouska*); David Burns (*Beretti*); Charles Carson (*Charles Cartwright*); Leslie Perrins (*Harper*); Ronald Shiner (*Spider Ferris*); Edward Lexy (*Inspector Elroyd*); Ballard Berkeley (*Detective in nightclub*). **Summary:** John Forrest (Jack Buchanan) ace investigator for an insurance company retires, only to be promptly recalled following the theft of a priceless collection of jewels belonging to Prince Homouska. —AFICFF. **Notes:** *TV Guide* had this to say regarding the film: "Supposed comedy about the breakup of a group of jewel thieves falls flat. But no amount of dreary material can conceal the undeniable comic genius of Horton."

That's Right—You're Wrong (November 24, 1939) RKO Radio Pictures, 94 minutes, comedy based on radio characters. **Producers:** David Butler, Fred Fleck. **Director:** David Butler. **Screenplay:** David Butler, David Conselman. **Music:** Roy Webb. **Camera:** Russell Metty. **Editor:** Irene Morra. **Cast:** Kay Kyser (*Himself*); Adolphe Menjou (*Stacey Delmore*); May Robson (*Grandma*); Lucille Ball (*Sandra Sand*); Dennis O'Keefe (*Chuck Deems, the Band Manager*); Edward Everett Horton (*Village, a screenwriter*); Roscoe Karns (*Mal Stamp*); Moroni Olsen (*Jonathan "J.D." Forbes*); Hobart Cavanaugh (*Dwight Cook, a screenwriter*); Charles Judels (*Luigi*); Appearing as Themselves: Ginny Simms; Harry Babbitt; Sully Mason; Merwyn Bogue (Ish Kabibble); Hedda Hopper; Sheilah Graham; Erskine Johnson; Harrison Carroll; Feg Murray. **Summary:** When a big Hollywood studio begins to see their box-office revenues slipping, studio head J.D. Forbes demands some down-to-earth yarns to fill the studio's coffers. They eventually decide to make a movie star out of bandleader Kay Kyser. Two screenwriters, Village (Eddie) and Cook (Hobart Cavanaugh) are given the daunting assignment of devising a star-making vehicle for Kyser. They turn in forty separate scripts, only to be turned down forty separate times. —AFICFF

You're the One (February 19, 1941) Paramount Pictures, 83 minutes, radio comedy. **Producer:** Gene Markey. **Director:** Ralph Murphy. **Screenplay:** Gene Markey. **Music:** Phil Boutelje. **Camera:** Ted Tetzleff. **Editor:** Archie Marshek. **Cast:** Bonnie Baker (*Bonnie Baker*); Orrin Tucker (*Orrin Tucker*); Albert Dekker (*Luke Laramie*); Edward Everett Horton (*Death Valley Joe Frink*); Lillian Cornell (*Miss Jones*); Renie Riano (*Aunt Emma*); Jerry Colonna (*Dr. Colonna*); Teddy Hart (*Julius, Luke's Chauffeur*); Tom Dugan (*Edgar Crump*); Walter Catlett (*Program Director*); Charles Lane (*Announcer*); Don Castle (*Tony Delmar*); Mariska Aldrich (*Mme. Ziffnidyiff*); Eddie Conrad (*Mr. Ziffnidyiff*);

Marie Blake (*Beauty Shop Operator*); Hal K. Dawson (*Male Secretary*); June Gaude (*Beauty Shop Manager*); Gerald Oliver Smith (*Hotel Clerk*); Sammy Cohen (*Bellboy*); Gilbert Wilson (*Hotel Clerk*); Foy Van Dolsen (*Chester Pugh*); Florine McKinney (*Archery Girl*). **Summary:** As bandleader Luke Laramie, "the Emperor of Rhythm," makes his last radio broadcast, agent "Death Valley" Joe Frink tries to interest Luke and his agent, Edgar Crump, in his latest find, small town singer, Bonnie Baker. —AFICFF. **Notes:** Bosley Crowther of the *New York Times* reviewed the musical negatively, criticizing it as "perilously close to being the most haphazard, pointless and dull motion picture shown on Broadway this season." He specifically critiqued the acting of Bonnie Baker and Orrin Tucker as being lackluster, and Jerry Colonna and Edward Everett Horton's roles for engaging in "meaningless and unfunny business."

Ziegfeld Girl (April 25, 1941) Metro-Goldwyn-Mayer / Loew's Inc., 132 minutes, all-star musical. **Producer:** Pandro S. Berman. **Director:** Robert Z. Leonard. **Screenplay:** Margurite Roberts, Sonya Levien. **Music:** Herbert Stothart. **Choreography:** Busby Berkeley. **Camera:** Ray June, Joseph Ruttinger. **Editor:** Blanche Sewell. **Cast:** James Stewart (*Gilbert Young*); Judy Garland (*Susan Gallagher*); Hedy Lamarr (*Sandra Kolter*); Lana Turner (*Sheila Regan*); Tony Martin (*Frank Merton*); Jackie Cooper (*Jerry Regan*); Ian Hunter (*Geoffre Collis*); Charles Winninger ("*Pop*" *Gallagher*); Edward Everett Horton (Noble Sage); Philip Dorn (*Franz Kolter*); Paul Kelly (*John Slayton*); Eve Arden (*Patsy Dixon*); Dan Dailey (*Jimmy Walters*); Al Shean (*Al*); Fay Holden (*Mrs. Regan*). **Summary:** In the 1920s, many girls dreamt of becoming "Glorified American Girls" in Florenz Ziegfeld's Broadway shows. Detailed in the film are the background stories for three of those girls. **Notes:** Although some footage from the earlier MGM film *The Great Ziegfeld* (1936) is used, the empresario is not depicted. As for Eddie, he plays Noble Sage, Ziegfeld's right-hand man. In an early scene, he hires Lana Turner, a beautiful elevator operator from Flatbush. And you thought she was discovered in Schwab's Drug Store.

Sunny (May 30, 1941) RKO Radio Pictures, 98 minutes, musical romance. **Producer:** Merrill G. White. **Director:** Herbert Wilcox. **Screenplay:** Sig Herzig; based on the musical play *Sunny* by Jerome Kern (music), Oscar Hammerstein II (lyrics), and Otto A. Harbach (libretto). **Music:** Anthony Collins. **Camera:** Russell Metty. **Editor:** Elmo Williams. **Cast:** Anna Neagle (*Sunny O'Sullivan*); Ray Bolger (*Bunny Bill-*

ings); John Carroll (*Larry Warren*); Edward Everett Horton (*Henry Bates*); Grace Hartman (*Juliet Runnymede*); Paul Hartman (*Egghead*); Frieda Inescort (*Elizabeth Warren*); Helen Westley (*Aunt Barbara*); Benny Rubin (*Maj. Montgomery Sloan*); Muggins Davies (*Muggins*); Richard Lane (*Reporter*); "Liltin'" Martha Tilton (*Queen of Hearts*); Torben Meyer (*Jean, head waiter*). **Summary:** In the crush of the Mardi Gras festivities, Larry Warren, the scion of a wealthy New Orleans family, is thrown together with Sunny O'Sullivan, a bareback rider in the circus. Commanded to kiss by the Queen of Hearts and her court, the two embrace, after which Sunny disappears into the night. **Notes:** Eddie plays the Warrens' family lawyer. —AFICFF

Bachelor Daddy (June 4, 1941) Universal Pictures, 61 minutes, comedy. **Producer:** Burt Kelly. **Director:** Harold Young. **Screenplay:** Robert Lees, Frederic I. Rinaldo. **Camera:** Milton Krasner. **Editor:** Paul Landres. **Cast:** Baby Sandy (*Sandy*); Edward Everett Horton (*Joseph Smith*); Donald Woods (*Edward Smith*); Raymond Walburn (*George Smith*); Evelyn Ankers (*Beth Chase*); Kathryn Adams Doty (*Eleanor Pierce*); Franklin Pangborn (*Williams*); Jed Prouty (*C.J. Chase*); Hardie Albright (*Ethelbert*); George Meader (*Judge McGinnis*); Bert Roach (*Louie*); Leonard Elliott (*Clark*); Juanita Quigley (*Girl*); Bobby Larson (*Boy*); Mira McKinney (*Landlady*). **Summary:** When Eleanor Pierce is arrested for selling homemade candy without a license, she tells the court that her name is "Jane Smith" and has her case held over for two weeks. Without any money for bail and realizing that her infant daughter Sandy is home alone, Eleanor sends a letter to the exclusive Bachelor's Club, addressed to "Mr. Smith." The letter is then presented to three men—Edward (Donald Woods), George (Raymond Walburn), and Joseph (Eddie)—all of whom have that common last name and none of whom believes himself to be the child's father. Edward, Joseph, and George take a cab to the incarcerated woman's apartment and take turns caring for Baby Sandy. Joseph takes her into a movie theatre catering to a rowdy group of kids watching an adventure serial. ("Oh, dear," he says upon witnessing the chaos.) Joseph is clearly as uncomfortable around children as they are around him. While battling to keep his seat, his adorable charge wreaks havoc, with Joseph being assigned the blame. We're fairly certain everything works out for all concerned parties, but we couldn't stay awake until the end of the picture.

Here Comes Mr. Jordan (August 7, 1941) Columbia Pictures, 94 minutes, fantasy-drama. **Producer:** Everett Riskin. **Director:** Alexander

Hall. **Screenplay:** Sidney Buchman, Seton I. Miller; based on the 1938 play *Heaven Can Wait* by Harry Segal. **Camera:** Joseph Walker. **Editor:** Violet Lawrence. **Cast:** Robert Montgomery (*Joe Pendleton*); Evelyn Keyes (*Bette Logan*); Claude Rains (*Mr. Jordan*); Rita Johnson (*Julia Farnsworth*); Edward Everett Horton (*Messenger 7013*); James Gleason (*Max "Pop" Corkle*); John Emery (*Tony Abbott*); Donald MacBride (*Inspector Williams*); Don Costello (*Lefty*); Halliwell Hobbes (*Sisk*); Benny Rubin (*"Bugsy," the handler*); Lloyd Bridges (*Mr. Sloan, the co-pilot*); Eddie Bruce (*Reporter*); John Ince (*Bill collector*); Bert Young (*Taxi driver*); Warren Ashe (*Charlie*); Ken Christy (*Plainclothesman*); Chester Conklin (*Newsboy*); Joseph Crehan (*Doctor*); Mary Currier (*Secretary*); Edmund Elton (*Elderly man*); Tom Hanlon (*Announcer*). **Summary, Review, and Notes:** "Excellent fantasy-comedy of prizefighter accidentally sent to heaven before his time, forced to occupy a new body on earth. Hollywood moviemaking at its best, with first-rate cast and performances. Harry Segal won an Oscar for his original story, as did Sidney Buchman and Seton I. Miller for their screenplay. Characters used again in *Down to Earth* (1947); film remade in *Heaven Can Wait* (1978) and *Down to Earth* (2001)" (****). —LMCMG. **Notes:** Eddie shines as the well-meaning but bumbling Messenger 7013.

The Body Disappears (December 6, 1941) Warner Bros. Pictures, 72 minutes, *Topper*-influenced farce. **Producers:** Bryan Foy, Ben Stoloff. **Director:** D. Ross Lederman. **Screenplay:** Scott Darling, Erna Lazarus. **Music:** Howard Jackson. **Camera:** Allen G. Siegler. **Editor:** Frederick Richards. **Cast:** Jeffrey Lynn (*Peter De Haven III*); Jane Wyman (*Joan Shotesbury*); Edward Everett Horton (*Professor Shotesbury*); Herbert Anderson (*George "Doc" Appleby*); Marguerite Chapman (*Christine Lunceford*); Craig Stevens (*Robert Struck*); David Bruce (*Jimmie Barbour*); Willie Best (*Willie*); Ivan F. Simpson (*Dean Claxton*); Tod Andrews (*Bill*); DeWolf Hopper (*Terrence Abbott*); Natalie Schafer (*Mrs. Lunceford*); Charles Halton (*Prof. Moggs*); Sidney Bracey (*Barrett*); Wade Boteler (*Inspector Deming*); Heinie Conklin (*Reporter*). **Summary:** At a courtroom hearing, "Doc" George Appleby recalls the events that led to the disappearance of Peter DeHaven III. —AFICFF. **Notes:** A review of the film in *TV Guide* described it as a "funny B movie" with "fine special effects [that] highlight this variation of the 'invisible man' theme," noting further that "Horton and wide-eyed Best [give] fine comic performances."

Week-End for Three (December 12, 1941) RKO Radio Pictures, 66 minutes, marital comedy. **Producer:** Tay Garnett. **Director:** Irving Reis. **Screenplay:** Dorothy Parker, Alan Campbell. **Music:** Roy Webb. **Camera:** Russell Metty. **Editor:** Desmond Marquette. **Cast:** Dennis O'Keefe (*Jim Craig*); Jane Wyatt (*Ellen*); Phillip Reed (*Randy*); Edward Everett Horton (*Stonebraker*); ZaSu Pitts (*Anna*); Franklin Pangborn (*Number Seven*). **Summary and Review:** "Hapless O'Keefe and manipulative wife Wyatt entertain her boorish old friend, who quickly proves to be the houseguest from hell. Considering cast and writers (Dorothy Parker and Alan Campbell, from Budd Schulberg's story), it's astonishing this isn't better than this." (**)—LMCMG. **Notes:** Although this film was (and continues to be) roundly panned, the performances of Franklin Pangborn, ZaSu Pitts, and Eddie remain above criticism.

The Magnificent Dope (July 1, 1942) 20th Century-Fox, 84 minutes, comedy. **Producer:** William Perlberg. **Director:** Walter Lang. **Screenplay:** George Seaton; based on a story by Joseph Schrank. **Music:** Emil Newman, Lee Harline, Cyril J. Mockridge, David Raksin. **Camera:** J. Peverell Marley. **Editor:** Barbara McLean. **Cast:** Henry Fonda (*Thaddeus Winship "Tad" Page*); Lynn Bari (*Claire Harris*); Don Ameche (*Dwight Dawson*); Edward Everett Horton (*Horace Hunter*); George Barbier (*James Roger Barker*); Frank Orth (*Messenger*); Roseanne Murray (*Dawson's Secretary*); Marietta Canty (*Jennie*); Hobart Cavanaugh (*Albert Gowdy*); Hal K. Dawson (*Charlie*); Josephine Whittell (*Mrs. Hunter*); Arthur Loft (*Mr. Morton, Fire Engine Salesman*); Paul Stanton (*Peters*); Claire Du Brey (*Peter's Secretary*); William B. Davidson (*Mr. J.D. Reindel*); Harry Hayden (*Frank Mitchel*); Pierre Watkin (*Bill Carson*). **Summary:** Energetic opportunist Dwight Dawson teaches a high powered system that promises to turn his pupils into successful businessmen. Meanwhile, his own business is suffering due to lack of enrollment. Eddie plays Horace Hunter, who runs an unsuccessful assertiveness training course along the principles of Dale Carnegie (*How to Win Friends and Influence People*). Originally, the film's title was "The Magnificent Jerk," but the Breen Office nixed it. Too edgy.

I Married an Angel (July 9, 1942) Metro-Goldwyn-Mayer, 84 minutes, fantasy-musical. **Director:** W.S. Van Dyke. **Cast:** Jeanette MacDonald (*Anna / Brigitta*); Nelson Eddy (*Count Willie Palaffi*); Edward Everett Horton (*Peter*); Binnie Barnes (*Peggy*); Reginald Owen ("*Whiskers*"); Douglass Dumbrille (*Baron Szigethy*); Mona Maris (*Marika*); Janis Carter (*Sufi*); Inez Cooper (*Iren*); Leonid Kinskey (*Zinski*); Anne

Jeffreys (*Polly*); Marion Rosamond (*Dolly*); Odette Myrtil (*The Modiste, uncredited*). **Summary and Review:** Count Willy Palaffi (Nelson Eddy), a bank executive, believes that no mortal woman is good enough for him; he feels that only an angel descended from Heaven would be suitable marriage material. As it happens, an actual angel (Jeannette MacDonald) appears and tells Willie that she is prepared to marry him. Things become complicated almost immediately. At a harp concert (!), Peter (Eddie), one of Willie's colleagues, informs him that the bank's stockholders are demanding an investigation of the new bride. It must be the wings that are making them nervous. **Notes:** This bizarre musical, with songs by Rodgers and Hart, features the lyrical "Spring is Here." The scenario was initially deemed unacceptable by the Breen Office, which stated that the idea of someone marrying an angel was "blasphemous and sacrilegious." Louis B. Mayer found the results to be so poor that he intentionally withheld publicity; as a result, the MGM film was the least profitable release of 1942. It also brought an end to the once-popular vehicles of Nelson Eddy–Jeanette MacDonald.

Springtime in the Rockies (November 6, 1942) 20th Century-Fox, 91 minutes, show business musical. **Executive Producer:** William Goetz. **Producer:** William LeBaron. **Director:** Irving Cummings. **Screenplay:** Walter Bullock, Ken Englund, Jacques Thery; based on "Second Honeymoon," a 1936 *Redbook* story by Philip Wylie. **Music:** Alberto Colombo. **Camera:** Ernest Palmer. **Editor:** Robert L. Simpson. **Cast:** Betty Grable (*Vicky Lane*); John Payne (*Dan Christy*); Carmen Miranda (*Rosita Murphy*); Cesar Romero (*Victor Prince*); Charlotte Greenwood (*Phoebe Gray*); Edward Everett Horton (*McTavish*); Harry James (*Himself*); Jackie Gleason (*Commissioner, uncredited*); Chick Chandler (*Stage Manager*); Iron Eyes Cody (*White Cloud*); Dick Elliott (*Mr. Jeepers*); Bess Flowers (*Mrs. Jeepers*); Harry Hayden (*Mr. Brown*); Russell Hicks (*Man in Dark with Lighter*); Aloísio de Oliveira (*Patrick Murphy, Jr.*); Frank Orth (*Mr. Bickel*); Charles Tannen (*Backstage Call Boy, voice*). **Summary and Review:** "Near definitive 1940s musical: Grable at her prettiest, Miranda at her silliest (doing a Brazilian 'Chattanooga Choo-Choo'). Technicolor at its lushest, and Harry James and His Band at their best, with Helen Forrest introducing 'I Had the Craziest Dream.' The 'plot'—about a bickering Broadway duo—is neither too tiresome nor too intrusive. Good fun all the way." (***) —LMCMG. **Notes:** Yet another film in which Eddie plays a valet, this time for John Payne's character, Dan Christy.

Forever and a Day (March 26, 1943) RKO Radio Pictures, 104 minutes, multi-star drama. **Producers:** René Clair, Edmund Goulding, Cedric Hardwicke, Frank Lloyd, Victor Saville, Robert Stevenson, and Herbert Wilcox. **Directors:** Herbert Wilcox, Rene Clair, Edmund Goulding, Cedric Hardwicke, Frank Lloyd, Victor Saville, and Robert Stevenson. **Screenplay:** Alan Campbell, Norman Corwin, C.S. Forester, Peter Godfrey, Jack Hartfield, Lawrence Hazard, S.M. Herzig, James Hilton, Michael Hogan, Christopher Isherwood, Emmet Lavery, W.P. Lipscomb, Gene Lockhart, Frederick Lonsdale, Alice Duer Miller, R.C. Sherriff, Donald Ogden Stewart, John Van Druten, Claudine West, Keith Winter and Alfred Hitchcock (uncredited). **Cast:** Kent Smith (*Gates Trimble Pomfret*); Reginald Gardiner (*Assistant Hotel Manager*); Victor McLaglen (*Archibald Spavin, hotel doorman*); Arthur Treacher (*Second Air Raid Watcher*); June Lockhart (*Girl in Air Raid Shelter*); Ruth Warrick (*Lesley Trimble*); Sir Cedric Hardwicke (*Mr. Dabb*); Herbert Marshall (*Curate in Air Raid Shelter*); Charles Irwin (*Corporal Charlie*); C. Aubrey Smith (*Admiral Eustace Trimble*); Edmund Gwenn (*Stubbs*); Lumsden Hare (*Fitch*); Ray Milland (*Lieutenant William Trimble*); Dame May Whitty (*Mrs. Lucy Trimble*); Gene Lockhart (*Cobblewick*); Anna Neagle (*Susan Trenchard*); Claud Allister (*William Barstow*); Alan Edmiston (Tripp, Pomfret's Lawyer); Claude Rains (*Ambrose Pomfret*); Clifford Severn (*Nelson Trimble*); Alec Craig (*Ambrose Pomfret's Butler*); Jessie Matthews (*Mildred Trimble*); Reginald Owen (*Simpson, solicitor*); Ian Hunter (*Dexter Pomfret*); Charles Laughton (*Bellamy, Dexter's butler*); Anna Lee (*Cornelia Trimble*); Buster Keaton (*Wilkins, plumber's helper*); Montagu Love (*Sir John Bunn*); Edward Everett Horton (*Sir Anthony Trimble-Pomfret*); Daphne Moore (*Elizabeth Trimble-Pomfret*); Patric Knowles (*Trimble-Pomfret son*); June Duprez (*Julia Trimble-Pomfret*); Cecil Kellaway (*Dinner Guest*); Isobel Elsom (*Lady Trimble-Pomfret*); Ida Lupino (*Jenny Jones, the maid*); Wendy Barrie (*Edith Trimble-Pomfret*); Wendell Hulett (*Augustus Trimble-Pomfret*); Eric Blore (*Charles, the butler*); Brian Aherne (*Jim Trimble*); Merle Oberon (*Marjorie Ismay*); Emily Fitzroy (*Mrs. Fulcher*); Una O'Connor (*Mrs. Caroline Ismay*); Richard Haydn (*Mr. Butcher*); Odette Myrtil (*Madame Gaby*); Nigel Bruce (*Major Garrow*); Elsa Lanchester (*Mamie, the hotel maid*); Ivan F. Simpson (*Dexter, the hotel tenant*); Anita Sharp-Bolster (*Mrs. Garrow*); Roland Young (*Henry Barringer*); Gladys Cooper (*Mrs. Barringer*); Marta Gale (*Miss Garrow*); Robert Cummings (*Ned Trimble*); Donald Crisp (*Captain Martin*); Doris Lloyd (*Trimble Maid*); Helena Pickard (*Trimble Maid*); Connie Leon (*Londoner in wartime*). **Summary:** During World War II, American reporter

Gates Trimble Pomfret is about to leave London for home when he receives a cable from his father in New York, instructing him to sell the ancestral house and acquire the Trimble portrait. Following his father's orders, Gates proceeds to the house at 6 Pomfret Street. As he knocks at the door, German bombs begin to fall, and he takes shelter in the cellar of the house. There he sees a plaque proclaiming that Eustace Trimble built the house. After the bombing ends, Gates returns upstairs and meets Lesley Trimble, the current occupant. Lesley resents Gates's blatant disrespect for the old house and after telling him to discuss the sale with her solicitor, she climbs up the stairs, leaving him behind. After Gates follows her and apologizes for his insensitivity, she explains that she was born in the house when it was a hotel, and later she and her mother lovingly restored the edifice to its original purpose as a single family residence. After admonishing Gates to respect the memories of those that lived in the house, Lesley recounts the history of the dwelling. —AFICFF. **Notes:** As Sir Anthony Trimble-Pomfret, Eddie has the following line upon receiving his knighthood: "I am of course gratified and flattered by the signal honour Her Majesty has done us."

Thank Your Lucky Stars (September 23, 1943) Warner Bros. Pictures, 127 minutes, musical variety show. **Producer:** Mark Hellinger. **Director:** David Butler. **Screenplay:** Norman Panama, Melvin Frank, James V. Kern; based on a story by Everett Freeman and Arthur Schwartz. **Music:** Heinz Roemheld. **Camera:** Arthur Edeson. **Editor:** Irene Morra. **Cast:** Eddie Cantor (*Himself / Joe Simpson*); Joan Leslie (*Pat Dixon*); Dennis Morgan (*Tommy Randolph*); Edward Everett Horton (*Farnsworth*); S.Z. Sakall (*Dr. Schlenna*); Mike Mazurki (*Olaf*); Noble Johnson (*Charlie, the Indian*); Ruth Donnelly (*Nurse Hamilton*); Ralph Dunn (*Marty*); Paul Harvey (*Dr. Kirby*); Don Wilson (*Radio Announcer*). **Guest stars:** Willie Best; Humphrey Bogart; Jess Lee Brooks; Jack Carson; Ben Corbett; Bette Davis; William Desmond; Olivia de Havilland; Errol Flynn; John Garfield; Alan Hale Sr.; Mark Hellinger; Ida Lupino; Hattie McDaniel; Ann Sheridan; Dinah Shore; Alexis Smith; Madame Sul-Te-Wan; George Tobias; Spike Jones and His City Slickers. **Summary:** Farnsworth (Eddie) and Dr. Schlenna (S.Z. Sakall), two producers who are planning a benefit extravaganza, want Dinah Shore, a singer on Eddie Cantor's radio show, to appear at their benefit, but they must first make a deal with Cantor, who holds her contract. —AFICFF

The Gang's All Here (December 24, 1943; released in the UK as *The Girls He Left Behind*) 20th Century-Fox, 103 minutes, super Technicolor musical. **Producer:** William LeBaron, William Goetz (executive producer, uncredited). **Director:** Busby Berkeley. **Screenplay:** Walter Bullock; based on a story by Nancy Wintner, George Root Jr., and Tom Bridges. **Music:** Leo Robin, Harry Warren. **Camera:** Edwin Cronjager. **Editor:** Ray Curtiss. **Cast:** Alice Faye (*Eadie Allen*); Carmen Miranda (*Dorita*); Phil Baker (*Himself*); Benny Goodman (*Himself*); Eugene Pallette (*Andrew Mason Sr.*); Charlotte Greenwood (*Blossom Potter*); Edward Everett Horton (*Peyton Potter*); Tony DeMarco (*Himself*); James Ellison (*Andy Mason*); Sheila Ryan (*Vivian Potter*); Dave Willock (*Sgt. Pat Casey*); Leon Belasco (*Waiter*); Brooks Benedict (*Club New Yorker Patron*); Jeanne Crain (*Chorus Girl / Pool Party Guest*); Frank Darien (*Stage Doorman*); Johnny Duncan (*Jitterbug Dancer*); Herbert Evans (*Club New Yorker Patron*); Frank Faylen (*Marine Sergeant*); June Haver (*Chorus Girl / Hat Check Girl*); Leyland Hodgson (*Butler*); Adele Jergens (*Chorus Girl*); Virginia Sale (*Miss Custer, Secretary*); Billie Seward (*Dancer*); Lillian Yarbo (*Maid, uncredited*). **Summary:** Wealthy businessman Andrew J. "A.J." Mason Sr. takes his nervous partner, Peyton Potter, to the Club New Yorker for a celebratory evening with his son, Sgt. Andrew J. Mason Jr., who is about to report for active duty in the Army. One online reviewer states: "The plot is mostly an excuse for some snappy repartee between major '40s stars (in particular, Eugene Pallette and Edward Everett Horton are hilarious)." —IMDb

Her Primitive Man (March 30, 1944) Universal Pictures, 79 minutes, romantic screwball comedy. **Producer:** Michael Fessier, Ernest Pagano. **Director:** Charles Lamont. **Screenplay:** Michael Fessier, Ernest Pagano; based on a story by Dick Irving Hyland. **Music:** Edward Ward. **Camera:** Charles Van Enger. **Editor:** Ray Snyder. **Cast:** Louise Allbritton (*Sheila Winthrop*); Robert Paige (*Peter Mathews*); Robert Benchley (*Martin Osborne*); Edward Everett Horton (*Orrin Tracy*); Helen Broderick (*Mrs. Winthrop*); Stephanie Bachelor (*Marcia Stafford*); Walter Catlett (*Hotel Clerk*); Ernest Truex (*Uncle Hubert*); Louis Jean Heydt (*Gerald Van Horn*); Nydia Westman (*Aunt Penelope*); Oscar O'Shea (*Jonathan*); Sylvia Field (*Aunt Martha*); Ian Wolfe (*Caleb*); Irving Bacon (*Mr. Smith*). **Summary:** A new book being written by "adventurer" Pete Matthews, entitled *Life and Death Among the Lupari Savages,* is making thousands of dollars in advanced sales due to the publicity efforts of its publisher, Martin Osborne. Unknown to the publisher and the treatise's prospective readers, however, is the fact that Peter is writing his book from the barstool of a Havana casino, where he is getting his information about the headhunters of Lupari Island from Orrin Tracy, a worldly bartender (Eddie). —AFICFF

Summer Storm (July 14, 1944) Seymour Nebenzal / United Artists, 106 minutes, Chekhovian drama ending in tragedy. **Producer:** Seymore Nebenzal, Rudolph F. Joseph. **Director:** Douglas Sirk. **Screenplay:** Douglas Sirk, Michael O'Hara, Rowland Leigh, Robert Thoeren; based on Anton Chekhov's 1884 play *The Shooting Party*. **Music:** Karl Hajos. **Camera:** Archie Stout (front for Eugen Schüfftan). **Cast:** George Sanders (*Judge Fedor Petroff*); Linda Darnell (*Olga Kuzminichna Urbenin*); Edward Everett Horton (*Count "Piggy" Volsky*); Anna Lee (*Nadena Kalenin*); Hugo Haas (*Anton Urbenin*); Laurie Lane (*Clara Heller*); John Philliber (*Polycarp, Petroff's Butler*); Sig Ruman (*Kuzma*); John Abbott (*Lunin, Public Prosecutor*); Mary Servoss (*Mrs. Kalenin*); André Charlot (*Mr. Kalenin*); Robert Greig (*Gregory, Volsky's Butler*); Nina Koshetz (*Gypsy Singer*); Paul Hurst (*Officer Orloff*); Charles Trowbridge (*Doctor*); Sarah Padden (*Beggar Woman*); Mike Mazurki (*Tall Policeman*). **Summary, Review, and Notes:** "Darnell gave one of her best performances as a peasant who victimizes every man she meets. Dreary adaptation of Chekov's 'The Shooting Party,' enlivened by Horton as an amoral Russian count." (**) —LMCMG

Arsenic and Old Lace (September 1, 1944; shot in 1941); Warner Bros. Pictures, 118 minutes, classic black comedy. **Producers:** Frank Capra, Jack L. Warner. **Director:** Frank Capra. **Screenplay:** Julius J. Epstein, Philip G. Epstein; based on the 1941 play *Arsenic and Old Lace* by Joseph Kesselring. The play remained on Broadway for nearly four years, from 1941 to 1944. Only when it closed could Warner Bros. finally release the three-year-old movie version. **Music:** Max Steiner. **Camera:** Sol Polito. **Editor:** Daniel Mandell. **Cast:** Cary Grant (*Mortimer Brewster*); Priscilla Lane (*Elaine Brewster*); Josephine Hull (*Aunt Abby Brewster*); Jean Adair (*Aunt Martha Brewster*); Raymond Massey (*Jonathan Brewster*); Peter Lorre (*Dr. Herman Einstein*); John Alexander ("*Teddy Roosevelt*" *Brewster*); Jack Carson (*Officer Patrick O'Hara*); John Ridgely (*Officer Sanders*); Edward McNamara (*Police Sgt. Brophy*); James Gleason (*Police Lt. Rooney*); Edward Everett Horton (*Mr. Witherspoon*); Grant Mitchell (*Reverend Harper*); Vaughan Glaser (*Judge Cullman*); Chester Clute (*Dr. Gilchrist*); Edward McWade (*Mr. Gibbs, the Old Man*); Garry Owen (*Taxicab Driver*); Charles Lane (*First Reporter*); Hank Mann (Second Reporter with Camera); Spencer Charters (*Marriage License Clerk*). **Summary, Review, and Notes:** "Hilarious adaptation of Joseph Kesselring's hit play (scripted by the Epstein brothers) about two seemingly harmless old ladies who poison lonely gentlemen callers. Frantic cast is excellent, particularly Lorre and Massey as unsuspecting murderers holed up in the Brooklyn household. Made in 1941. Hull, Adair, and Alexander repeat their Broadway roles." (***½) —LMCMG. Notes: Eddie would reprise his role as Mr. Witherspoon on television in 1955.

San Diego, I Love You (September 29, 1944) Universal Pictures, 83 minutes, romantic comedy. **Producers:** Michael Fessier, Ernest Pagano. **Director:** Reginald Le Borg. **Screenplay:** Richard Bransten, Michael Fessier, Ruth McKenney, Ernest Pagano. **Music:** Hans J. Salter. **Camera:** Hal Mohr. **Editor:** Charles Maynard. **Cast:** Jon Hall (*John Thompson Caldwell IV*); Louise Allbritton (*Virginia McCooley*); Edward Everett Horton (*Philip McCooley*); Eric Blore (*Nelson, the Butler*); Buster Keaton (*Bus Driver*); Irene Ryan (*Sheila Jones*); Rudy Wissler (*Walter McCooley*); Peter Miles (*Joel McCooley*); Charles Bates (*Larry McCooley*); Donald Davis (*Pete McCooley*); Florence Lake (*Miss Lake*); Chester Clute (*Percy Caldwell*); Sarah Selby (*Mrs. Lovelace*); Fern Emmett (*Mrs. Callope*); Harry Barris (*Clarinetist*); Leon Belasco (*Violinist*); Hobart Cavanaugh (*Mr. McGregor*); William B. Davidson (*General*); Vernon Dent (*Mr. Fitzmaurice*); Eddie Dunn (*Stevedore*); Mabel Forrest (*Mrs. Fresher*); John Gannon (*Soldier*); Edward Gargan (*Policeman*); Victoria Horne (*Mrs. Allsop*); Esther Howard (*Mother*); Teddy Infuhr (*Brat*); Tom Keene (*Reporter*); George Lloyd (*Moving Man*); Matt McHugh (*Man on Street*); George Meader (*Mr. Applewaite*); Clarence Muse (*Porter*); Sarah Padden (*Mrs. Gulliver*); Jack Rice (*Hotel Clerk*); Dewey Robinson (*Stevedore*); Gene Roth (*Stevedore*); Almira Sessions (*Mrs. Mainwaring*); Jerry Shane (*Sailor*); Harry Tyler (*Mr. Carruthers*); Jan Wiley (*Receptionist*). **Summary:** Schoolteacher Philip McCooley returns home to discover that his daughter Virginia has offered his resignation at Waterville High School so that the family can move to San Diego and Philip can present his new invention, a lifeboat, to the International Research Bureau. **Notes:** At one point in the film, Buster Keaton flashes a warm, beautiful smile. Bosley Crowther, the cranky movie critic for the *New York Times*, detested this charming film, calling it "worse than terrible." He opined that Buster's supporting role was an insult to him and described Eddie's performance as "embarrassing."

Brazil (November 30, 1944; a.k.a. *Stars and Guitars*) Republic Pictures, 91 minutes, musical set in South America. **Producer:** Robert

North. **Director:** Joseph Santley. **Screenplay:** Richard English, Frank Gill Jr., Laura Kerr. **Music:** Walter Scharf. **Camera:** Jack A. Marta. **Editor:** Murray Seldeen, Harry Gerstad (uncredited). **Cast:** Tito Guízar (*Miguel Soares*); Virginia Bruce (*Nicky Henderson*); Edward Everett Horton (*Everett St. John Everett*); Robert Livingston (*Rod Walker*); Veloz and Yolanda (*Themselves*); Fortunio Bonanova (*Señor Renaldo Da Silva*); Richard Lane (*Edward Graham*); Frank Puglia (*Señor Machado*); Aurora Miranda (*Ballerina*); Alfredo de Sa (*Master of Ceremonies*); Henry De Silva (*Comerciante*); Rico De Montez (*Airport Official*); Leon Lenoir (*Reporter*); Roy Rogers (*Himself*); Trigger, Roy's horse (*Himself*); Billy Daniels (*Dancer*). **Summary:** American writer Nicky Henderson travels to Rio de Janeiro to spend two weeks researching a new book on Brazil. When the local reporters discover that Nicky is the author of the unflattering *Why Marry a Latin?*, they treat her coldly, but she is happily greeted by Rod Walker, a diplomat and former boyfriend. —AFICFF. **Notes:** In what is likely a play on his own name, Eddie is Everett St. John Everett.

The Town Went Wild (December 15, 1944) Producers Releasing Corporation, 77 minutes, small town comedy. **Producer:** Clarence Greene, Bernard B. Roth, Russell Rouse. **Director:** Ralph Murphy. **Screenplay:** Bernard B. Roth, Clarence Greene, Russell Rouse. **Music:** Gerald Carbonara. **Camera:** Philip Tannura. **Editor:** Thomas Neff. **Cast:** Freddie Bartholomew (*David Conway*); Jimmy Lydon (*Bob Harrison*); Edward Everett Horton (*Everett Conway*); Tom Tully (*Henry Harrison*); Jill Browning (*Carol Harrison*); Minna Gombell (*Marian Harrison*); Maude Eburne (*Judge Bingle*); Charles Halton (*Mr. Tweedle*); Ruth Lee (*Lucille Conway*); Roberta Smith (*Millie Walker*); Ferris Taylor (*Mr. Walker*); Jimmy Conlin (*Lemuel Jones, Justice of the Peace*); Monte Collins (*Oscar, Public Defender*); Olin Howland (Bit); Charles Middleton (*Sam, Midvale District Attorney*); Emmett Lynn (*The Watchman*); Dorothy Vaughan (*Nurse Irma Reeves*). **Summary:** Next-door neighbors Henry Harrison (Tom Tully) and Everett Conway (Eddie) have been feuding for twenty years. Despite their fathers' discord, Henry's daughter Carol and Everett's son David have fallen in love. After David, a young engineer, learns that he is being shipped to Alaska for six months to work on a government project, he decides to elope with Carol. When David goes to City Hall to get a copy of his birth certificate to send to Washington, Mr. Tweedle, the head of the Bureau of Vital Statistics, makes an amazing discovery which he decides to investigate further. —AFICFF

Steppin' in Society (July 9, 1945) Republic Pictures, 72 minutes, comedy-drama. **Producer:** Joseph Berchoiz. **Director:** Alexander Esway. **Screenplay:** Bradford Ropes, based on the French novel *Les vacances singulieres* by Marcel Arnac (Paris, 1929). **Music:** Joseph Dubin. **Camera:** Reggie Lanning. **Editor:** Harry Keller. **Cast:** Edward Everett Horton (*Judge Avery Webster*); Gladys George (*Penelope Webster*); Ruth Terry (*Lola Forrest*); Robert Livingston (*Montana*); Jack La Rue (*Bow Tie*); Lola Lane (*The Duchess*); Isabel Jewell (*Jenny the Juke*); Frank Jenks (*George*); Paul Hurst (*Cookie*); Harry Barris (*Ivory*); Iris Adrian (*Shirley*); Tom Herbert (*Hilliard*). **Summary:** Howard "Ten Spot" Rocky, convicted of stealing an automobile, is sentenced by Judge Avery Webster to serve time in the state penitentiary. The sentence devastates Ten Spot's girlfriend, "Jenny the Juke," who tells the judge that her boyfriend has reformed, and that he stole the car to take her to the hospital when she suffered from an appendicitis attack. The judge refuses to accept Jenny's arguments, and she accuses him of lacking feeling and understanding. Later, Avery and his wife Penelope leave for a vacation in Hot Springs, but their plans go awry when George Baxter, their chauffeur, quits. Stranded halfway between their home and Hot Springs, Penelope takes over the driving and crashes the car. A thunderstorm then forces the couple to take refuge at the Jungle Club inn, which, unknown to the Websters, is a front for jailed gangster Aloysius "Cookie" Blaine's operation. The Websters sense danger and decide to leave but are prevented from doing so by Cookie's henchmen. Later, the gangsters read about their pal Ten Spot's sentence and vow to take revenge on the judge who sentenced him, unaware that Avery was that judge. —AFICFF. In a perceptive review on IMDb, the writer provides some insight into the film's literary source and Eddie's character, Judge Avery Webster:

> It's a remake of Jean Boyer's *Circonstantes Attenuantes* and I regret to inform you that is a much better movie, because of Michel Simon in the same role as Horton; as much as I enjoy Horton, no one is a better comically monstrous performer than Simon. However, the character is rewritten for Horton, and he offers his usual excellent comedy performance. So by all means enjoy this but see if you can find the other movie.

Lady on a Train (August 3, 1945) Universal Pictures, 94 minutes, mystery-comedy. **Producer:** Felix Jackson. **Director:** Charles David. **Screenplay:** Edmund Beloin, Robert O'Brien. **Music:** Miklós Rózsa. **Camera:** Woody Bredell. **Editor:** Ted J. Kent. **Cast:** Deanna Durbin (*Nicki Collins*); Ralph Bellamy (*Jonathan Waring*); David Bruce (*Wayne Mor-*

gan); George Coulouris (*Mr. Saunders, Circus Club Manager*); Allen Jenkins (*Danny*); Dan Duryea (*Arnold Waring*); Edward Everett Horton (*Mr. Haskell*); Jacqueline de Wit (*Miss Fletcher*); Patricia Morison (*Joyce Williams*); Elizabeth Patterson (*Aunt Charlotte Waring*); Maria Palmer (*Margo Martin*); Samuel S. Hinds (*Mr. Wiggam*); William Frawley (*Desk Sgt. Brennan*); Thurston Hall (*Josiah Waring, uncredited*); Kathleen O'Malley (*Photographer*); Lash LaRue (*Club Waiter, uncredited*); Ben Carter (*Maxwell, Wayne Morgan's Valet, uncredited*); Sam McDaniel (*Train Porter, uncredited*); Chester Clute (*Train Conductor, uncredited*); Matt McHugh (*Drunk, uncredited*). **Summary:** Arriving in New York City for a Christmas visit with her aunt; Nicki Collins sees through her train window the murder of shipping magnate Josiah Waring. Because of her known addiction to mystery novels, the debutante is unable to convince the police that she witnessed a crime and decides to begin her own investigation. —AFICFF. **Notes:** When Eddie's character, Mr. Haskell, leaves Grand Central Station with Nikki Collins, they call for a taxi. When a taxi pulls up, however, Nikki's luggage is already piled in the front seat though she did not walk out with any bags nor did a porter load any luggage into the taxi. The taxi wasn't there waiting for them; it was just a random taxi that happened to pull up. The sequence, therefore, doesn't make any sense, and it interrupts the flow of the story. —IMDb

Cinderella Jones (March 9, 1946) Warner Bros. Pictures, 91 minutes, comedy. **Producer:** Alex Gottlieb. **Director:** Busby Berkeley. **Screenplay:** Charles Hoffman; based on the 1943 *Redbook Magazine* story "Judy Adjudicates," by Philip Wylie. **Music:** Friedrich Hollender. **Camera:** Sol Polito. **Editor:** George Amy. **Cast:** Joan Leslie (*Judy Jones*); Robert Alda (*Tommy Coles*); Julie Bishop (*Camille*); William Prince (*Bart Williams*); S.Z. Sakall (*Gabriel Popik*); Edward Everett Horton (*Keating*); Charles Dingle (*Minland*); Ruth Donnelly (*Cora Elliot*); Elisha Cook, Jr. (*Oliver S. Patch*); Hobart Cavanaugh (*George*); Charles Arnt (*Mahoney*); Chester Clute (*Krencher*); Edward Gargan (*Riley*); Margaret Early (*Bashful Girl*); Johnny Mitchell (*Soldier*); Mary Dean (*Singer*); Monte Blue (*Jailer*); Marianne O'Brien (*Marie*); Marion Martin (*Burlesque Queen*). **Summary:** Having failed to locate heiress Judy Jones, the law firm of Minland, Mahoney and Krencher decide to advertise. One of the many people who sees the ad is band leader Tommy Coles, whose girlfriend, an addlepated singer, is named Judy Jones. Tommy has proposed many times to Judy, but she refuses to marry him until they have more money. —AFICFF. **Notes:** For a change, Eddie plays a surprisingly clear-thinking role as Keating.

Faithful in My Fashion (August 22, 1946) Metro-Goldwyn-Mayer, 82 minutes, comedy. **Producer:** Lionel Houser. **Director:** Sidney Salkow. **Screenplay:** Lionel Houser. **Music:** Nathaniel Shilkret. **Camera:** Charles Salerno Jr. **Editor:** Irvine Warburton. **Cast:** Donna Reed (*Jean "Chunky" Kendrick*); Tom Drake (*Jeff Compton*); Edward Everett Horton (*Hiram Dilworthy*); Spring Byington (*Miss Mary Swanson*); Harry Davenport (*Great Grandpa*); Sig Ruman (*Professor Boris Riminoffsky*); Margaret Hamilton (*Miss Applegate*); Warner Anderson (*Walter Medcraft*); Hobart Cavanaugh (*Mr. Wilson*); Connie Gilchrist (*Mrs. Murphy*); Fred Essler (*Nikolai*); Wilson Wood (*Henry Stute*); William "Bill" Phillips (*1st Barfly*); Jack Overman (*2nd Barfly*); Phyllis Kennedy (*Miss Dale, Walter's Secretary*); Barbara Billingsley (*Mary*); Lillian Yarbo (*Celia*). **Summary:** Hoping to find everything just as he had left it four years ago, soldier Jeff Compton, who is home on a two-week furlough, visits the New York City department store in which he worked and surprises his former co-worker and sweetheart Jean Kendrick with a kiss. Jean, who is now an executive with the store, has since fallen out of love with Jeff, however, and is dating Walter Medcraft in the accounting department. As Jean never returned the engagement ring that Jeff sent to her while he was away, Jeff believes that she is still his fiancée. Realizing that Jeff is about to get his heart broken, Hiram Dilworthy (Eddie) and other department employees band together and, with Jean's consent, work diligently to prevent Jeff from learning the truth about his failed engagement. —AFICFF

Earl Carroll Sketchbook (August 22, 1946) Republic Pictures, 90 minutes, musical. **Producer:** Robert North. **Director:** Albert S. Rogell. **Screenplay:** Frank Gill Jr., Parker Levy. **Music:** Nathan Scott. **Camera:** Jack A. Marta. **Editor:** Richard L. Van Enger. **Cast:** Constance Moore (*Pamela Thayer*); William Marshall (*Tyler Brice*); Bill Goodwin (*Rick Castle*); Johnny Coy (*Johnny*); Barbara Jo Allen (*Sherry Lane*); Edward Everett Horton (*Dr. Milo Edwards*); Hillary Brooke (*Lynn Stafford*); Dorothy Babb (*Babs*); Robert Homans (*Pop Edgar*); Ray Walker (*Agent Sammy Harris*); Sarah Padden (*Mrs. Murphy*); Russell Hicks (*John Hawks*); Frances Morris (*Nurse*); Bobbie Dorree (*Blonde*). **Summary:** Songwriter Tyler Brice makes a handsome living composing jingles for radio commercials, much to the dismay of his loyal secretary, Pamela Thayer, who thinks that Ty is wasting his talent. Ty reminds Pam, who once aspired to a career as a professional singer, that she, too, is caught in the "jingle jungle," which keeps her employed. Ty also tries to lessen Pam's jealousy as he pays an increasing amount of attention to

Lynn Stafford, an attractive advertising executive who is interested in more than Ty's songs. **Notes:** Earl Carroll (1893–1948) was a producer, composer, playwright, and nightclub owner; he was best known for his "Vanities" and "Sketchbook" musical revues. Eddie is cast as Dr. Milo Edwards, who warns Pam about the potential danger of amnesia, following her being struck by a car. —AFICFF

The Ghost Goes Wild (March 8, 1947) Republic Pictures, 66 minutes, comedy-mystery. **Producer:** Armand Schaefer. **Director:** George Blair. **Screenplay:** Randall Faye, Taylor Caven. **Music:** Joseph Dubin. **Camera:** John Alton. **Editor:** Fred Allen. **Cast:** James Ellison (*Monte Crandall*); Anne Gwynne (*Phyllis Beecher*); Edward Everett Horton (*Eric*); Ruth Donnelly (*Aunt Susan Beecher*); Stephanie Bachelor (*Irene Winters*); Grant Withers (*Bill Winters*); Lloyd Corrigan (*The Late Timothy Beecher*); Emil Remeau (*Prof. Jacques Dubonnet*); Jonathan Hale (*Max Atterbury*); Charles Halton (*T. O'Connor Scott*); Holmes Herbert (*Judge*); Edward Gargan (*Newsstand Man*); Eugene Gericke (*Reporter*); Michael Hughes (*Reporter*); William Austin (*Barnaby*); Robert J. Wilke (*Burglar*). **Summary:** When painter Monte Crandall works for a trashy magazine published by Max Atterbury, he meets Susan Beecher and asks her if she will pose for him. She agrees, and when the painting, a grotesque caricature of Susan and her French poodle, François, is published on the front page of the magazine, Susan complains to her lawyer, T. O'Connor Scott. Scott then tries to contact Monte and learns that he has gone to stay at his home in Connecticut, Haunted Hill Farm. Monte, who is intrigued by parapsychology, recently purchased the house, which is supposed to be haunted by the ghost of Benedict Arnold. **Notes:** Eddie portrays Monte Crandall's butler, Eric, in this tepid comedy for Republic Pictures. —AFICFF

Down to Earth (August 21, 1947) Columbia Pictures, 101 minutes, musical comedy-drama. **Producer:** Don Hartman. **Director:** Alexander Hall. **Screenplay:** Edwin Blum, Don Hartman; based on characters from the 1938 play *It Happened Like That* by Harry Segal. **Music:** Allan Roberts, Doris Fisher (songs); ballet choreographed by Mario Castelnuovo-Tedesco. **Camera:** Rudolph Maté. **Editor:** Viola Lawrence. **Cast:** Rita Hayworth (*Terpsichore / Kitty Pendleton; singing voice dubbed by Anita Ellis*); Larry Parks (*Danny Miller; singing voice dubbed by Hal Derwin*); Marc Platt (*Eddie*); Roland Culver (*Mr. Jordan*); James Gleason (*Max Corkle*); Edward Everett Horton (*Messenger 7013*); Adele Jergens (*Georgia Evans / New Terpsichore; singing voice dubbed by Kay Starr*);

George Macready (*Joe Manion*); William Frawley (*the police lieutenant*); Kathleen O'Malley (*Dolly, uncredited*); William Haade (*Spike, uncredited*); James Burke (*Detective Kelly, uncredited*); Arthur Blake (*Nathaniel Somerset, uncredited*); Frank Darien (*the janitor, uncredited*); Ethan Laidlaw (*the stagehand, uncredited*). **Summary:** When questioned by the police about the murder of gambler Joe Mannion, Broadway theatrical agent Max Corkle professes his innocence and tells the police lieutenant the story of how he came to know one of the gambler's associates, Danny Miller. While Danny, the director and leading actor of a musical show about the nine Greek muses, rehearses his play, Terpsichore, a real muse, high in the heavens on Mount Parnassus, becomes angered by the vulgar portrayal of herself by actress Georgia Evans and vows to destroy Danny. Mr. Jordan, the man who oversees all travel from the heavens to earth, assigns Messenger 7013 (Eddie) to be Terpsichore's guide, and sends the two to earth, specifically New York City. **Notes:** Due to the acclaim Eddie received for his performance as Messenger 7013 in 1941's *Here Comes Mr. Jordan*, he was asked to reprise his role in this musical sequel. —AFICFF

Her Husband's Affairs (November 12, 1947) Columbia Pictures, 85 minutes, marital comedy. **Producer:** Rapheal Hakim. **Director:** S. Sylvan Simon. **Screenplay:** Ben Hecht, Charles Lederer. **Music:** George Duning. **Camera:** Charles Lawton Jr. **Editor:** Al Clark. **Cast:** Lucille Ball (*Margaret Weldon*); Franchot Tone (*William Weldon*); Edward Everett Horton (*J.B. Cruikshank*); Mikhail Rasumny (*Prof. Emil Glinka*); Gene Lockhart (*Peter Winterbottom*); Nana Bryant (*Mrs. Winterbottom*); Jonathan Hale (*Gov. Fox*); Paul Stanton (*Dr. Frazee*); Mabel Paige (*Mrs. Josper*). **Summary:** Margaret Weldon, bride of advertising man William Weldon, finds her honeymoon constantly delayed by her husband's marketing schemes. Their latest planned trip is postponed when the Tappel hat account rejects Bill's slogan and insists on a celebrity endorsement instead. **Notes:** At one point in the film, Eddie appears bald due to a plastic head-piece. He had a Ball working with Lucille. —AFICFF

The Story of Mankind (November 8, 1957) Warner Bros. Pictures, 100 minutes, historical-fantasy comedy-drama. **Producer:** Irwin Allen, George E. Swink. **Director:** Irwin Allen. **Screenplay:** Irwin Allen, Charles Bennett; based on the 1921 novel *The Story of Mankind* by Hendrik Willem van Loon. **Music:** Paul Sawtell. **Camera:** Nicholas Musuraca. **Editor:** Gene Palmer. **Cast:** Ronald Colman (*The Spirit of Man*); Vincent Price (*Mr. Scratch*); Hedy Lamarr (*Joan of Arc*);

Groucho Marx (*Peter Minuit*); Harpo Marx (*Sir Isaac Newton*); Chico Marx (*Monk*); Virginia Mayo (*Cleopatra*); Agnes Moorehead (*Queen Elizabeth I*); Peter Lorre (*Nero*); Charles Coburn (*Hippocrates*); Sir Cedric Hardwicke (*High Judge*); Cesar Romero (*Spanish Envoy*); John Carradine (*Khufu*); Dennis Hopper (*Napoleon Bonaparte*); Marie Wilson (*Marie Antoinette*); Helmut Dantine (*Mark Antony*); Edward Everett Horton (*Sir Walter Raleigh*); Reginald Gardiner (*William Shakespeare*); Marie Windsor (*Joséphine de Beauharnais*); George E. Stone (*Waiter*); Cathy O'Donnell (*Early Christian Woman*); Franklin Pangborn (*Marquis de Varennes*); Melville Cooper (*Major Domo*); Henry Daniell (*Bishop Cauchon*); Francis X. Bushman (*Moses*); Jim Ameche (*Alexander Graham Bell*); Austin Green (*Abraham Lincoln*); Bobby Watson (*Adolf Hitler*). **Summary:** Two angels, appearing as stars in the heavens, discuss how man has invented the super H-bomb sixty years ahead of schedule. Noting that all of mankind will be destroyed if the bomb is detonated, the stars report the news to the High Tribunal of Outer Space, which is then called into session. Their agenda is to determine whether to prevent the bomb from detonating or allow it to go off. To present a defense, the Spirit of Man is called and The Devil, Mr. Scratch, who arrives with his apprentice, is appointed prosecutor of the case. The High Judge instructs Man and Scratch to visit any time or place on Earth to present supporting evidence, adding that their travels will be watched by the tribunal. **Notes:** In a cameo lasting mere seconds, Eddie appears wordlessly as Sir Walter Raleigh. This was Eddie's sole movie role of the 1950s. — AFICFF

Pocketful of Miracles (December 19, 1961) Franton Productions / United Artists, 137 minutes, sentimental comedy-drama. **Producer:** Frank Capra. **Director:** Frank Capra. **Screenplay:** Hal Kanter, Harry Tugend; based on a 1929 *Cosmopolitan Magazine* story "Madame la Gimp" by Damon Runyon, and the screenplay for the 1933 film *Lady for a Day* by Robert Riskin. **Music:** Walter Scharf. **Camera:** Robert J. Bronner. **Editor:** Frank P. Keller. **Cast:** Glenn Ford (*Dave the Dude*); Bette Davis (*Apple Annie*); Hope Lange (*Queenie Martin*); Arthur O'Connell (*Count Alfonso Romero*); Peter Falk (*Joy Boy*); Thomas Mitchell (*Henry G. Blake*); Edward Everett Horton (*Hudgins*); Mickey Shaughnessy (*Junior*); David Brian (*Governor*); Sheldon Leonard (*Steve Darcey*); Ann-Margret (*Louise*); Jerome Cowan (*Mayor*); Peter Mann (*Carlos Romero*); Ellen Corby (*Soho Sal*); Jack Elam (*Cheesecake*); Mike Mazurki (*Big Mike*); Barton MacLane (*Police Commissioner*); John Litel (*Police Chief*); Doodles Weaver (*Pool Player*); Frank

Ferguson (*Newspaper Editor*); George E. Stone (*Shimkey, the Blind Man*); Jay Novello (*The Spanish Consul*); Benny Rubin (*Flyaway, Dude's lawyer*). **Summary:** In 1930 New York, shortly after debt-ridden nightclub owner Rudy Martin dies, his daughter Elizabeth, whom he called "Queenie," shows up to hand the deed to his club to kindhearted bootlegger Dave the Dude. Attracted to Queenie, the Dude decides to help her turn the club into a popular speakeasy, and two years later she has paid off all of her father's debts. Everything is going right for the Dude, who thinks that his luck comes from his daily purchase of an apple from "Apple Annie," a disheveled old apple vendor who leads the Broadway panhandlers. **Notes:** This was Eddie's third and final film for Frank Capra. It was also the director's last film. —AFICFF

It's a Mad, Mad, Mad, Mad World (November 7, 1963); United Artists, 202 minutes (original cut proposed by Stanley Kramer); 192 minutes (Cinerama Dome Premiere); 159–163 minutes (general release); 197 minutes, all-star comedy about unbridled greed. **Producer:** Stanley Kramer. **Director:** Stanley Kramer. **Screenplay:** William Rose, Tania Rose. **Music:** Ernest Gold. **Camera:** Ernest Laszlo. **Editor:** Frederic Knudtson, Robert C. Jones, Gene Fowler Jr. **Principal Cast:** Spencer Tracy (*Captain T. G. Culpeper*); Milton Berle (*J. Russell Finch*); Sid Caesar (*Melville Crump*); Buddy Hackett (*"Benjy" Benjamin*); Ethel Merman (*Mrs. Marcus*); Mickey Rooney (*Ding Bell*); Dick Shawn (*Sylvester Marcus*); Phil Silvers (*Otto Meyer*); Terry-Thomas (*Lt. Col. J. Algernon Hawthorne*); Jonathan Winters (*Lennie Pike*); Edie Adams (*Monica Crump*); Dorothy Provine (*Emeline Marcus-Finch*). **Supporting Cast:** Eddie "Rochester" Anderson (*cab driver*); Jim Backus (*airplane owner Tyler Fitzgerald*); Jack Benny (*derby-wearing motorist in desert*); Ben Blue (*vintage biplane pilot*); Joe E. Brown (*the union official giving a speech at a construction site*); Alan Carney (*a sergeant with the Santa Rosita Police Department*); Chick Chandler (*a policeman outside Ray & Irwin's Garage*); Barrie Chase (*Sylvester Marcus's dancing, bikini-clad paramour*); Stanley Clements (*reporter*); Lloyd Corrigan (*the mayor of Santa Rosita*); William Demarest (*Aloysius, Chief of the Santa Rosita Police Department*); Andy Devine (*the sheriff of Crockett County, California*); Selma Diamond (*voice of Ginger Culpeper*); Jimmy Durante (*Smiler Grogan*); Minta Durfee (*woman in crowd*); Peter Falk (*cab driver*); Norman Fell (*primary detective at the Smiler Grogan accident site*); Paul Ford (*Col. Wilberforce*); Stan Freberg (*deputy sheriff of Crockett County*); Louise Glenn (*voice of Billie Sue Culpeper*); Nicholas Georgiade (*detective at crash site*); Leo Gorcey (*the cab driver bringing Melville and Monica to the hardware store*);

Sterling Holloway (*the Santa Rosita Fire Department fireman*); Edward Everett Horton (*Mr. Dinkler, owner of the hardware store*); Allen Jenkins (*police officer*); Marvin Kaplan (*service station co-owner Irwin*); Buster Keaton (*Jimmy the Crook*); Tom Kennedy (*manic traffic conductor*); Don Knotts (*the nervous motorist*); Charles Lane (*the airport manager*); Jerry Lewis (*idiot motorist who runs over Culpeper's hat*); Mike Mazurki (*the miner bringing medicine to his wife*); Charles McGraw (*Lt. Mathews of the Santa Rosita Police Department*); ZaSu Pitts (*Gertie, the Santa Rosita Police Department Central Division's switchboard operator*); Carl Reiner (*the Rancho Conejo airport tower controller*); Madlyn Rhue (*secretary Schwartz of the Santa Rosita Police Department*); Roy Roberts (*policeman outside Irwin & Ray's Garage*); Eddie Ryder (*tower radioman*); Jean Sewell (*woman in migrant truck*); Arnold Stang (*service station co-owner Ray*); Nick Stewart (*the migrant truck driver forced off the road*); The Three Stooges (*Moe Howard, Larry Fine, and Curly Joe DeRita as Rancho Conejo Airport firemen*); Sammee Tong (*a laundryman*); Doodles Weaver (*hardware store employee*); Jesse White (*a Rancho Conejo air traffic controller*); and others. **Summary:** Passengers from four vehicles rush to the scene of an accident after a fast-moving car sails off the edge of a mountain road and tumbles down a steep embankment. They include J. Russell Finch, president of the Pacific Edible Seaweed Company, who is traveling with his wife, Emmeline, and his shrewish mother-in-law, Mrs. Marcus; dentist Melville Crump and his wife, Monica; gag-writers Benjy Benjamin and Ding Bell; and furniture mover Lennie Pike. Smiler Grogan reveals with his dying breath that he has buried $350,000 in stolen money under the "Big W" at Santa Rosita Beach State Park. Unable to determine the identity of the "Big W" or even to decide on a way to divide the cash, the greedy witnesses disperse and head for the park.

Sex and the Single Girl (December 25, 1964) Warner Bros. Pictures, 114 minutes, feminist comedy. **Producer:** William T. Orr. **Director:** Richard Quine. **Screenplay:** Joseph Heller, David L. Schwartz; based on the 1962 book *Sex and the Single Girl* by Helen Gurley Brown. **Music:** Neal Hefti. **Camera:** Charles Lang. **Editor:** David Wages. **Cast:** Tony Curtis (*Bob Weston, managing editor of* Stop Magazine); Natalie Wood (*Dr. Helen Brown, psychologist and author of* Sex and the Single Girl); Henry Fonda (*Frank Broderick, owner of a stocking manufacturing firm, Bob's friend*); Lauren Bacall (*Sylvia Broderick, Frank's wife*); Mel Ferrer (*Rudy DeMeyer, psychiatrist, Helen's colleague*); Fran Jeffries (*Gretchen, Bob's girlfriend*); Leslie Parrish (*Susan, Bob's secretary*); Edward Everett Horton (*The Chief*); Larry Storch (*The Motorcycle Cop*); Stubby Kaye (*Helen's*

Cabbie); Otto Kruger (*Dr. Anderson*). **Summary:** Bob Weston, managing editor of scandal magazine *STOP,* writes a sensational and highly successful article on research psychologist Helen Gurley Brown, whose recently published book, *Sex and the Single Girl,* has become a national bestseller. Bob is assigned to interview Dr. Brown, but she refuses to see him. In order to meet her, Bob impersonates one of his neighbors, Frank Broderick, and goes to Helen for marriage counseling. — AFICFF. **Notes:** At one point in the film, Eddie delivers "a long address in the boardroom scene with undiminished time and delivery, and every appearance of relish." (Source: Jeanie Stein, "'Fusspot' and 'Fortune's Fool,' Edward Everett Horton," *Focus on Film*, no. 1, 1970.)

The Perils of Pauline (August 7, 1967) Universal Pictures, 102 minutes, satirical comedy-adventure. **Producer:** Herbert B. Leonard. **Directors:** Herbert B. Leonard and Joshua Shelley. **Screenplay:** Albert Beich; based on the 1914 silent movie serial *The Perils of Pauline* and a play by Charles W. Goddard. **Music:** Vic Mizzy. **Camera:** Jack A. Marta. **Editor:** Sam E. Waxman. **Cast:** Pat Boone (*George Stedman*); Pamela Austin (*Pauline*); Terry-Thomas (*Sten Martin*); Edward Everett Horton (*Caspar Coleman*); Hamilton Camp (*Thorpe*); Doris Packer (*Mrs. Carruthers*); Kurt Kasznar (*The Consul General*); Vito Scotti (*Frandisi*); Leon Askin (*The Commissar*); Rick Natoli (*Prince Benji*). **Summary:** Two orphans, Pauline and George, fall in love at the Baskerville Foundling Home. Before leaving the orphanage, George vows to return as a millionaire and marry Pauline. Seven years later he fulfills his promise, only to find that Pauline has gone to Arabia as the governess of twelve-year-old Prince Benji. Arriving in Arabia, George learns that Pauline, having frustrated the precocious prince's plan to make her the first member of his harem, has been sold to white pygmies in the Congo. Abducted by a gorilla, Pauline is rescued by the renowned hunter Sten Martin. While George is recovering in New York City from an African disease, Pauline falls into a sewer. Her elderly savior, millionaire Caspar Coleman, freezes Pauline in anticipation of his grandson's maturity. —AFICFF

2000 Years Later (March 11, 1969) Warner Bros. Seven Arts, 80 minutes, fantasy-comedy. **Producer:** Bert Tenzer. **Director:** Bert Tenzer. **Screenplay:** Bert Tenzer. **Music:** Stu Phillips. **Camera:** Mario Di Leo. **Editor:** Donn Cambern. **Cast:** Terry-Thomas (Goodwyn); Edward Everett Horton (*Evermore*); Pat Harrington, Jr. (*Franchot*); Lisa Seagram (*Cindy*); John Abbott (*Gregorius*); John Myhers (*Air Force General*); Tom Melody (*Senator*); Myrna Ross (*Miss Forever*); Monti Rock

III (*Tomorrow's Leader*); Murray Roman (*Superdude*); Michael Christian (*The Piston Kid*); Casey Kasem (*Disk Jockey*); Bert Tenzer (*Mercury's Voice*); Rudi Gernreich (*Himself*). **Summary:** During the fall of Rome, the god Mercury transforms citizen Gregorius into a ball of fire. Centuries later, Mercury, alarmed by contemporary trends, dispatches the Roman to Hollywood. Horrified by American hedonism, Gregorius is unable to speak. The Roman's silence, however, does not prevent his discovery and exploitation by Goodwyn and Evermore, hosts of the televised *International Culture Hour*. —AFICFF

Cold Turkey (January 30, 1971) Tandem-DFI / Artists, 101 minutes, bombastic comedy about smoking. **Producer:** Norman Lear. **Director:** Norman Lear. **Screenplay:** Norman Lear, William Price Fox Jr.; based on the unpublished novel "I'm Giving Them Up for Good," by Margaret and Neil Rau. **Music:** Randy Newman. **Camera:** Charles F. Wheeler. **Editor:** John C. Horger. **Cast:** Dick Van Dyke (*Rev. Clayton Brooks*); Bob Newhart (*Merwin Wren*); Pippa Scott (*Natalie Brooks*); Tom Poston (*Edgar Stopworth*); Edward Everett Horton (*Hiram C. Grayson*); Bob Elliott (*Hugh Upson / David Chetley / Sandy Van Andy*); Ray Goulding (*Walter Chronic / Paul Hardly / Arthur Lordly*); Vincent Gardenia (*Mayor Quincey L. Wappler*); Barnard Hughes (*Dr. Proctor*); Graham Jarvis (*Amos Bush*); Jean Stapleton (*Mrs. Wappler*); Barbara Cason (*Letitia Hornsby*); Judith Lowry (*Odie Turman*); Sudie Bond (*Cissy*); Helen Page Camp (*Mrs. Watson*); Paul Benedict (*Zen Buddhist*); Simon Scott (*Mr. Kandiss*); Raymond Kark (*Homer Watson*); Peggy Rea (*Mrs. Proctor*); Woodrow Parfrey (*Tobacco Executive*); George Mann (*Bishop Manley*); Charles Pinney (*Col. Galloway*); M. Emmet Walsh (*Art*); Gloria LeRoy (*Lottie Davenport, the Masseuse*); Eric Boles (*Dennis*); Jack Grimes (*TV Stage Manager*); Walter Sande (*Tobacco Executive*); Harvey Jason (*Hypnotist*). **Summary:** Public relations director Merwin Wren (Newhart), inspired by the irony that the Nobel Peace Prize's founder made his fortune manufacturing explosives used in rifles, schemes to promote the elderly owner of Valiant Tobacco Company, Hiram C. Grayson (Horton), as a great humanitarian in the tradition of Alfred Nobel. To accomplish this, Wren convinces the company's board of directors to offer $25 million to any town that can stop smoking "cold turkey" for thirty days, certain that none will ever claim the prize. In Eagle Rock, Iowa, where the closing of an airbase has caused economic depression, Rev. Clayton Brooks hopes his church will re-assign him to the wealthy community of Dearborn, Michigan. The vainly handsome Brooks is popular with everyone except his meek wife Natalie, who stoically submits to his constant criticism and his accusations that she subconsciously sabotages his ambitions. Brooks preaches to his congregation that God has plans for their town and when he learns about the prize, decides that Valiant's offer is the "purpose" God intended for them. With the approval of the town council, the dynamic preacher leads a campaign to persuade the townspeople to pledge to quit smoking for one month. **Notes:** In their feature film debut, Bob Elliott and Ray Goulding, better known as Bob & Ray, portray such contemporary television and radio commentators as Arthur Godfrey, Paul Harvey, Chet Huntley, and Walter Cronkite, using slightly altered names. According to June 1969 *Hollywood Reporter* and *Daily Variety* news items, the film was shot on location in Winterset, Greenfield, and Des Moines, IA, in the summer of 1969; it was not released to theatres until January 1971. Many Iowan citizens were cast as extras. Tandem Productions was owned by Lear and his partner, Bud Yorkin. Although Dick Van Dyke is not personally credited onscreen as producer, his company, DFI Productions (Dramatic Features, Inc.), was a co-producer, as noted by the ending credits. *Cold Turkey* marked the feature film directorial debut for writer-producer Lear and marked the final film of Edward Everett Horton. —AFICFF

Unrealized film projects

As prolific as Eddie's screen career was, there were a number of projects that didn't come off as planned. In various trade magazines, he was announced as a cast member in *Under Two Flags*, *Rainbow on the River*, *One Rainy Afternoon* (all 1936), and *Hi Diddle Diddle* (1943), but does not appear in any of these films. Originally, the screenplay for *The Milky Way* (also 1936) was intended as a Paramount vehicle for Jack Oakie as Burleigh "Tiger" Sloan, Gertrude Michael as Ann Westley, and Eddie as Gabby Sloan. But when Harold Lloyd was cast in the lead role, Horton was considered too similar in style, and both he and Gertrude Michael were cut. William Frawley was the second choice for Gabby, but Adolphe Menjou ultimately played the part. Eddie was also signed to portray Alphonsus Mannering, a finicky editor of a home and garden magazine in Universal-International's *Ma and Pa Kettle at Home* (1954). Because of a schedule conflict with the New Orleans Opera, Eddie was replaced in the picture by his friend and two-time co-star Alan Mowbray.

Radio & TV Credits
1934-1970

The Rudy Vallée Show (NBC Radio, 1929–1939), also known as *The Fleischmann Yeast Hour*, was one of network radio's earliest musical-variety programs. Rudy Vallée had become a popular crooner during the "Vo-De-O-Do" fad of the late twenties. His appeal is difficult to fathom from a modern-day perspective. He was a brazenly egocentric man with a nasal tenor voice that was magnified by the use of a hand-held megaphone. One of his biggest fans was NBC executive Bertha Brainard, who strongly believed that Vallée deserved his own radio program and predicted that he would likely have a huge female listenership. She was correct. In 1936, the program lost its sponsor and gained a new one. Now known as *The Royal Gelatin Hour*, that iteration lasted until 1939. Eddie, who had recently gained some solid recognition from his role in *The Gay Divorcee*, was one of Vallée's on-air guests on October 25, 1934, along with former silent screen actress Carmel Myers and Warner Bros. star James Cagney.

Shell Chateau (NBC Radio, 1935–1937) also known as *The Shell Show*, was a musical-comedy variety series broadcast on Saturday evenings at 9:30, beginning on June 29, 1935. The show's host was Al Jolson, a powerful singer who is best known for his star turn in the seminal part-talkie *The Jazz Singer* (1927), although his movies are said to be but a pale shadow of his electrifying live performances. Before Bing Crosby became the most popular entertainer in every available form of media, Jolson was a major star on radio. *Shell Chateau*, in fact, was designed especially to display his talents. His guests on September 28, 1935, included Ginger Rogers and Eddie, who were then promoting their recent film, *The Gay Divorcee*. A difficult man, Jolson abruptly left the program on March 6, 1936. Despite a major dip in ratings, it remained on the air until the following year, with intermittent hosts Wallace Beery, Walter Winchell, Lionel Barrymore, Smith Ballew, Joe Cook, and Eddie.

The Chase and Sanborn Hour (NBC Radio, 1929–1948) began life as *The Chase and Sanborn Choral Orchestra*. The show hit its peak in the late thirties when the stars were Edgar Bergen and his wooden figure Charlie McCarthy. Despite the seeming folly of building a radio show around a ventriloquist act, Charlie's wisecracking personality captured the collective imagination of his countless listeners while raking in the profits for the show's sponsor, Chase and Sanborn coffee. Bergen and McCarthy began their eleven-year run on the NBC network on May 9, 1937. In the show's initial incarnation, the cast was made up of master of ceremonies Don Ameche, singers Dorothy Lamour and Nelson Eddy, and for the first sixteen weeks, comedian W.C. Fields; there was also a different guest star each week. In 1940, the regular cast, apart from Bergen and McCarthy, was dropped and the show was cut to a half-hour and retitled *The Chase and Sanborn Program*. Eddie and Constance Bennett were the guest stars on October 1, 1939.

Forecast (CBS Radio, 1940) was a summer replacement series for the long-running *Lux Radio Theatre*. It was a well-calculated gamble for the network. *Forecast*'s opener for the first of its two seasons was a half-hour variety show, followed by a half-hour drama, which was usually an adaptation of a literary work. On August 8, 1940, *Forecast* presented "Leave It to Jeeves," based on the characters of P.G. Wodehouse. In this proposed pilot for a half-hour comedy series, the main characters, the girl-chasing Bertie Wooster and his faithful valet, Jeeves, were played by Eddie and Alan Mowbray, respectively. Unfortunately, the pilot did not sell.

The Pepsodent Show (NBC Radio, 1938–1948), with its emphasis on entertaining the troops during wartime, provided reassurance to anxious American families and those serving overseas during the turbulent war years. The show was hosted by Bob Hope. Known affectionately as "Rapid Robert," Hope earned the sobriquet with his rat-a-tat delivery of topical jokes, courtesy of his team of gag writers. These speed-comedy monologues set Hope's show apart from others on the radio at the time. Hope's cast of regulars included comic Jerry Colonna, singer Frances Langford, bandleader Skinnay Ennis, and announcer Bill Goodwin. Eddie was one of Bob's guest stars on January 20, 1942.

The Screen Guild Theatre (NBC Radio, 1939–1952) was a weekly radio anthology series featuring leading Hollywood stars in adaptations of popular motion pictures. Fees that would ordinarily have been paid to the stars and studios were instead donated to the Motion Picture Relief Fund, and were used for the construction and maintenance of the Motion Picture Country House and Hospital. Originating on CBS Radio, the show was known at various times as *The Gulf Screen Guild Show*, *The Gulf Screen Guild Theatre*, *The Lady Esther Screen Guild Theatre* and *The Camel Screen Guild Players*. Regardless of how it was billed, the show was a success, lasting for fourteen seasons and 527 episodes.

Hosted by Roger Pryor, the roster of guest stars included Ethel Barrymore, Lionel Barrymore, Ingrid Bergman, Humphrey Bogart, Eddie Cantor, Gary Cooper, Bing Crosby, Bette Davis, Douglas Fairbanks Jr., Gregory Peck, Fred Astaire, and Frank Sinatra. Eddie took his turn, appearing in a dramatisation of the 1942 romantic comedy *Take a Letter Darling*, on November 9, 1942.

Front Line Theatre (AFRS program, 1943–1944) was a commercial-free presentation of the Armed Forces Radio Service (AFRS), whose mission was to help improve the morale of American troops overseas by bringing them a slice of home over their radio sets. The service produced some of the best original programming of the era, including *Command Performance*, *G.I. Journal*, and *Mail Call*. These shows were recorded at the AFRS Hollywood Studios with a live audience (usually servicemen stationed nearby) and pressed onto high-quality phonograph discs. The discs were then shipped to AFRS stations in every theatre of the War. On March 6, 1944, *Front Line Theatre* presented a heavily revised, shortened adaptation of *The Gay Divorcee*, the 1934 musical comedy starring Fred Astaire, Ginger Rogers, Eddie, and Alice Brady. The plot is essentially the same in that a popular American entertainer named Guy Holden (Frank Sinatra, taking over for Fred Astaire) and his lawyer, Egbert (Eddie, reprising his original role) are vacationing in Paris. There, Guy meets and falls for a pretty young lady named Mimi, who is in the process of divorcing her husband (Gloria DeHaven, taking over for Ginger Rogers). Mimi's Aunt Hortense, a flighty social butterfly, is delighted to again be in the company of Egbert, to whom she was once engaged (Spring Byington, standing in for Alice Brady). The script, containing Cole Porter's lyrics and surprisingly suggestive dialogue, was clearly a hit with the soldiers (and their dates) in the studio audience.

The Sealtest Village Store (CBS Radio, 1943–1945) was unique in that it was set in an imaginary tea shop in the fictional community of Smallville. The co-hosts (or proprietor and manager) were comedic actors Joan Davis and Jack Haley. Davis carried the show so capably that she went on to her own solo series in mid-1945, *Joan Davis Time*, leaving Haley (the Tin Man in *The Wizard of Oz*) to mind the store until he left in 1947. The supporting cast featured Verna Felton, Hans Conried, and Harry von Zell as the announcer. Eddie visited the tea shop on episode no. 49, which originally aired on August 24, 1944.

Command Performance (AFRS program, 1942–1949) was yet another commercial-free radio program designed exclusively for the military. Troops sent in their requests of various movie and radio stars, with such familiar names as Bob Hope, Bing Crosby, Frank Sinatra, Jack Benny, Fred Allen, and glamour girls Lucille Ball, Carole Landis, Ann Miller, and Ginger Rogers. Eddie appeared as a guest on February 8, 1945.

The Kraft Music Hall (NBC Radio, 1933–1949), also known as *The Kraft Program* and *The Kraft Musical Revue*, was initially a musical-variety show featuring orchestra leader Paul Whiteman, then known as "The King of Jazz." Whiteman remained the host until December 6, 1935. One of his protégés, Harry Lillis "Bing" Crosby, took over as master of ceremonies on January 2, 1936. Bing hosted such musical guests as Connie Boswell, Victor Borge, Mary Martin, Spike Jones, the Andrews Sisters, Nat "King" Cole, and Peggy Lee. A review in *Billboard* magazine commented, "It is a tribute to Bing Crosby … that the *Music Hall* seems to survive all talent changes—these changes simply pointing up the fact that the show is completely dependent on Crosby." For the advertising managers at Kraft Foods, it was imperative that advertising and entertainment be kept separate. For this reason, Kraft insisted that an announcer, not cast members, read its commercials. Crosby, with his easygoing manner and extensive vocabulary, was the longest-running *Kraft Music Hall* host, from 1936 through 1946, at which time he began hosting his own series, *Philco Radio Time*, which remained on the network until 1962. *Kraft Music Hall* went through a handful of short-lived hosts. Edward Everett Horton, Eddie Foy, and Frank Morgan took turns hosting from 1945 through 1947. Eddie's documented hosting dates were July 26, August 30, September 6, September 13, September 20, September 27, 1945, and February 10, 1946. He was a guest star on January 14, 1937, November 30, 1947, and March 11, 1948.

The Fred Allen Show (NBC and CBS Radio, 1932–1949) was a long-running American radio comedy program starring the brilliantly witty Fred Allen and his annoying wife, Portland Hoffa. Over the course of the program's seventeen-year run, the show's format (and title) varied. It was known, at one time or another, as *The Lint Bath Club Revue*, *The Salad Bowl*, *The Sal Hepatica Revue*, *The Hour of Smiles*, *Town Hall Tonight*, and *Texaco Star Theatre with Fred Allen*. The show's best-remembered segment is "Allen's Alley." The premise of the recurring sketch had Allen going door-to-door, visiting his ethnically diverse neighbors, such as Pansy Nussbaum (Minerva Pious), Falstaff Openshaw (Alan Reed, later the voice of Fred Flintstone), Ajax Cassidy (Peter Donald), Titus Moody (Parker Fennelly), and Senator Beauregard Claghorn (announcer Kenny Delmar). Some prominent guest stars on Allen's program included Frank Sinatra, Orson Welles, Roy Rogers, Bela Lugosi, Ed Gardner, Norman Corwin, Edgar Bergen & Charlie McCarthy, and on February 10, 1946, Eddie. The premise of the episode was "Edward Everett Horton wants to change his name."

Request Performance (CBS Radio, 1945–?), sponsored by the makers of Campbell's Soup, earned its solid reputation with a series of well-done audio plays. Eddie appeared on episode no. 10, although no date is listed in his records.

The Greatest Story Ever Told (ABC Radio, 1947–1950) was a 30-minute drama inspired by Christian writings. The episode on which Eddie appeared, "The Idle Word," was broadcast on September 26, 1948.

MGM Musical Comedy Theatre, an hour-long syndicated anthology radio program, staged audio versions of the Tiffany studio's latest movies. Eddie appeared on the episode "On an Island With You" (broadcast by electrical transcription on March 11, 1952.) Polly Bergen was the show's hostess.

The Candid Microphone (ABC Radio, 1947–1948), created by Allen Funt, was the audio precursor to the popular television show *Candid Camera*. The premise involved average citizens being recorded without their knowledge. Of course, the more embarrassing their statements are, the funnier it is to the listener (or later, the viewer). Various celebrities took part in some practical jokes. Eddie's sole appearance on the show was on January 22, 1948.

The Edward Everett Horton Collection contains documentation of several little-known radio shows on which he appeared. They include: *The Adventures of Horace Jenks* (January 17–18, year unknown); *Stage Door Canteen* (April 4, 1944); *The Edward Everett Horton Show* (Summer 1945); *American Iron and Steel: Armstrong's Theatre of Today, Presents* "Party Line," *starring Edward Everett Horton* (October 8, 1949); *Fifty and Over* (Cline Broadcasting, Australia, April 29, 1962); *The Fran Harris Show* (January 27, 1951); *General Mills Betty Crocker Radio Show* (n.d., 1949); *Get It in Writing* (July 14, 1959); *Hollywood Party* (July 1935); *KDKA Home Forum* (June 13, 1951); *KGO: ABC Home Digest*

(October 9, 1952); *Leicester Square to Broadway* (April 27, 1954); *The Crime Society* (July 11, 1948); *The Northerners* (January 4, 1954); *Old Milwaukee Beer* (September 28, 1948); *The Prize Maid* (September 28, 1948); *Betty Crocker Magazine on the Air* (July 5, 1948; April 3, 1951); *Theatre USA* (February 10, 1948). Eddie also recorded a number of radio and television commercials for The National Biscuit Company, makers of Milk Bone dog treats (February 13–14, 1950); Greenland Company, Inc., producers of Red E. Frozen Foods (October 30, 1960); Laboratory Products (August 5, 1960); and General Foods Corporation, makers of Prime Dog Food (February 2, 1966).

The Margaret Arlen Show (WCBS-TV, 1943–1952) was a morning talk show, which ran from 8:30 to 9:00 on Monday through Saturday. After station WCBS was left in the lurch by their popular female commentator, they invented Margaret Arlen, a name owned by the station. Playing this role for several years was Margaret Hollowell Hains. Eddie was her guest on April 2, 1946.

The Chevrolet Tele-Theatre (NBC-TV, 1948–1950) was an anthology series that aired on Monday nights from 8 to 8:30; it was also known as *Chevrolet on Broadway* and *The Broadway Playhouse*. Eddie appeared in two of the televised one-act plays, Frank G. Tompkins's "Sham" (1948) and James L. Daggert's "Good Night, Please" (1949). His co-star on both episodes was Natalie Schafer, who later gained sitcom immortality as Mrs. Lovey Howell on *Gilligan's Island* (1964–1967). He also appeared on *The Chevrolet Theatre Radio Show*'s presentation of "The Head Man" (January 22, 1951).

We the People (CBS-TV, 1948–1949; NBC, 1949–1953) was an early television talk show. The hosts were Dwight Weist and Dan Seymour; Eddie and Dr. Arthur Twomey were guests in an episode from the show's inaugural year.

Hollywood Screen Test (ABC-TV, 1948–1953) was a talent show with the distinction of being the first regularly scheduled series by the American Broadcast Company (ABC). The initial host was Bert Lytell; he was succeeded by Neil Hamilton. Such promising young thespians as Grace Kelly, Jack Lemmon, Pernell Roberts, and Jack Klugman gained some of their earliest exposure by appearing on the show. Eventually, the most exceptional aspirants were given the opportunity to play opposite established stars in a half-hour playlet. Eddie was one of those stars.

The original broadcast dates of his episodes include December 15, 1949; September 5, 1950; March 1, 1951; September 14, 1951; and December 29, 1952. Six episodes of *Hollywood Screen Test* have been preserved in the collection of the UCLA Motion Picture and Television Archive.

The Eyes Have It (NBC-TV, 1949–1950; CBS-TV, 1950–1952) was a game show with a complicated history. In addition to changing networks mid-run, it underwent several name changes, including *Celebrity Time*; *Goodrich Celebrity Time*; *Stop, Look, and Listen*; and *Riddle Me This*. It also had several different hosts, including Douglas Edwards, novelist Paul Gallico, and former silent film star Conrad Nagel. Conceived as a "battle of the sexes" game show, it morphed into a musical variety program. Eddie appeared on episodes nos. 7, 10, and 22. The only confirmed date is May 20, 1951.

The Ed Sullivan Show (CBS-TV, 1948–1971) is a legendary variety series, originally titled *Toast of the Town*. *The Ed Sullivan Show* is best remembered for introducing The Beatles to America in 1964, but there were innumerable other acts that captivated viewers, everything from acrobats, comedians, highlights from hit Broadway shows, operatic and popular singers, and a lovable mouse puppet named Topo Gigio. For its entire twenty-three-year run, the hour-long program's timeslot was Sunday evenings on CBS, from 8 to 9. It was hosted by newspaper columnist Ed Sullivan, whose awkward hosting style was widely (and affectionately) ridiculed. Eddie guest-hosted the show, episode nos. 11 and 47, in the second season.

The Milton Berle Show (NBC-TV, 1948–1956), also known as *Texaco Star Theatre*, was one of the first major TV broadcasts. It aired live on Tuesday nights beginning in 1948. Essentially a vaudeville show, complete with ancient jokes and comedy routines, the aggressive host (who later earned the nickname of "Mr. Television") tended to insinuate himself into many of his guest stars' acts—without their prior consent. Eddie appeared in episode no. 11 of the show's second season, in 1949. Berle often said he was responsible for more television sets being sold than anyone: "My uncle sold his; my brother sold his …"

The Ford Theatre Hour (CBS-TV, 1948–1953) was one of the many anthology programs of early television, showcasing hour-long adaptations of popular plays and films. Taped in New York City, the show's status attracted top-flight guest stars from motion pictures and the Broadway stage, all of whom appeared in condensed versions of popular plays. In his television debut in 1949, Eddie essayed the role of the insufferable Sheridan Whiteside in the George S. Kaufman / Moss Hart comedy *The Man Who Came to Dinner*.

Holiday Hotel (Star-Telegram TV Station, 1950–1951) was a single-season flop combining music and comedy. The regular cast included Don Ameche, singer Betty Brewster, The Charles Tate Dancers, and The Bernie Green Orchestra. Set in a hotel lobby, the half-hour show features Eddie as the nervous manager, constantly fretting over what the often referred to but never seen Mr. Holiday will say about the latest mishap.

The Magnavox Theatre (CBS-TV, 1950) was an anthology show comprised of seven hour-long episodes, both comedies and dramas. *Magnavox Theatre* alternated weekly with another anthology series, *Ford Theatre*. The first episodes were performed live; the later ones were filmed at the Hal Roach Studios in Culver City, California. According to CBS, episode six, an adaptation of Alexander Dumas's *The Three Musketeers*, was supposedly the first hour-long film made in Hollywood specifically for television. *Magnavox Theatre* was produced by Garth Montgomery, directed by Budd Boetticher and Richard L. Bare, and featured such guest stars as Robert Clarke, Leslie Nielsen, Marjorie Lord, Dane Clark, and Cecil Kellaway. Eddie had the title role in Ludwig Bemelmans's comedy *Father, Dear Father*, which was adapted by William Kendall Clarke. Co-starring Kim Stanley and Leora Thatcher, the teleplay aired live over CBS on November 10, 1950.

Penthouse Party (ABC-TV, 1950–1951) was a Manhattan-based talk show set in the chic penthouse apartment of television spokesmodel Betty Furness. Her guests were from the worlds of entertainment and high society. Furness's questions were non-intrusive; for instance, she routinely asked her guests about any theretofore unknown talents they possessed, like cooking, which they would then demonstrate. Eddie appeared as himself on two episodes, nos. 5 and 12, which aired respectively on November 10 and December 1, 1950.

Robert Q's Matinee (CBS-TV, 1951) was an hour-long daily musical variety program broadcast from the CBS studio in New York City. Robert Q. Lewis was a well-known television personality at the time. His cohorts on this short-lived program were the singing Clooney sisters,

Rosemary and Betty. Eddie was a guest on one of the show's thirty-one episodes.

Showtime, U.S.A. (ABC-TV, 1950–1951) was a talk / variety show bearing the tag line, "The Who's Who of Show Business." It was hosted by Victor Freedley, president of the American National Theatre Company. As a result, the show featured many luminaries from the Broadway stage, including Helen Hayes (revered as The First Lady of the American Stage), Gertrude Lawrence, and playwright Moss Hart. There were entertainers from the music world as well, such as clarinetist Benny Goodman and jazz singer Sarah Vaughan; movie actors Henry Fonda, Lee Tracy, Jack Carson, Thomas Mitchell, and the great silent film comedian Buster Keaton performing his classic pantomime skit, "A Day in the Park." Eddie was a guest on two episodes, nos. 8 and 25.

General Electric Guest House (CBS-TV, 1951) was yet another short-lived talk show featuring movie actors as themselves. Eddie took his turn as a guest on no. 8 of the program's measly nine episodes. The host was Garry Moore's second banana Durward Kirby. There is a connection between Kirby and Eddie regarding *The Rocky and Bullwinkle Show*. In 1961, when Eddie was lending his distinctive voice to the show's "Fractured Fairy Tales," Kirby threatened to file a suit against Jay Ward Productions for a storyline involving the elusive Kirwood Derby.

The James Melton Show (NBC-TV, 1951–1952) was initially a sitcom depicting the behind-the-scenes machinations of a television variety show. This concept would be implemented far more effectively by Jack Benny, Dick Van Dyke, and even later by Garry Shandling. The host, veteran broadcaster James Melton, was shown interacting with his regular cast, which included a vaudeville comedy team called the Wiere Brothers, opera singer Dorothy Warenskjold, and comedienne Vera Vague, whose actual name was Barbara Jo Allen. When the ratings sank, the producers changed the format, transforming it into a standard variety show. The Wiere Brothers were dropped, only to be replaced by the diminutive Billy Barty. After sixty-five unimpressive episodes, two of which featured Eddie, *The James Melton Show* was replaced by another Ford Motor Company–sponsored program, *Ford Television Theatre*, which lasted from 1952 to 1956.

Where Was I? (DuMont TV, 1952–1953) was an American panel show which aired on the DuMont Television Network Tuesdays at 9 p.m. eastern time from September 2, 1952, to October 6, 1953. The panelists' objective was to guess a location based on clues and photos. Hosts included Dan Seymour, Ken Roberts, and John Reed King; the panelists were Bill Cullen, Nancy Guild, Virginia Graham, Skitch Henderson—and on at least one occasion, Eddie. Like the majority of DuMont's programs, no episodes of *Where Was I?* are known to exist.

I Love Lucy (CBS-TV, 1951–1957) There are many hilarious episodes of *I Love Lucy*, one being "Lucy Plays Cupid," the series' fifteenth episode, which was filmed on December 13, 1951, and made its network debut on January 21, 1952. The cast includes Lucille Ball, Desi Arnaz, Bea Benaderet (the original choice to play Ethel Mertz), and Eddie. The storyline is a variation on "Valentine's Day," an episode of the CBS Radio program *My Favorite Husband*, starring Lucille Ball and Richard Denning.

Broadway Television Theatre (WOR-TV, 1952–1954) was an hour-long anthology series, performed live over WOR-TV in New York City; kinescopes were then made available for syndication. Eddie starred in the following adaptations: "The Night-Cap" (1952); "Whistling in the Dark" (1953); and "Your Uncle Dudley" (also 1953). In the 1931 movie version of *The Front Page*, Eddie portrayed the prissy columnist Ray V. Bensinger; in the 1953 *Broadway Television Theatre* version he took on a very different role, that of the ruthless editor Walter Burns. Jack Gould, television critic for the *New York Times*, said, "Mr. Horton imparts the stylized fussiness and gentleness that practically have become his trademark." He also called the interpretation "a mistake."

Medallion Theatre (CBS-TV, 1953–1954), also known as *Chrysler Medallion Theatre*, was another anthology series, a shorter one, running a mere 30 minutes per episode. Vintage stories were adapted by such top writers as Rod Serling and Robert Armstrong, and starred both rising and established names as Jack Lemmon, Helen Hayes, Zachary Scott, Rod Steiger, Claude Rains, and Janet Gaynor. Eddie portrayed the cowardly Sir Simon de Canterville in an adaptation of Oscar Wilde's humorous short story *The Canterville Ghost*. The episode's airdate was November 21, 1953.

The Philco Television Playhouse (NBC-TV, 1948–1955), briefly known as *Repertory Theatre* and *Arena Theatre*, was an anthology program that is credited as one of the reasons shows from that period are often referred to collectively as "The Golden Age of Television." Throughout its celebrated seven-season run, the Philco-sponsored program received eight Emmys and a Peabody Award. Among its many notable guest stars was Eddie, who performed in the live presentation of "The Velvet Mitten."

The Name's the Same (ABC-TV, 1951–1955) was a game show from the production team of Mark Goodson & Bill Todman. Robert Q. Lewis was the host, and the panelists were comedian Jerry Lester, socialite Joan Alexander, and composer Meredith Willson. The premise of the game was for the panelists to guess what person the visiting star wanted to be. In Eddie's case, he wanted to be Mr. America. Not surprisingly, no one guessed it. That particular episode aired on November 17, 1955.

On Your Way (DuMont TV, 1953–1954; ABC, January–April 1954) was initially a travel-oriented game show, hosted by the bow-tie-wearing Bud Collyer. At ABC, the host was John Reed King, who was soon joined by Kathy Godfrey. Pairs of everyday contestants who correctly answered as many questions as possible were rewarded with a bus trip to their preferred destination. Certain winners were given the option of flying, which was then considered a rare privilege. Eddie was a special guest on season one, episode eight, on October 28, 1953.

Four Star Revue (NBC-TV, 1950–1953), also known as *All Star Revue*, was an hour-long weekly variety show. The original set of revolving hosts were Ed Wynn, Danny Thomas, Jack Carson, and Jimmy Durante, hence the title *Four Star Revue*. Other hosts, including Bob Hope and Martha Raye, took over in subsequent seasons. With production costs reaching $50,000 per episode, it was considered the second-most expensive program on network television; the most expensive show was the similarly formatted *Colgate Comedy Hour*. Despite the expenditure, *Four Star Revue* never became a ratings juggernaut. The episode (date unknown) to feature Eddie was hosted by Phil Harris and co-starred Ann Sheridan, Jim Backus, Eartha Kitt, Red Nichols & His Five Pennies, and Les Brown and His Band of Renown.

Omnibus (CBS-TV, 1952–1957; NBC-TV, 1957–1961) was one of the most prestigious television programs of its time. Created by the Ford Foundation, the show's intent was to raise the education level of the American public. Scheduled at the unlikely time slot of 4 p.m. EST, on Sundays, the 90-minute variety show was a massive hit. At its peak in 1957, it drew an estimated viewership of 5.7 million. Those watching were treated to live performances by some of the country's most prominent entertainers, interviews with public figures, and original plays. Eddie narrated one such play, James Thurber's *The Remarkable Case of Mr. Bruhl*.

The Colgate Comedy Hour (NBC-TV, 1950–1955), alternately known as *Colgate Summer Comedy Hour* and *Colgate Variety Hour*, was a hugely popular program, airing live on Sunday evenings at 8 p.m. EST. Like its less successful sister series, *Four Star Revue*, *Colgate Comedy Hour* featured revolving hosts, in this case Eddie Cantor, Dean Martin & Jerry Lewis, and Bud Abbott & Lou Costello. On October 24, 1954, Eddie co-starred with Anna Maria Alberghetti, Illona Massey, Harpo Marx, and Jerry Colona in a truncated version of the Howard Dietz–Arthur Schwartz 1934 Broadway show *Revenge with Music*.

The Best of Broadway (CBS-TV, 1954–1955) was an anthology series with a short but memorable run of only nine episodes. One of its hour-long (including commercials), abridged productions was Joseph Kesselring's timeless farce, *Arsenic and Old Lace*, which was presented live and in color on January 5, 1955. Directed by Herbert B. Swope, Jr., the program's cast includes Orson Bean as Mortimer Brewster; Helen Hayes and Billie Burke as Mortimer's seemingly harmless spinster aunts, Abby and Martha Brewster; and Eddie, reprising his role from the 1944 film as Mr. Witherspoon, the agreeable owner of Happy Dale sanitarium. Two other refugees from the movie version are John Alexander as Teddy "Roosevelt" Brewster, and Peter Lorre as the murderous Dr. Einstein. This time around, Boris Karloff, who was portraying Jonathan Brewster in the Broadway show when the film was shot in 1941, appears in the role that routinely mentions his real name, as in "He said I look like Boris Karloff!" Jonathan most assuredly does not take this as a compliment. A kinescope of the episode has survived but is not currently available for home viewing.

Max Liebman Presents (NBC-TV, 1954–1956) was a 90-minute musical variety special (then known as a *spectacular*) that appeared monthly on either Saturday or Sunday evenings. Liebman produced and directed the lavish shows, one being *The Merry Widow*, the 1905 operetta by the Austro-Hungarian composer Franz Lehár. The libretto, by Victor Leon and Leo Stein, is based on Henri Meilhac's 1861 comedy play, *L'attaché d'ambassade* (*The Embassy Attaché*). The story concerns a wealthy but discontented widow who is planning to relocate. Determined to keep the widow (and especially her substantial holdings) within their principality, the citizens join forces to find her a husband. Eddie had played Ambassador Popoff in the 1934 movie version of *The Merry Widow*; in this instance, he was Baron Zelta. Although it is a musical, Eddie made it clear to the producers beforehand that he would not (because he could not) sing.

Damon Runyon Theatre (CBS-TV, 1955–1956), initially a radio program in the late forties, was a television series in which Damon Runyon's short stories were enacted. Runyon's world was Broadway in the era of Prohibition. The characters, most of whom are gangsters, have names like Harry the Horse and Sam the Gonoph. They speak in a distinctive manner: in the present tense and without contractions, e.g., "I long ago come to the conclusion that life is six to five against." Runyon and his characters have been immortalized by Frank Loesser's Broadway musical-comedy *Guys and Dolls*. One of the television show's thirty-nine episodes is "A Light in France," in which Eddie plays Thaddeus. It originally aired on July 30, 1955.

Shower of Stars (CBS-TV, 1954–1958), also known as *Chrysler's Shower of Stars*, was an anthology series broadcast live and in color for four successful seasons. The show was critically acclaimed for its hourlong presentations of both straight plays and rousing musical-comedies. Many Hollywood stars took part in the productions, including Fredric March, Van Johnson, Betty Grable, and especially Jack Benny, who was the show's most frequent guest star. Eddie played Ed Hoffman in "Time Out for Ginger." William Lundigan was the show's host.

I've Got a Secret (CBS-TV, 1952–1967) was a game show produced by Mark Goodson & Bill Todman and hosted by Garry Moore. The premise of the show is that a special guest—Eddie, for instance—reveals a secret to the host, after which a panel of celebrities ask questions of the guest in hopes of learning what that secret is. Unfortunately, this particular episode (no. 118), which originally aired on January 12, 1955, is not readily available, so we don't know *what* Eddie's secret was.

The Stork Club (UHF, 1950–1955) was a unique concept, if nothing else. A fifteen-minute program aired on a UHF channel, it was shot in a specially constructed room, outfitted with tables and chairs, at the famous Stork Club, located at 3 East 53rd Street in New York City. The club's owner, Sherman Billingsley, was the host. He would roam from table to table and interact with his celebrity guests, including Betty Clooney, The Satisfiers, Frank Fontaine, Joe E. Howard, Edie Adams, Morey Amsterdam, and on one episode during 1955, Eddie.

General Electric Theatre (NBC-TV, 1953–1962) was an anthology series hosted by Ronald Reagan. Each weekly half-hour program presented a different playlet and a different cast. Appearing on the show were many stars from Hollywood's Golden Age (Ronald Colman, Joan Crawford, Bette Davis, Greer Garson, Myrna Loy). There were also stars on the rise (James Dean, Walter Matthau, Gena Rowlands, Natalie Wood). These are but a handful of the hundreds of guest stars who graced the small screen during the show's nine-year run. Eddie played the title role in "The Muse and Mr. Parkinson," produced by Desilu (Lucille Ball and Desi Arnaz), directed by Don Medford, with a screenplay by Miriam Balf (based on a story by James B. Gidney). Eddie plays a prosaic individual who suddenly discovers his inner poet. The supporting players are Vera Vague and Russell Hicks. The episode originally aired on January 26, 1956.

Saturday Spectacular: **"Manhattan Tower"** (NBC-TV, October 27, 1956) was a dramatisation of composer / arranger Gordon Jenkins's suite "Manhattan Tower," a two-disc 78 rpm Decca Records album that had remained on the bestseller list for a decade. In 1956, Jenkins co-produced (with Elliott Lewis) one of the first made-for-television movies, based on his composition; he also wrote the book and lyrics, and staged the production with director Boris Sagal. "Manhattan Tower" tells the romantic story of a young man named Steven (Peter Marshall), who travels to New York City, where he meets a girl named Julie (Helen O'Connell); together, they take a large bite out of the Big Apple. Eddie plays a character named Noah. Other supporting cast members include Phil Harris, Hans Conried, Tommy Farrell, Cesar Romero, and Ethel Waters.

The Linkletter Show (CBS-TV, 1952–1970), originally titled *House Party*, was a popular daytime variety show. The genial host, Art Linkletter, developed a reputation as an ideal interviewer of children, best exemplified by his 1959–1967 television series *Kids Say the Darndest Things*. But Linkletter was every bit as proficient at interviewing adults, particularly celebrities like Eddie, who appeared in one episode of *House Party* on March 6, 1956.

The Helen O'Connell Show (NBC-TV, 1956-1957) was a fifteen-minute program that aired twice weekly on NBC. Helen O'Connell was well known for her vocal recordings with the Jimmy Dorsey Band in the early 1940s, including "Tangerine," "Green Eyes," and "Brazil." At the time of her eponymous program, she was also the co-host (with Dave Garroway) on NBC's *The Today Show*, from 1956 to 1958). Eddie was a guest on *The Helen O'Connell Show* in 1956.

Matinee Theatre (NBC-TV, 1955–1958) was a true phenomenon in the annals of television. It was a heavily promoted anthology series that aired daily, with a viewing audience of seven million! Of the series' 576 episodes, all but a handful were broadcast live. It was also in color— never mind that only a small percentage of the public owned color sets. Eddie was but one of the countless Hollywood stars to take part in multiple productions. His episodes were entitled "The Egoist" (1956); "Mr. Pim Passes By" (1957); "Dandy Dick" (1958); and "Town in Turmoil" (also 1958).

Playhouse 90 (CBS-TV, 1956–1960) set the standard for all of the many anthology series that populated the airwaves during the 1950s. No other program was as ambitious or possessed more top talent both behind, and in front of, the camera. Some of the most heralded movie directors of the 1960s and '70s cut their teeth helming the ninety-minute episodes. The best writers imagined bold new stories as well as adapting the classics. Stage and screen veterans, some of whose careers dated back to the silent era, chanced working without a net, performing live before an increasingly discerning audience of millions. Even more daring were the less-experienced actors whose ambition was to one day rule the screen. The sheer number of *Playhouse 90*'s guest stars is staggering. In the midst of that list is Eddie, who starred in the teleplay, "Three Men on a Horse," as Mr. Carver. The technology that determined the quality of transmission improved significantly during the show's four-season run; this made it possible to preserve stunning recordings of such episodes as The "Days of Wine and Roses," "Judgment at Nuremberg," and "Requiem for a Heavyweight." These will no doubt be studied, and appreciated, by future generations.

The Lux Show (NBC-TV, 1957–1958) was a variety program hosted by the marvelous singer Rosemary Clooney, who frequently performed with Bing Crosby. The show only stayed on the air for one season, which consisted of thirty-six episodes. Eddie was the hostess's special guest on the third episode, which aired on October 10, 1957. Miss Clooney (at that time she was Mrs. Jose Ferrer) produced the show through The Maysville Corporation, named for her birthplace of Maysville, Kentucky.

December Bride (CBS-TV, 1954–1959) is a sitcom that was adapted from the 1952–1953 network radio series of the same name. It stars Spring Byington as Lily Ruskin, a feisty widow who would consider remarrying if the right man came along. The supporting cast includes Frances Rafferty as Lily's daughter, Ruth Henshaw; character actress Verna Felton as Lily's close friend Hilda Crocker; Dean Miller as Ruth's husband, Matt Henshaw (in an uncharacteristic twist on the old joke, Matt and his mother-in-law get along famously); and Harry Morgan as Pete Porter, Lily's unhappily married next-door neighbor. Due to its fortuitous time slot, following the enormously popular *I Love Lucy*, *December Bride* had an impressive rating through most of its run. Incidentally, the show's creator and head writer, Parker Levy, owned 50 percent of the property, while Desilu and CBS each owned 25 percent. Eddie guest-starred in the episode "The Butler Show," which aired on December 16, 1957.

The Steve Allen Plymouth Show (NBC-TV, 1956–1960), "brought to you in living color on NBC," is one of the many programs hosted by the multi-talented Steve Allen during his long career in television; he was the author of more than fifty books, a game show host and panelist, a comedian, an actor (*The Benny Goodman Story*), a pianist, a singer, and a prolific songwriter (8,500 songs by his own count), although his only well-known song is "This Could Be the Start of Something Big." According to one of his acolytes, David Letterman, Allen all-but-single-handedly created the late-night talk show format. He was even the co-creator and first host of NBC's *The Tonight Show*. Eddie appeared as a guest on the Plymouth show on November 17, 1957, along with Marie McDonald, Walter Chiari, Ferlin Husky, and The King Sisters.

Gerald McBoing-Boing (CBS-TV, 1956–1957), also known as *The Boing-Boing Show*, was apparently the first cartoon to be regularly scheduled in prime time. Although well received by the public, the program, narrated by radio announcer Bill Goodwin, was deemed too expensive to produce, severely limiting its run to three months. Gerald McBoing-Boing is a cutely drawn little boy who communicates exclusively through sound effects. The limited, minimalist animation, known as Abstract Modernism, was a bold, stylistic alternative to the strictly realistic approach taken by Walt Disney. United Productions of America, better known as UPA, produced theatrical and television cartoons for Columbia Pictures and its subsidiary, Screen Gems, the most famous example being *The Nearsighted Mr. Magoo*. The simple line drawings, suggested backgrounds, jazz music, and use of vivid color (although the television episodes were broadcast in black and white) became emblematic of the late fifties and early sixties "Beat" culture. A one-off experiment, "Edward Everett Horton Tells a Story: 'The Unenchanted Princess,'" is a three-minute fairy tale with a moral: Do not judge others by their physical appearance. It was but one of the December 16, 1956, episode's segments, the others being Dusty of the Circus in "The Five-Cent Nickle," and "Be Quiet, Kind, and Gentle." Each of these stories was written by Dr. Seuss, Theodor Geisel's pseudonym. This was the precursor to Horton's regular role as the narrator of "Fractured Fairy Tales," a staple of *The Rocky and Bullwinkle Show*. About which, *much* more anon.

The Red Skelton Hour (CBS-TV, 1951–1971) served as a showcase for Richard "Red" Skelton, clown and pantomimist. This family-friendly, comedy-themed variety show was warmly welcomed into America's collective living room for twenty consecutive years. Eddie appears in several episodes, playing opposite Skelton in the host's Freddie the Freeloader sketches. In two sketches from 1957, "Freddie's Surprise Party" and "Freddie's Thanksgiving," Eddie portrays Smitty, a hobo character. In a 1959 sketch, "Munson's Red Herring or Freddie and the Spies," he is Sir Alfred Hangeron. And he is back with Freddy, this time as a character called Muggsy, in two sketches from 1960: "Freddie in Las Vegas" and "Freddie, Willing, and Able."

The Ford Show Starring Tennessee Ernie Ford (NBC-TV, 1956–1961) was named, *not* for the host, but for the show's sponsor, the Ford Motor Company. Ernie Ford was a singer ("Sixteen Tons" was his big hit) and a comedian of the cornpone variety; for instance, he referred to himself as "The Old Pea Picker." This rustic approach was antithetical to Eddie's, which may be why he was selected as a guest on the February 20, 1958, episode.

The George Gobel Show (NBC-TV, 1954–1960) was a half-hour variety program, hosted by a comedian who referred to himself as "Lonesome George." TV fans of a certain age may remember him best as a hesitant older man seated in the lower-right-hand cubicle on the first incarnation of *The Hollywood Squares* game show. But when Gobel broke onto the scene, he was considered fresh and innovative. An anti-show business type, he wore his hair in a brush cut. His delivery was awkward and unpolished, and his humor was self-deprecating (he once remarked that life was a tuxedo, and he was a pair of brown shoes). His favorite topic, apparently, was his wife, "Spooky Old Alice," who was based on his real-life wife; she was portrayed in various skits by actress Jeff Donnell. There was a resident vocalist, Peggy "I've Come a Long Way from Saint Louie" King, and John Scott Trotter was the show's musical director. Gobel favored certain guests, inviting them back repeatedly. Singer Eddie Fisher, for instance, was on a total of seventeen times. Another Eddie—Edward Everett Horton—made three guest appearances: on December 11, 1954; November 17, 1956; and January 3, 1960.

Pillsbury Advertising Campaign (1957). According to a press release in Eddie's collection, he was hired by the Pillsbury company in 1957 to be their television spokesman. If indeed the campaign began, it obviously did not catch on with the viewing public.

The Tonight Show Starring Jack Paar (NBC-TV, 1957–1962) was a must-watch late-night program in its time, primarily due to the emotional volatility of its thin-skinned host. Eddie was Paar's guest on three episodes in 1959 and one in 1960.

The Real McCoys (ABC-TV, 1957–1962; CBS-TV, 1962–1963) was a rural sitcom featuring the McCoys, a close-knit family from the Appalachian Mountains of West Virginia, who inherit a farm in Southern California. The family patriarch is Grandpa Amos (three-time-Oscar-winning character actor Walter Brennan); Amos's grandson is Luke (Richard Crenna); Luke's wife is Kate (Kathleen Nolan); Luke's younger brother, also named Luke, goes by the moniker Little Luke (Michael Winkelman); their teenaged sister Tallahassee, known as Hassie (Lydia Reed); and their Mexican farmhand, Pepina Garcia (Tony Martinez). Eddie appears in one of the show's 225 episodes, "Teenage Wedding" (October 3, 1960). The IMDb synopsis reads: "When sixteen-year-old Hassie and her boyfriend Jerry (Barry McGuire) impetuously announce their engagement, Grandpa's apparent approval causes much consternation among Luke, Kate, and Jerry's fastidious grandfather J. Luther Medwick (Edward Everett Horton)."

The Adventures of Rocky and Bullwinkle (ABC-TV, 1959–1961; NBC-TV, 1961–1964), known at various times as *Rocky and His Friends, The*

Bullwinkle Show, *The Rocky and Bullwinkle Show*, *The Adventures of Bullwinkle and Rocky*, and *Bullwinkle's Moose-O-Rama*, is Jay Ward's hilariously wacky Cold War cartoon series. The three main actors supplying the characters' voices are Daws Butler, Bill Scott, and June Foray. Each episode is superbly narrated—or, as the opening title card reads, "'Fractured Fairy Tales,' As Told by Edward Everett Horton." Keith Scott, author of *The Moose That Roared*, the definitive study of this idiosyncratic cartoon, has graciously allowed us to reprint his evocative synopses for each of the ninety-one episodes.

Goldilocks—Goldilocks learns a valuable lesson about misusing people's property.

Jack and the Beanstalk (Title onscreen: *Fee Fi Fo Fum*)—A slow-witted giant can't remember how to say, "Fee Fi Fo Fum," thus allowing Jack to escape.

Rapunzel—Rapunzel and a charming prince foil a wicked witch.

Puss in Boots—A clever cat accomplishes the impossible: His master, The Marquis, finally takes a bath.

The Enchanted Fish—A poor fisherman meets a mermaid who grants wishes, but his greedy wife makes trouble.

The Little Tailor—The king offers his daughter's hand in marriage to a tailor, who must first kill a unicorn in the woods.

Rumpelstiltskin—PR man Rumpelstiltskin becomes Gladys's agent, in exchange for her first child.

The Princess and the Pea—A greedy court jester disguises his friend Clyde as a missing princess.

Beauty and the Beast—A hideous beast must get kissed by a beauty if he is to become handsome.

Sweet Little Beet—The invisible Prince Fascinato wants a bride; Beet and her two ugly sisters audition.

Dick Whittington—In London, a sharp-talking cat becomes ambitious Dick Whittington's manager.

Tom Thumb—Miniscule Tom forms a juvenile delinquent gang and is subsequently psychoanalyzed. (This is the only episode in which Eddie has a minor role in addition to his narration duties; as Citizen no. 4, he says just three words: "The King's fault!")

The Elves and the Shoemaker—A depressed artist wants to be a shoemaker like his idol Hermann Cappuccino, but first he must "suffer."

Cinderella—Bankrupt Prince Fascinato needs to marry an heiress but instead meets Cinderella, who is selling pots and pans on commission for the Good Fairy.

Snow White—A sarcastic Magic Mirror tells the Wicked Queen about Snow White, but first the Queen must join the Seven Dwarves' Health Club.

Sir Galahad—Young Sir wants to be a knight over the objections of his father, who wants the boy to follow him into the clown biz.

King Midas—Greedy Midas craves the love of his subjects—so he can tax them even more.

Pinocchio—Pinocchio wants to be brave so he can become a real boy, but "kindly" old Geppetto gets him a TV show, begging him to "stay wood."

Little Red Riding Hood—Red, who sells riding hoods in Hollywood, needs a wolf skin and snares naïve Walter Wolf, who must dispose of his grandma.

Sleeping Beauty—A prince realizes he can make money out of Sleeping Beauty; instead of awakening her, he markets her comatose form by building a theme park called Sleeping Beauty-land.

Hansel and Gretel—Hansel and Gretel find the Witch's gingerbread house, but the Witch turns the boy into an aardvark.

Cinderella Returns—After embarrassing herself by trying to snag Prince Edgar the Mild, Cinderella discovers he's already married to her fairy godmother, Bertie.

Snow White, Incorporated—A tale of corporate climbers: the wicked queen is head of the Witchpak; Snow runs Consolidated Dwarfs, an agency for showbiz midgets.

Jack and the Beanstalk—When Jack joins baseball club the Boston Beavers they win all their games.

The Pied Piper—A musician who rids the kingdom of mice is asked by the king to exterminate his mother-in-law, but piper and victim fall in love.

Puss in Boots no. 2—A cunning cat grants three wishes to a gullible young man.

Leaping Beauty—A witch turns the popular Leaping Beauty into a crashing bore, and she is banished to the forest.

Tom Thumb no. 2 (also called *Tiny Tom*)—A woodchopper tries in vain to get his microscopic son to grow. The lad finally leaves to seek a bride.

Slipping Beauty—A witch forgets her appointment to cast a sleeping spell on a girl who is meant to be awakened by a prince.

Aladdin's Lamp—Aladdin's lamp shop is a front for a gambling joint, but the king demands a lamp.

Rumpelstiltskin Returns—A contest-crazy girl is helped by Rumpelstiltskin, who wants her child—until he realizes the boy is a lummox.

The Enchanted Fish (title on-screen: *The Magic Fish*)—A poor chimney sweep buys a supposedly magic fish, then suffers nothing but bad luck.

The Frog Prince—An oversupply of witches results in a fight over a frog; the frog has so many spells cast on him he angrily confronts the witches' union.

The Pied Piper no. 2—A mute man blows pies from his pipe, until his tempting tobacco-leaf pie causes all who eat it to disappear.

Prince Darling—A good fairy turns a wicked boy into a "horrid kind of thing," until he learns to be kind.

The Ugly Duckling—A talented but ugly duck wants to be a movie star and undergoes plastic surgery.

Son of Rumpelstiltskin—To get her child back, a princess must guess a funny little man's name, but even *he's* forgotten it.

Beauty and Her Beast—An ugly girl becomes beautiful every time she sits on her mule.

The Golden Goose—A dullard is rewarded with a golden goose; but everyone in the kingdom becomes stuck to the bird.

The Enchanted Frog—Philbert Frog grows to human size and thinks he's an enchanted prince.

The Goose and the Golden Egg—A goose pretends to lay a golden egg in order to avoid being cooked, but when war breaks out she discovers she really can lay golden ones.

Robin Hoods Anonymous—A wolf is trying to "kick the riding hood" habit, but Red and her equally violent grandma don't believe him.

The Shoemaker and the Elves no. 2—A shoemaker is ordered by the king to stop making shoes, but two overzealous elves try to help him.

Speeding Beauty—A beauty is changed into a horse and a prince decides to race her. But she constantly falls asleep short of the finish line.

The Three Little Pigs—Henry Q. Wolf tries courting the three wealthy Pigg sisters, but his greed goes unrewarded.

Goldilocks and the Three Bears—Goldie opens her winter resort in summer, and the Three Bears take over in her absence.

Son of Beauty and the Beast—Prince Fletcher, son of the famous beast, can't follow in his father's footsteps; he decides to get a book written about his life.

Androcles and the Lion—Androcles pulls a thorn from the paw of a Bert Lahr-type lion; years later they meet again.

The Fisherman and His Wife—A struggling fisherman is granted three wishes by a talking fish, but the man and his wife soon lose everything.

The Goblins—The goblins move into a mountain and terrorize the populace, then abduct Irene, the King's daughter.

Snow White Meets Rapunzel—A witch cuts off Rapunzel's hair so that she can't let it down; the prince must learn how to fly in order to reach her.

The Little Princess—When a little princess grows to giant size, the heavily taxed citizens advertise for a suitor in order to marry her off.

Thom Tum—Thom Tum is a tiny lad until a good fairy turns him into a giant with a ravenous appetite.

Slow White and Nose Red—A miller has two daughters, whose love for the forest animals is almost their father's undoing.

Prince Hyacinth and the Dear Little Princess—Fairy 53 helps poor King Dom, whose son has a nose like a casaba melon.

The Giant and the Beanstalk—A sequel to "Jack and the Beanstalk," twenty years later. Jack is wealthy from his golden harp business.

The Enchanted Fly—An enchanted fly grants the king's every wish; finally the king becomes a fly (until he meets a certain tailor).

Felicia and the Pot of Pinks—A woodcutter leaves a chicken to his son Bruno, and a pot of pinks to his daughter Felicia.

Hans Klinker—Hans is a born musician; this story involves a pair of silver skates and the Zuyder Zee race.

The Witch's Broom—Grizelda, Witch of the Year, falls hopelessly in love with a handsome prince.

Son of King Midas—Midas's son finds it impossible to follow in his father's footsteps.

The Magic Chicken—The path to the hand of a merchant's daughter includes a magic chicken, golden axes, and an ogre.

Aladdin and His Lamp—Aladdin must look for a new lamp when his old one is stolen by an evil sorcerer.

The Enchanted Gnat—A tinker has three sons, each of whom is granted a magic wish; the son named Nathaniel is a real menace.

Milo and the Thirteen Helmets—At Dragon U, poor Milo the Dragon has been a senior for forty years and still hasn't graduated.

The Prince and the Popper—In the town of Tootsie Lavendur, a popper overthrows an evil prince, saving the kingdom's champagne.

Booty and the Beast—Handsome Alden Farquhar, sick of being pursued by all the beautiful maidens, wants to be turned into a beast.

Little Fred Riding Hood—Little Fred Riding Hood is granted a wish after helping two strange little people.

Goldilocks and the Three Bears—Goldilocks, a home economist, helps the three bears move into an apartment.

The Ugly Almond Duckling—An ugly duck from the Yangtze River in China takes up music and tours as a bandleader.

John's Ogre Wife—Prince John and Princess Tinsel are deliriously happy until mean witch Grumpira turns Tinsel into an ogre.

The Absent-Minded King—A forgetful king wants to find a bride, but to do so he must remember a magic word; he must also face a giant, some vicious thorns, and a witch.

The Mysterious Castle—In the castle of Easy Pickins, man of the year Schuyler Sugg must determine who dwells in a spooky black castle.

The Little Tinker—A tinker confronts a giant troll who wants his "People Pot" repaired.

Tale of a Frog—Julius Frog is unhappy, believing "people have more fun than frogs." But after his fairy frogmother turns him into a "people," he's not so sure.

The Teeth of Baghdad—A set of false teeth provides the clue to the identity of the rightful ruler of Baghdad.

The Little Man in the Pub—A poor man with the unfortunate name Delicia finally scrapes up some money but ends up with mother-in-law problems.

Red White—A duke and a fair maiden are both endowed with hair that's "redder than red."

Cutie and the Beast—Cutie tries to turn a beast into a prince, but the tables are eventually turned.

The Flying Carpet—A rug seller tells the king that a carpet with a hole in it is really a magic carpet that can fly.

The Count and the Bird—A gullible count is a dupe for the local charlatans; he finds a bird that lays eggs containing gold coins but loses his fortune on a wager.

The Tale of a King—Nothing-Ham is a kingdom where nothing ever happens, so the king decides to make up a "keen story" about his daughter.

Sweeping Beauty—A frumpish castle maid discovers that a series of catnaps will make her beautiful.

The Wishing Hat—A boy named Booby helps a Brownie and is rewarded with a red wishing hat; he finally turns into an owl.

Son of Snow White—Joe White, handsome son of Snow White, faces his opponent, a handsome prince.

Jack B. Nimble—A sly caretaker is banished; he enters into a prosperous magic fountain business.

Potter's Luck—A potter's boiling temper does him in when he is used as a guinea pig by a group of witches.

The Magic Lychee Nut—A young man asks his honorable father's permission to marry; an old man gives him some magic lychee nuts.

The King and the Witch—A king is tricked into marrying an ugly witch but is saved by a magic wishbone.

The Seven Chickens—A prince meets the king's six beautiful daughters, who have all been changed into chickens—the seventh chicken is a witch.

A Youth Who Set Out to Learn What Fear Was—A young boy named Swinburne knows no fear, but he must learn how to shudder.

Dennis the Menace (CBS-TV, 1959–1963) is a live-action sitcom based on Hank Ketcham's comic strip character that was based on his own five-year-old son Dennis. It stars Jay North as Dennis (the menace) Mitchell; Herbert Anderson and Gloria Henry play Dennis's overwhelmed parents, Henry and Alice; Joseph Kearns is the Mitchells' harassed next-door neighbor, Mr. George Wilson; Sylvia Field is George's more tolerant wife, Martha; Jeannie Russell and Billy Booth are Dennis's friends, Margaret Wade and Tommy Anderson; Gale Gordon is Mr. John Wilson, the late George's brother; and Sara Seegar is John's wife, Eloise. Eddie portrays the Wilson Brothers' elderly uncle Ned Matthews in three episodes: "Mr. Wilson's Uncle" (February 18, 1962); "Dennis's Lovesick Friend" (May 20, 1962); and "My Uncle Ned" (January 13, 1963).

Here's Hollywood (NBC-TV, 1960–1962) was a daily show in which various television personalities (Dean Miller, Helen O'Connell, Jack Linkletter, and Joanne Jordan) interviewed movie actors, often in their homes. Eddie was the subject of back-to-back episodes, nos. 210 and 212, in 1961.

Our Man Higgins (ABC-TV, 1962–1963) was a 30-minute sitcom starring Stanley Holloway in the title role of an English butler. Higgins is inherited by the MacRoberts household, an American family living in the suburbs. Eddie portrays Rawley in the May 8, 1963, episode "Who's on First?"

Saints and Sinners (NBC-TV, 1962–1963) is purported to have been an excellent hour-long drama. It began life as "Savage Sunday," an episode of *The Dick Powell Theatre* in 1961. *Saints and Sinners* takes place at a newspaper plant in New York City. Nick Adams plays Nick Alexander, an investigative reporter with no family ties, who does whatever it takes to get his story. Despite being a critical success, the show failed to complete even a single season due to network politics and poor scheduling.

Joining the many fine character actors then working in television, Eddie played a Mr. Hollister in the episode "A Night of Horns and Bells," which aired on Christmas Eve, 1962.

Mr. Smith Goes to Washington (ABC-TV, 1962–1963) has former *Davey Crockett* (and future *Daniel Boone*) star Fess Parker as Eugene Smith, an idealistic young senator in this adaptation of the Frank Capra–directed 1939 film of the same name. Eddie portrays Senator Crabtree in the episode "The Senator Baits a Hook," which aired on November 24, 1962.

Fractured Flickers (Syndicated, 1963–1964) is a live-action, half-hour comedy series produced by Jay Ward and Bill Scott, who were also responsible for "Fractured Fairy Tales." Joining forces with the notorious film pirate Raymond Rohauer, they recut prints of silent comedies and dramas from the 1920s, adding wacky dialogue, music, and sound effects. The resulting parodies are, at best, uneven. Hans Conried, portraying the cynical host, introduces the clips and conducts pseudo interviews with television actors and pop singers. Eddie was the only such guest who had actually starred in silent films. That particular episode originally aired on September 5, 1963.

The Tonight Show Starring Johnny Carson (NBC-TV, 1962–1992) will likely remain the definitive version of that television staple. In the first decade of Johnny Carson's rein, *The Tonight Show* was set in New York City; he didn't relocate to "beautiful downtown Burbank" in NBC's West Coast Studio One until 1972, taking with him his faithful announcer Ed McMahon (whose introduction "Heeeeeeeeeeeeeer's Johnny!" never varied) and his flamboyant bandleader Doc Severinsen. Johnny's on-camera image may not have inspired the constant drama of his mercurial predecessor Jack Paar, but he was an assured monologist and ad-lib artist. He also knew how to play straight for guests like his idol Jack Benny, Benny's best friend George Burns, and the original "reality star" Zsa Zsa Gabor. Eddie was Johnny's guest when all three of those television icons were guests on one special episode in 1963.

One Got Fat (Interlude Films, 1963) is a fifteen-minute educational short about bicycle safety. It was written by Dale Jennings and narrated by Eddie. Perhaps to draw attention to itself, the film is populated by juvenile actors wearing monkey masks and tails. Evidently, this gimmick worked: *One Got Fat* was shown widely in grammar schools in the sixties and seventies and has become an oft-viewed curiosity on YouTube.

The Mike Douglas Show (Syndicated, 1961–1981) was a popular afternoon talk show that was taped first in Cleveland, then Philadelphia, and finally, in Hollywood; it was produced by the Westinghouse Broadcasting Company. The show's genial host was Mike Douglas, who began his career as a singer with Kay Kyser's big band. He also provided the singing voice of Prince Charming in the 1950 Walt Disney animated classic *Cinderella*. Douglas would usually open the ninety-minute show with a song; he had a few notable hits during his career, e.g., "Ol' Buttermilk Skies" (1946), "The Old Lamp-Lighter" (1947), and "The Men in My Little Girl's Life" (1966). Throughout its twenty-year run, there were more than four thousand episodes, featuring thousands of guests, one of whom was Eddie. The episodes on which he appears are, from season two, nos. 8 and 38 (both 1963); season three, nos. 147 and 152 (both 1964); and season five, episode no. 97 (1966).

Burke's Law (ABC-TV, 1963–1966) is a detective series starring Gene Barry. His character, Amos Burke, is a wealthy captain of the Los Angeles Police Department Homicide Division. Instead of riding around town in a squad car, he has a chauffeur-driven Rolls Royce Silver Cloud. In the third and final season, he changed professions, which was reflected by the show's new title, *Amos Burke, Secret Agent*. The series featured innumerable guest stars, including Eddie. He appears in two episodes: "Who Killed Eleanora Davis?" as Grover Leander Smith, and in "Who Killed Hamlet?" as Wilbur Starlington.

The Merv Griffin Show (CBS-TV, 1962–1963; Syndicated, 1965–1969; CBS, 1969–1972; Syndicated, 1972–1986) was a successful talk-and-variety show. Like Mike Douglas, Merv Griffin had been a big band singer (he had a major hit with the 1950 novelty song, "I've Got a Lov-e-ly Bunch of Coconuts"). In addition to being an engaging interviewer, Griffin was a successful producer, creating two television game shows that remain popular to the present day: *Jeopardy* and *Wheel of Fortune*. Merv's onscreen sidekick in the sixties was Arthur Treacher, an English character actor known for his many movie roles as haughty butlers and manservants. He and Eddie were often up for the same roles in the 1930s, and even appeared together in three films. The two must have had a lot to talk about when Eddie was one of Merv's guests, once in 1963, twice in 1965, and once in 1966.

Valentine's Day (ABC-TV, 1964–1965) is a half-hour, single-season sitcom created by Hal Kanter. The title refers to Farrow Valentine (Anthony "Tony" Franciosa), a swinging Manhattan publishing executive who doesn't chase women—they chase *him*. His private secretary is named Libby (Janet Waldo), and his best friend is Sam Sin (Jack Soo), a poker-playing con man. In episodes nos. 21 and 22, "All Right, Louie, Drop That Blue Pencil" (February 5, 1965) and "For Me and My Sal" (February 12, 1965), special guest star Eddie plays Charles Marks, a lonely English professor who has not slept well in fifty years. In an earlier episode, no. 18, "The Sweet Smell of Wampum" (January 15, 1965), Eddie is cast as Chief Wampum, an elderly Indian chief. This led to a minor case of typecasting, as he would soon play the same basic character on two other ABC shows, *F Troop* and *Batman*.

The Cara Williams Show (CBS-TV, 1964–1965) is a single-season, half-hour sitcom created and developed by Keefe Brasselle. Cara Williams, the former co-star (with Harry Morgan) of an earlier sitcom, *Pete and Gladys*, plays Cara Bridges. She and her husband, Frank Bridges (Frank Aletter), secretly married when their workplace, Fenwicke Diversified Industries, issued a "no-inter-office dating" policy. In episode 20, "How to Be Happy Though Married" (February 10, 1965), Eddie guest stars as old Fenwick himself.

Camp Runamuck (NBC-TV, 1965–1966) is a single-season, half-hour sitcom created by David Swift. Some of the characters and situations on the show were inspired by Allan Sherman's then-popular song, "Hello Mudda, Hello Fadduh! (A Letter From Camp)." One episode, "Spiffy Quits: Part 2," features Eddie as Henry Saunders.

F Troop (ABC-TV, 1965–1967) is a half-hour sitcom that takes place in the Old West at the fictional Fort Courage, during the post American Civil War years. The cast includes Ken Berry (*Captain Wilton Parmenter*); Forrest Tucker (*Sergeant Morgan O'Rourke*); Larry Storch (*Corporal Randolph Agarn*); Frank de Kova (*Chief Wild Eagle*); and Melody Patterson (*Angelica Thrift*). In 1965, Eddie played the recurring character Chief Roaring Chicken, an elderly medicine man. The episodes in which Roaring Chicken are featured include "Scourge of the West" (September 14); "Don't Look Now, One of Our Cannon is Missing" (September 24); "Corporal Agarn's Farewell to the Troops" (October 5); "The Girl from Philadelphia" (October 26); "Me Heap Big Injun" (November 9); and "A Gift from the Chief" (November 23).

Batman (ABC-TV, 1966–1968) is a hugely popular camp superhero series, based on the DC comic book character created by Bob Kane and Bill Finger. Starring as Bruce Wayne / Batman is Adam West, and Dick Grayson / Robin, the Boy Wonder is Burt Ward. Others in the cast include Neil Hamilton as the earnest Commissioner James Gordon; Stafford Repp as Chief O'Hara; and Alan Napier as Alfred Pennyworth. The show is bursting with color, expressionistic sets, and tongue-in-cheek performances from the cast of regulars and the numerous guest stars in the guise of surrealistic villains attempting to take over the fictional Gotham City. In the back-to-back episodes, "An Egg Grows in Gotham" and "The Yegg Foes in Gotham," Eddie portrays Chief Screaming Chicken. The episodes were originally aired on consecutive nights, on October 19–20, 1966.

The Steve Allen Show (Syndicated, 1968–1969) is another of the talented multi-hyphenate host's talk shows. This one, produced by Filmways, was broadcast in color and aired every weeknight in the 11:15–1:00 time slot. On October 29, 1968, his guests were Barrie Chase, Denny McLain, Pat Harrington, and Eddie.

The Ed Nelson Show (Syndicated, 1969) starred Edwin Stafford Nelson, an actor best known for his role as Dr. Michael Rossi on all 243 episodes of the nighttime soap opera *Peyton Place*, which ran from 1964 to 1969. Less than a month after that show's finale, Nelson was hosting his own syndicated half-hour talk show. On July 29, 1969, his guests were Hollywood columnist Shirley Eder and Eddie. The show lasted for only thirty-nine episodes.

It Takes a Thief (ABC-TV, 1968–1970) was one of the last spy dramas that had been so popular since the mid-sixties. Handsome movie star Robert Wagner made his television debut with the series, starring as Alexander Mundy. Not unlike Cary Grant in the 1955 Alfred Hitchcock feature *To Catch a Thief*, Alexander is a dashing cat burglar and a smooth ladies' man. (Although the series was said to have been inspired by the Hitchcock thriller, it was not based on it.) During the late sixties and throughout the seventies, noted actors of Hollywood's Golden Age began turning up regularly as guest stars on television dramas. In the third season of *It Takes a Thief*, Fred Astaire had the recurring role of Alexander's father, Alistar Mundy. Other industry veterans who appeared on the series included Bette Davis, Gale Sondergaard, Joseph Cotten, Elsa Lanchester, Paul Henreid, and Ida Lupino. Eddie is seen to good advantage as Lord Pelham-Gifford in "A Matter of Grey Matter: Part 1," which aired on February 4, 1969.

Cinema (Granada Television, United Kingdom, 1964–1975) was a series of filmed interviews on various aspects of motion picture industry, hosted by Michael Parkinson. Eddie, who was often mistaken for an Englishman—even by the English—was the subject of one episode in 1969.

The David Frost Show (Syndicated, 1969–1972) was a ninety-minute daytime talk show starring the renowned British interviewer David Paradine Frost. While enjoying a successful career as a chat show host in the United Kingdom, he fronted an American talk show that was aired on the Westinghouse Broadcasting stations. Frost's interview with Eddie (episode 2.188) took place in 1970.

The Name of the Game (NBC-TV, 1968–1971) was the highest-budgeted series of its time. Derived from the 1966 made-for-television movie, *Fame is the Name of the Game*, it is set in the then-thriving world of magazine publishing. Each ninety-minute episode of the series featured one of three main characters: Jeff Dillon (Tony Franciosa); Dan Ferrell (Robert Stack); and Greg Howard (Gene Barry, taking over the role for the TV movie's star, George Macready), each of whom works for Howard Productions. (The exterior used for establishing shots was actually the Universal Studios headquarters building.) This was yet another series to feature stars from an earlier era, including Charles Boyer, Yvonne de Carlo, Dorothy Lamour, Boris Karloff, Hoagy Carmichael, Robert Young, and the biggest of them all, Frank Sinatra. Eddie guest stars as Philip Armistead in season two, episode 42, "The Island of Gold and Precious Stones," which aired January 16, 1970.

Love, American Style (ABC-TV, 1969–1974) is an hour-long anthology comedy series. Each episode is made up of three or four stories, all of which include the word *Love* in the title. The show was part of a popular ABC Friday night primetime lineup featuring *The Brady Bunch*, *The Partridge Family*, *Room 222*, and *The Odd Couple*. Eddie appears in the second season episode entitled "Love and Las Vegas / Love and the Good Samaritan / Love and the Marriage Counselor" (February 27, 1970). He is cast as Elmo in the "Love and Las Vegas" segment. His co-stars are Bill Dana, Patricia Stich, Nellie Burt, Jim Connell, and Ann Prentiss.

Nanny and the Professor (ABC-TV, 1970–1971) is a half-hour sitcom that capitalized on the popularity of the P.L. Travers character, Mary Poppins. Professor Harold Everett (Richard Long), a single father of three spirited children, is at a loss when the kids go through five au pairs in less than a year. Enter Phoebe Figalilly, an ambiguously "magical" British nanny, who sets to work, bringing the children to heel and restoring peace and unity to the Everett household. The show was successful enough when it was scheduled among ABC's family comedy lineup, but when it was moved to Monday nights it was trounced by *Gunsmoke* on CBS and *Rowan & Martin's Laugh-In* on NBC. Episode no. 8 in *Nanny and the Professor*'s first season, "Strictly for the Birds," features three beloved character actors: Eddie, J. Pat O'Malley, and Cecil Kellaway. The story revolves around some motherless ducklings that Nanny and the children come across in a park. Concerned for the animals' well-being, they take them home. This is witnessed by an elderly zoologist, Professor Clarendon (Eddie), who then contacts the police to report the do-gooders for stealing city property. Nanny arranges a meeting with the professor, who patiently explains to her and the children the proper way to care for the ducklings. This heartwarming episode first aired on March 11, 1970.

The Governor and J.J. (CBS-TV, 1969–1970) is a half-hour sitcom starring former song-and-dance man Dan Dailey as William Drinkwater, the widowered governor of an unidentified Midwestern state. Julie Sommars is Jennifer Jo, the conservative Drinkwater's liberal twentysomething daughter and de facto "first lady." (Ironically, Sommars in real life has been an active supporter of the Republican Party.) In season two's episode "File Safe," the governor's mansion is in an uproar when the main inhabitant's birth certificate goes missing. As that legal document is required for the governor to qualify for re-election, it is incumbent on ninety-seven-year-old Doc Simon (played by eighty-four-year-old Eddie) to remember having delivered the candidate. In real life, Julie Sommars was one of Eddie's protégées in summer stock. In the guise of the elderly doctor, Eddie uses a cane. This was not an affectation; it was because Eddie had pulled a muscle while playing tennis. The episode first aired on October 14, 1970, approximately two weeks after Eddie's passing.

Johnny Carson Presents the Sun City Scandals, '70 (NBC-TV, December 1970) is one of two comedy-variety specials highlighting performers from an earlier era; the sequel aired in 1972. As the title indicates,

Johnny Carson serves as master of ceremonies, introducing such veteran entertainers as Gladys & Will Ahern, Benny Rubin, Gloria Swanson, Louis Armstrong, Frankie Carle, Fifi D'Orsay, Wilbur Hall, and Billy Gilbert (who hilariously demonstrates his famous sneezing routine). Eddie coaches Johnny on how to do a double-take. He also participates in some blackout sketches, including one in which he and his equally elderly wife are in bed together. Feeling amorous, she asks her husband to give her a hickey. Immediately, he begins to get out of the bed. When his wife asks him where he is going, he tells her, "I have to put in my teeth." On *The Tonight Show*, Johnny Carson eulogized Eddie as a total, no-nonsense professional.

Sources

Books

AFI Catalog of Feature Films, 1921–1930 (2-volume set). Edited by Patricia King Hanson. University of California Press, 1993 (reprint of the 1971 edition).

AFI Catalog of Feature Films, 1931–1940 (3-volume set). Edited by Patricia King Hanson. University of California Press, 1993.

AFI Catalog of Feature Films, 1941–1950 (3-volume set). Edited by Patricia King Hanson. University of California Press, 1999.

AFI Catalog of Feature Films, 1951–1960 (3-volume set). Edited by Patricia King Hanson. University of California Press, 1999.

AFI Catalog of Feature Films, 1961–1970 (2-volume set). Edited by Richard Krafsur. University of California Press, 1997 (reprint of the 1976 edition).

Alistair, Rupert. *The Name Below the Title: 65 Classic Movie Character Actors from Hollywood's Golden Age.* "Edward Everett Horton," pp. 125–128; "Franklin Pangborn," pp. 212–214. Published independently, UK, 2018.

Astor, Mary. *My Story: An Autobiography.* Garden City, NY: Doubleday & Co., 1959.

Blum, Daniel C. *A Pictorial History of the Silent Screen.* New York: G.P. Putnam's Sons, 1953.

Brownlow, Kevin. *The Parade's Gone By …* New York: Knopf, 1969.

Cary, Diana Serra. *What Ever Happened to Baby Peggy?* New York: St. Martin's Press, 1996.

Curtis, James. *W.C. Fields: A Biography.* New York: Knopf, 2003.

Davis, Lon. *Silent Lives: 100 Biographies of the Silent Film Era* (with a foreword by Kevin Brownlow). Albany, GA: BearManor Media, 2008.

Dennis, Charles. *There's a Body in the Window Seat: A History of* Arsenic and Old Lace. Essex, CT: Applause Books, 2022.

Eyman, Scott. *Ernst Lubitsch: Laughter in Paradise.* Baltimore, MD: Johns Hopkins University Press, 2000.

Gehring, Wes D. *Leo McCarey: From Marx to McCarthy.* Lanham, MD: The Scarecrow Press, 2005.

Golden, Eve. *Bride of Golden Images: 42 Essays on Film Stars of the 1930s–60s.* (Essay on Edward Everett Horton, pp. 178–184.) Albany, GA: BearManor Media, 2009.

Gunter, Matthew C. *The Capra Touch: A Study of the Director's Hollywood Classics and War Documentaries, 1934–1945*. Jefferson, NC: McFarland & Co., 2012.

Harmon, Jim. *The Great Radio Comedians*. New York: Doubleday, 1970.

Higby, Mary Jane. *Tune in Tomorrow; Or How I Found the Right to Happiness with* Our Gal Sunday, Stella Dallas, John's Other Wife, *and Other Sudsy Radio Serials*. New York, NY: Cowles, 1968.

Katula, Richard A. *The Eloquence of Edward Everett: America's Greatest Orator* (new edition). Lausanne, Switzerland: Peter Lang Inc., International Academic Publishers, 2010.

Lahue, Kalton C. *World of Comedy: The Motion Picture Comedy Short, 1910–1930*. Norman: Oklahoma University Press, 1966.

Levy, Benn W. *Springtime for Henry: A Farce in Three Acts*. New York, NY: Samuel French, 1931. This play is in the public domain. The text on the back cover reads: "Scholars believe, and we concur, that this work is important enough to be preserved, reproduced, and generally made available to the public."

Maltin, Leonard (ed.). *Classic Movie Guide: More Than 10,000 Movies From the Silent Era Through 1965*. New York: Plume, a member of the Penguin Group, 2005.

Mann, William J. *Beyond Paradise: The Life of Ramon Novarro*. Jackson: University Press of Mississippi, 2002.

———. *Wiseacre: The Life and Times of William Haines, Hollywood's First Openly Gay Star*. New York: Penguin Books, 1999.

Massa, Steve. *Lame Brains and Lunatics 2: More Good, Bad, and Forgotten of Silent Comedy* (Chapter 8: "Edward Everett Horton: Silent Clown?" pp. 551–588). Orlando, FL: BearManor Media, 2022.

McBride, Joseph. *Frank Capra: The Catastrophe of Success*. Jackson: University Press of Mississippi, 1992.

McCabe. John. *Charlie Chaplin*. New York: Doubleday, 1978.

Plummer, Christopher. *In Spite of Myself: A Memoir*. New York: Vintage Press (a Division of Random House), 2012.

Rosenberg, Bernard, and Harry Silverman. *The Real Tinsel*. (Chapter on Edward Everett Horton, pp. 219–235.) New York: The Macmillan Company, 1970.

Scott, Keith. *The Moose That Roared: The Story of Bill Scott, Jay Ward, a Flying Squirrel, and a Talking Moose*. New York: Thomas Dunne Books, 2001.

Slide, Anthony. *Eccentrics of Comedy.* (Chapter on Edward Everett Horton, pp. 57–73.) Lanham, MD: The Scarecrow Press, 1998.

Wilde, Larry. *Great Comedians Talk About Comedy*. Mechanicsburg, PA: Executive Books, 2000. (Originally published in 1968.)

Periodicals

"Actor Edward Everett Horton Dies at 84." *Dayton Beach Morning Journal*, October 1, 1970.

Aliperti, Cliff. "Edward Everett Horton – Biography of the Beloved Character Actor." *Immortal Ephemera* (December 7, 2011).

Bernstein, Neil. "Notable City College Knights." Baltimore, MD: The Baltimore City College Alumni Association, 2008.

Bradford, Serena. "Squire of Belleigh Acres: With something less than complete seriousness, Edward Everett Horton, matinee idol and farmer, discusses life in the great out-doors on the ranch, one of the show places of the Valley," *Hollywood* (1939).

Canal, Marie. "Edward Everett Horton Learned to Like the Oregon Mist: Noted Comedian Played Stock in Portland for 88 Successive Weeks; During the War he Doled out Food to Cafes and Restaurants." *The Sunday Oregonian* (Portland), September 30, 1934.

Carr, Jeremy. "There Seems to Be a Slight Mistake": Edward Everett Horton—8 Silent Comedies," *Film International Magazine*, November 20, 2021. (filmint.nu)

Desowitz, Bill. "Something 'Fractured,' Something New." *Los Angeles Times*, August 27, 1999.

"Edward Everett Horton." *Moving Picture World*, April 9, 1927.

"Edward Everett Horton is 79 and as Roaring Chicken is One Active Bird." *TV Guide*, October 16, 1965.

"Edward Everett Horton Is Dead; Comic Character Actor Was 83 (*sic*). Star of Stage, Film and TV Played 'Befuddled' Role in a 60-Year Career." *New York Times*, October 1, 1970.

"Edward Everett Horton Will Make 'Em Laugh: Horton Featured in Picture Made From Famous Play." *Universal Weekly* (32), May 22, 1926.

"Edward Everett Horton's Encino Ranch Estate and the 101 Freeway; How A Celebrity Lost His Ranch to Suburbanization." *San Fernando Valley Blog* (April 4, 2012).

Eligible Mr. Bangs, The. William K. Everson notes, September 29, 1960. (https://wke.hosting.nyu.edu/wke/notes/huff/huff_600929.htm).

Fowler, James. "Horton's House Grew with Film Career." *Los Angeles Times*, April 12, 1997.

Green, John. "Play Title a Perfect Fit: [Edward Everett Horton] To Appear in 'Springtime for Henry.'" *Lansing* (MI) *State Journal*. August 24, 1960.

Gussow, Mel. "Stage: 'Springtime for Henry.'" *New York Times*, August 2, 1985.

"Hailing a New Horton," *New York Times*, June 19, 1938.

Hall, Mordaunt. "Lonely Wives: The Lawyer and His Double." *New York Times*, March 16, 1931.

"Horton to Play on Orpheum." *Moving Picture World*, October 6, 1923.

Irwin, Virginia. "He's Having the Time of His Life: Comedian Edward Everett Horton Enjoys Ordering Women Around in Stage Play." *St. Louis* (MO) *Dispatch*, January 1, 1940.

Kerr, Walter. "A Show in Search of Edward Everett Horton," *The Baltimore Sun*, September 26, 1976.

Kirby, Walter. "Better Radio Programs for the Week." *The Decatur Daily Review* (March 16, 1952).

Kirkley, Donald. "'Springtime for Henry' Returns with Edward Everett Horton," *The Baltimore Sun*, October 20, 1939.

MacCormac, John. "The Terror" (1928) [Review], *New York Times*, November 18, 1928.

McManus, Margaret. "Edward Everett Horton to Make TV Series Debut," *Portland Press Herald* (Maine), September 16, 1965.

Meredith, Jack. "Edward Everett Horton … Sage, Actor, Raconteur." *The Windsor Star* (Detroit, Michigan), November 18, 1967.

Reid, James. "The Lord of Belleigh Acres: His Lordship, Edward Everett Horton, founded his estate on belly laughs." *Motion Picture Magazine* (July 1937).

Reid, Larry. "Accidentally Funny: Edward Everett Horton can't understand why producers pay him $5,000 a week just to be funny—but as he says, '[I] can take it.'" *Movie Classic* (September 1936–February 1937).

Reid, Margaret. "A Prophet of Honor: Edward Everett Horton, whose service to the stage means as much to the stars as his comedy on the screen does to fans." *Picture Play Magazine* (July–December 1930).

Rhodes, Robert J. " 'Alice' Finds that Wonderland Proved Just a Myth, After All: Charlotte Henry, Who Tasted Fame and Fortune Six Years Ago in Child Film Fantasy, Is Trying to Convince Hollywood She Can Act." *The Times* (Hammond, Indiana), Thursday, July 28, 1939.

Stein, Jeanne. "Fusspot and Fortune's Fool: Edward Everett Horton." *Focus on Film* (UK) (January 1, 1970).

Wallace, Irving. "Nurseries for Newcomers." *Modern Screen* (October 1940), 21 (5): 26–27 – via The Internet Archive, archive.org.

Wilson, Scott (August 19, 2016). *Resting Places: The Burial Sites of More Than 14,000 Famous Persons*, 3d ed. McFarland. p. 353. ISBN 978-1-4766-2599-7.

Websites

AFI Catalogs of Feature Films: The First Hundred Years, 1893–1993. https://aficatalog.afi.com/

Callahan, Dan. "Double-Takes," https://stolenholiday.substack.com/ June 2, 2024

"Famed Actor Edward Everett Horton Was Born and Bred in Brooklyn." https://stuffnobodycaresabout.com/2019/01/07/edward-everett-horton/

Doctor Macro's High Quality Movie Scans. https://www.doctormacro.com/Galleries.htm

Everything Lucy
hollywoodsgoldenage.com
Internet Archive https://archive.org/
Internet Broadway Database (IBDb) https://www.ibdb.com/
Internet Movie Database (IMDb) https://www.imdb.com/
It's About TV https://www.itsabouttv.com/
Media History Digital Library https://mediahistoryproject.org
Newspaper.com
The Socratic Method
Old-Time Radio Downloads, https://www.oldtimeradiodownloads.com/
Once Upon a Screen … a classic film and TV blog: "The Serious Domestic Charms of Eric Blore," October 21, 2021 / by Aurora.
Wisconsin Center for Film and Theatre Research
YouTube: Various movies; filmed interviews from 1961, 1963, and 1968.

Index